Napoleon's Heavy Cavalry

To Ian James Smith

Thank you for your friendship, encouragement and support of my research.

Napoleon's Heavy Cavalry

Uniforms and Equipment of the Cuirassiers and Carabiniers, 1805–1815

Paul L. Dawson

FRONTLINE BOOKS

First published in Great Britain in 2024 by
Frontline Books
An imprint of Pen & Sword Books Limited
Yorkshire – Philadelphia

Copyright © Paul L. Dawson 2024

ISBN 978 1 52678 419 3

The right of Paul L. Dawson to be identified as
Author of this Work has been asserted by him in accordance
with the Copyright, Designs and Patents Act 1988.

A CIP catalogue record for this book is
available from the British Library

All rights reserved. No part of this book may be reproduced or
transmitted in any form or by any means, electronic or mechanical
including photocopying, recording or by any information storage and
retrieval system, without permission from the Publisher in writing.

Typeset by Mac Style
Printed and bound in India by Replika Press Pvt. Ltd.

Pen & Sword Books Limited incorporates the imprints of After the Battle,
Atlas, Archaeology, Aviation, Discovery, Family History, Fiction, History,
Maritime, Military, Military Classics, Politics, Select, Transport, True Crime,
Air World, Frontline Publishing, Leo Cooper, Remember When, Seaforth
Publishing, The Praetorian Press, Wharncliffe Local History, Wharncliffe
Transport, Wharncliffe True Crime and White Owl.

For a complete list of Pen & Sword titles please contact:

PEN & SWORD BOOKS LIMITED
47 Church Street, Barnsley, South Yorkshire, S70 2AS, England
E-mail: enquiries@pen-and-sword.co.uk
Website: www.pen-and-sword.co.uk
or
PEN AND SWORD BOOKS
1950 Lawrence Rd, Havertown, PA 19083, USA
E-mail: uspen-and-sword@casematepublishers.com
Website: www.penandswordbooks.com

Contents

Acknowledgements		vi
Chapter 1	The Cavalry Regiments	1
Chapter 2	Clothing the *Cuirassiers* 1801–05	6
Chapter 3	Armour and Helmets 1801–05	18
Chapter 4	*Cuirassier* Horse Equipment 1801–05	28
Chapter 5	Continuity and Change 1805–08	31
Chapter 6	1808 Reviews	41
Chapter 7	1812 Campaign Preparations	56
Chapter 8	Bardin Regulations	62
Chapter 9	Regulations in Practice 1812–15	68
Chapter 10	Bardin and the *Cuirassiers* – Myth and Reality	147
Chapter 11	The *Carabiniers* 1802–10	157
Chapter 12	The *Carabiniers* 1810–15	168
Chapter 13	Regulations in Practice	174
Chapter 14	*Carabiniers* – Myth and Reality	184
Notes		195
Bibliography		204

Acknowledgements

This book and its companion volumes marks the culmination of almost two decades of research, and a combined period of almost four months of daily study in the French army archives in Paris. In December 2001 I first walked through the gate house of *Château de Vincennes* as the clock above me chimed 9 o'clock. I turned left and passed through a large wooden door and climbed a staircase. I explained the nature of my visit, and was guided by an army officer through an arched doorway and up a flight of stairs in what was an 1830s barrack block. Waiting for me was the muster list of the 1ᵉ regiment of Grenadiers a Pied of the Imperial Guard. I was visiting the archives to find out as much as I could about Grenadier Simplet, whose uniform is on display in the Musée de l'Armée, and what source material existed to tell me about what the regiment wore: a whole new world of primary sources was opened up to me, most of them I had never seen referenced before. Thus began my love affair with wanting to find out exactly how Napoléon's men were dressed. Since then I have made annual pilgrimages to Vincennes.

For the last 200 years, it has been assumed that army-level regulations had been the primary source for the appearance of the armed forces. However, this did not answer key questions of how the regulations were interpreted, how the regulations were changed and above all how each regiment introduced the regulations, this far outweighs the dictates of the War Ministry or other official publication. To answer these questions, perhaps, 1,000 archive boxes needed to be consulted. Such an extensive degree of research was only possible through collaboration with a core team of friends who supported me in my endeavour.

I am indebted to Jean-Charles Lair, Sally Fairweather and Yves Martin for their most generous and gracious assistance with, and photographing of, archival material at the Archives Nationale and Service Historique de la Défense Armée de Térre in Paris. Without their help, this book could not have been written. Yves is also to be thanked for his friendship, advice and most generous provision of illustrative material. My esteemed friend and research colleague Robert Cooper is to be thanked for his steadfast friendship and comments on my essay and critical comments on my thought processes in understanding the archive sources and supply issues for the army. I must thank Olivier Lapray for provision of notes on the 8ᵉ *Cuirassiers*. The regimental archive has not been accessible for a number of years: *bravo mon ami*!

Jerome Croyet must be thanked for his permission to reproduce the photographs I have taken of the former Brunon collection. He is also to be thanked for the provision of research notes.

Also to be thanked is Bertrand Malvaux for permission to use images of items in his collection.

The long-suffering staff at Service Historique de la Défense Armée de Térre in Paris need to be thanked for answering questions and locating items of research that have made this book possible.

To Jose Luis Canibe I am eternally grateful. His digital artworks have brought to life what the archive documents say in his wonderful graphics. Without these many hundreds of illustrations, the book would not be the 'ultimate reference book' that I hope it is for the *cuirassiers* and *carabiniers*.

Paul L. Dawson, Paris, 5 December 2023

Chapter 1

The Cavalry Regiments

Upon becoming First Consul, Napoléon inherited twenty-five regiments of heavy cavalry and two of *carabiniers*. They were the shock troops of the army. Armed with a straight sabre, a pair of pistols and sometimes a carbine, these men had been the French nation's principal mounted combat arm throughout the eighteenth century. These were in theory the big men on big horses who were held in reserve exclusively for service in battle. Due to their large size and heavy armour, which increased their protection and survivability, the heavy cavalry was Napoléon's decisive combat arm that could deliver a devastating blow upon enemy units when properly employed. While other types of cavalry had their important roles to play during battle, Napoléon's heavy cavalry was typically held in reserve to be committed at the critical place and time to deliver the decisive blow against the enemy. Thus, the cavalry's commitment to the main battle tended to prove decisive. The *cuirassiers* were the descendants of the medieval knights, who could turn a battle with their sheer weight and brute force. In order to preserve the combat effectiveness of the heavy cavalry in battle, the tasks of courier duty, screening, reconnaissance and pursuit typically fell to lighter cavalry units so that the heavy cavalry could be employed with maximum effectiveness at the critical time.

Dressed in cutaway *habits*, with felt *chapeaux*, their appearance was markedly similar to their infantry counterparts, with differing lace and facing colour combinations marking out each regiment. These regiments, with over 100 years of tradition behind them, would be swept away in a whirlwind of army reforms.

During the Treaty of Amiens, Napoléon had time to rebuild the French army in the form he envisioned for it. New equipment regulations were issued, and army-wide inspections were carried out. The great innovation of 1801 to 1803 was the formation of twelve regiments of *cuirassiers* – the iconic French heavy cavalryman, whose uniform changed little from Austerlitz to the Marne in a period of over 100 years.

The decree of 9 September 1799 (*23 Fructidor An VII*) tells us the 8e *régiment de cavalerie* had the denomination 8e *régiment cavalerie-cuirassiers*. The regiment had been wearing the *cuirass* since 'time immemorial'. A second regiment of *cuirassiers* was created when the 1e *régiment de cavalerie* became the 1e *régiment de 'cavalerie-cuirassiers'* by a decree of 10 October 1801 (*18 Vendémiaire An X*). Colonel Merlin of the 8e complained bitterly to the war minister that HIS regiment should be the 1e as they had been wearing armour far longer. He argued that his regiment had been formed in 1665 as *cuirassiers* and although the 1e *Cavalerie* had been raised in 1635, if another regiment was to become *cuirassiers*, then the 8^e should become the 1^e regiment of the new arm. The war minister refused Merlin's request.[1] To bring both units up to strength, the 1e, 3e and 5^e

2 Napoleon's Heavy Cavalry

companies of the 24ᵉ *Cavalerie* were passed to the 1ᵉ *Cavalerie-Cuirassiers* and the 2ᵉ, 4ᵉ 6ᵉ to the 8ᵉ *Cavalerie-Cuirassiers*.[2] Three more regiments were created when the 2ᵉ, 3ᵉ and 4ᵉ followed suit with a decree dated 12 October 1802 (*20 Vendémiaire An XI*). Two months would pass before a third decree was issued, 23 December 1802 *(2 Nivôse An X)*, which ordered that the 5ᵉ, 6ᵉ and 7ᵉ *Cavalerie* were also added to the new arm that, with the 8th, comprised eight regiments.

Less than a year later, 24 September 1803 (*1 Vendémiaire An XIII*), the arm was increased to twelve with the addition of 9ᵉ, 10ᵉ, 11ᵉ and 12ᵉ regiments of cavalry. This number remained unchanged until the end of 1807, when three more regiments were formed:[3]

1ᵉ provisional regiment was formed at the end of 1807 from detachments of the 1ᵉ and 2ᵉ *Carabiniers* and the 1ᵉ, 2ᵉ and 3ᵉ *Cuirassiers*.
2ᵉ provisional regiment formed from parts of the 5ᵉ, 9ᵉ, 10ᵉ, 11ᵉ and 12ᵉ *Cuirassiers*.
3ᵉ provisional regiment formed in 1808 from detachments of the 4ᵉ, 6ᵉ, 7ᵉ and 9ᵉ.

The 1ᵉ and 2ᵉ provisional regiments became the 13ᵉ *Cuirassiers* in 1813 and the 3ᵉ provisional was unofficially known as the 14ᵉ *Cuirassiers* for a matter of months.

In September 1810, the 2ᵉ regiment of Dutch *cuirassiers* was incorporated into the French army and took the number 14.

Spring 1813 witnessed three more regiments being formed in Hanover, taking the tally to seventeen regiments of *cuirassiers*. The 1ᵉ provisional regiment became consolidated as the 15ᵉ *cuirassiers* at the end of the year. With the 1st Restoration in spring 1814, the 13ᵉ, 14ᵉ, 15ᵉ as well as 2ᵉ and 3ᵉ provisional *Cuirassiers* were disbanded into the remaining twelve regiments.

Forming the twelve new regiments of *cuirassiers* took time. The paper archive allows us to reconstruct the process in great detail. The starting point was what the regiments were authorised to wear as cavalry regiments.

The 1802 Dress Regulations

The basic building block for the dress of the heavy was laid out in 1802. No uniform regulation had been issued since 1791 that addressed all aspects of the uniform of the army. To try and create some order from chaos, at the start of the Napoléonic period, the decree of 22 February 1802 was introduced:

Cavalerie, Carabiniers, Dragoons

Objects	*Duration*
Cloth *habit*:	4 years
Cloth *surtout*:	4 years
Manteaux:	10 years
Hat:	2 years
Helmet:	8 years

The Cavalry Regiments   3

White buff leather waist belts:	20 years
Giberne:	20 years
White buff leather *Giberne* belt:	20 years
Musket sling:	20 years
Porte-manteaux:	8 years
Saddle:	20 years
Housse:	8 years
Chaperons:	8 years
Boots:	2 years

For Year X, there will be provided a sheepskin *culotte* to each man of the cavalry and dragoons. As of the year XI, each *sous-officier*, cavalryman and *dragon*, will have two pairs of hide *culotte* one in sheepskin, and one in doe hide. They will supply these two *culottes* with a sum of six francs, which will be issued to them as part of the clothing mass. All in accordance with the provisions of the instruction to be drafted and addressed to the Minister of War.

Each *sous-officier*, cavalryman and dragoon will receive, each year, a *veste*, which will be worn with the old *surtout*.

The *sous-officier* and soldiers will provide, at their expense, the repair and maintenance of the boots.

The above provisions prescribed for infantry, in Articles IV, VI, VIII, IX and X, will be common to cavalry and dragoons, Viz.

IV. *sous-officier* and soldiers will be required to provide *bonnets de police* at their expense.

VI. The clothes and jackets that will be replaced in year X, will belong to the regiment; the best will be kept for the clothing of the new soldiers, for the guard – house, the prison and the discipline room.

VII. *sous-officier* and soldiers will be allowed to provide white linen *pantalons* for the summer, while complying with the provisions of the instruction, which will be written and addressed to each regiment by the Minister of War.

VIII. The boards of directors will take steps to procure for each ordinary or barrack room, a number of canvas smocks for the men to wear on fatigues.

IX. *sous-officier* and soldiers who will have to obtain their final discharge during the course of the year X, will have no part in the distribution, which will have to be made during the course of this year, in effects of clothing. Their clothes will be repaired with care at the moment of their departure.

X. The men who can be reformed will have a *habit*, a *surtout*, a pair of *culottes* and a hat, taken from those who will be in their last year of service.[4]

Of interest, *bonnets de police* were non-army issue, so we are left to wonder as to their exact appearance. As summer ended in 1802, another decree was issued on 23 September. Point 9 elaborated on the *bonnets de police*: 'sous-officiers and soldiers will be provided

4 Napoleon's Heavy Cavalry

with a *bonnet de police*, which will be made with offcuts from making the new clothing and the best pieces of the debris of the old clothing.' An early case of recycling! Point 13 introduced loose-fitting linen overalls for fatigue duties to be worn with the smock.[5] Officially the decree of 8 December 1802 ordered that *surtouts* were to be used to provide materials to make stable coats – we assume either the tails were lopped off to make stable coats or they were taken to pieces and remade. Stable coats as specific garments came back into use until 1806.[6]

The men's uniform was provided for through stoppages in their pay. In consequence the soldier's uniform and equipment was tightly regulated and was issued on a controlled basis. Each item of clothing had a specified duration period. A *habit* had to last two years, a bearskin twenty years, a pair of *culottes* a matter of months. Every year a regiment would be inspected, and the condition of the clothing assessed. A return of all the clothing to be struck off/disposed of was made, and the appropriate number of new items ordered. Clothing and equipment needing repairs was also logged, as was how many items had been repaired since the last inspection. The soldier was responsible for the repair of his own clothing and any costs associated. Likewise, if he lost items, he had to purchase replacements – in many ways a soldier ended up paying to be in the army when these deductions were taken into consideration. Every year half the regiment's cloth work was replaced, so every twenty-four months a soldier received a new *habit*. It was very much make do and mend by the time the cloth items of equipment were coming to the end of their service life. These inspection returns are a fantastic resource for outlining what a regiment actually wore rather than the theory based on the regulations. The two often did not agree in practice. The regiment's clothing and equipment was overseen by the regiment's clothing officer. His work was overseen by an inspector general. Items of clothing had a specific lifespan. Each time an item was inspected it was classed as either new, in need of repair, due to expire, or expired and in need of replacement. Upon joining the army, a soldier was issued his first complete set of uniform (*1e Messe*), which came from stoppages in pay. From the *masse d'habillement* or literally clothing fund which set a yearly quota of money available to a colonel to pay for clothing renewals and repairs. In addition, the regimental Council of Administration drew its necessary funds to buy raw materials, equipment and headdress, as well as to pay the regimental workmen. It also covered sundry items such as the epaulettes of the *adjutant-sous-officiers*, lace for rank stripes, service chevrons, musicians and drummers lace, plumes and pompoms. The fund was to provide a soldier with his full issue of uniform and equipment. A solider in addition to his basic issue, needed more than a single shirt, stock and pair of shoes. This was paid for with more stoppages from his pay being sent to the Linen and Shoe Fund. The fund was paid for at the rate of 12 centimes a day for *sous-officiers* and 7 centimes for other ranks.[7] The men were paid, in theory, weekly, according to rank and status. In all cases, the pay was subject to a number of deductions for communal funds (*masse d'habillement*), which left very little actual pay. The purpose of the pay was actually not to give the soldier pocket money to spend on wine, women and gambling but so he could pay for fines, meet repair bills for his clothing and equipment, purchase soap and cleaning

The Cavalry Regiments 5

Trooper's helmet of the 1ᵉ *Cuirassiers* dating to 1814–15. (*Private collection Switzerland*)

equipment and if needed buy new items of clothing. All repairs were carried out under the auspices of the *caporal-fourrier*. Minor repairs were to be carried out to clothing and equipment by the soldier. For more major repairs, the *caporal-fourrier* took the solider and his damaged items to the captain clothing officer, who authorised the regimental workmen to undertake the repair. If the repair was judged to be due to negligence by the soldier he had to pay for the work or a replacement item from his pay.[8]

Chapter 2

Clothing the *Cuirassiers* 1801–05

Having looked at the basic dress regulations, we turn our attention to how the *cavalerie* regiments became *cuirassiers*.

The dress of the *cuirassiers* is a complex subject, and it is one that is greatly confused by writers taking an overtly simplistic overview relying solely on official decrees, and not using archive research, or consulting the Bardin regulation proper as opposed to the heavily redacted copy printed in 1812.

It is easy to understand why so much misinformation is in print. From the various decrees, it is straightforward. Regiments replaced the old long-tailed *cavalerie habits* with the single-breasted, short-tailed *surtout*, and this was replaced in 1806 with a short-tailed *habit*. However, the subject is far more complex than the formation decree made allowances for and is far more complex than artists, historians and re-enactors have presumed the subject matter to be.

Untangling the truth about what the *cuirassiers* actually wore is complex and time-consuming, and can only be achieved by conducting original archive research. Many questions arise out of the two different Bardin regulations!

The War Ministry issued a decree on 10 October 1801 outlining the dress of the new *cuirassier* arm. The contents of this has been lost to time.

In response to this dictate, *Chef de Brigade* (Colonel) Margaron of the 1ᵉ, wrote to General Berthier, the Minister for War, and expressed his concerns about becoming *cuirassiers* in a letter of 9 December 1801. He wondered if the War Ministry had fully thought through the idea. He noted that the minister's intention was to adopt a *habit-veste* that buttoned closed without *revers*, and was cut to conceal the second button from the top of the breeches, and to have scarlet collar and cuffs: this garment was to be worn in full dress. In other orders of dress the *surtout* was to be kept in use but cut longer in front. He felt that with the adoption of armour, the officers' epaulettes would be concealed, so asked would not a large coloured waist sash denoting rank be of more use?

To stop the hilt of the sabre rattling on the *cuirass*, he urged that a sabre belt with slings was essential rather than retaining the old *cavalerie* sabre belts as the minister urged. He also noted that *bottes forte* (rigid riding boots) should be cut to 'come a little distance above the knee' and *culottes de peau*, made from first-class materials, were ideal rather than *bottes à la écurie*. The finest quality of wax was needed to maintain the boots. Margaron also noted that a *giberne* and belt was totally useless for *cuirassiers* and it was much simpler to convert a pistol holster to take a wooden cartridge block holding twelve rounds of ammunition, as the pistols were almost never used. Margaron told the minister that he examined a helmet of the 8ᵉ *Cavalerie*, which was in the form of a dragoon helmet, made to the same dimensions but with a bearskin turban. However, the colonel felt that the bearskin was the proper headdress of elite cavalry: it was more imposing, and as effective at warding off sabre blows as a helmet. He also noted it was cheaper than the helmet. He asked the minister that whatever was chosen for headdress, the *chapeau* had to be dispensed with. Furthermore, he urged that *cuirassiers* were not be armed with *mousquetons* as they did not fight on foot. For sentinels on campaign 15 *mousquetons* per company was sufficient, giving the regiment a total of 100 such weapons. He also asked that a sheepskin *schabraque* was adopted to replace *chaperons*.

Margaron in addition requested that the *manteau* was replaced with a large, sleeved *capote* with an ample collar – I assume a shoulder cape – cut long and buttoned along the front, and with the back cut open like a *redingote* but able to be buttoned closed. If, he urged the minister, the *habits long* were to be replaced, then the *cuirassiers* must replace the *manteaux* at the same time. Because of the weight of the *cuirass*, he requested that he was allowed the tallest and most robust conscripts and horses.[1] Clearly it seems that from day one the *cuirassiers* were to have a single-breasted *habit de cuirass*.

At this stage, just a brigade was envisioned of *cuirassiers*, but that all changed with the decree of 23 December 1802, which created more *cuirassier* regiments. The decree left the old cavalry regiment uniforms unchanged. The men were to simply adopt a *cuirass*, and the *habit* adapted as needed. The next document to detail the dress of the new arm of *cuirassiers* was a draft decree of 31 July 1803, of which Article 26 states that:

> The clothing of *cuirassiers* will consist of a *habit* in blue broadcloth, cut short, with no *revers*, closed with a single row of buttons to the waist, cut short in such a manner to display the waistbelt plate. The buttons are in tin. The twelve regiments will have the following distinctive colours to cuffs and collars: 1st scarlet, 2nd crimson; 3rd rose, 4th yellow, 5th white, 6th sky blue, 7th light brown, 8th violet, 9th iron grey, 10th yellow, 11th aurore, 12th chamois. Lining will be in the colour of the *habit*. The tails will be ornamented with fascines. The *gilet* of *cuirassiers* will be in white broadcloth. They will have *culotte de peau*. The *surtout* will be replaced with a stable coat cut from broadcloth and in the same form as the *grenadiers à cheval*. The *chapeau* will be substituted for a helmet in iron and bronze, in the form of that used by the dragoons, ornamented with a cockade and a white plume. The turban will be of bearskin, the chinstrap will be in copper fish scales and will carry to the depth of the chin to preserve the face from sabre cuts.[2]

The decree in essence replaces the *habit* with a *surtout,* the *surtout* is then replaced with a stable coat. All very easy to understand. New facing colours were potentially introduced. But did this happen? Arguably no, as just a matter of weeks later, the decree of 24 September 1803 states that the facing colours as they then existed were to be retained and 'the *habits* were to be cut so as to accommodate wearing the *cuirass*'.[3] It says nothing about the *habit* having or not having *revers*, indeed it says nothing as to how it actually looked. Ian Smith comments:

8   Napoleon's Heavy Cavalry

Officially, only two garments were regulation, the cavalry *habit* of 4 Brumaire AnX, and the Bardin 1812 *habit*.

The 1803 formation decree, in theory states that the uniform was basically a dark blue *surtout* if we follow Rousselot and Margerand, with dark blue epaulette straps and grenades on the turnbacks; the lining and the turnbacks, the piping to the pockets and the piping on the epaulette straps were in the regiment's facing colour; the collars and the cuffs and flaps were piped in the opposing colour. The tin uniform buttons bore the regimental number. However, the decree itself only states that the cut of the *habit* was to be changed to allow the wearing of a *cuirass*. Not a single document exists that describes the cut of this garment.[4]

We have no clue as to what this *habit* looked like in reality, but we can make informed, educated guesses. It is likely that the *habit* of 31 July 1803 is the single-breasted 'new model' or the '*habit de cuirass*'. The September garment is likely to be the *habit à revers*, or at least giving sanction to altering existing *cavalerie habits* to accommodate the *cuirass*. Thus, in theory, the colonels had a huge amount of leeway in how to dress their men.

Habits à Revers or Habits de Cuirass?

Only archive research can inform us to as how the process of dressing the men actually proceeded.

Key to this process is remembering that all items made pre-24 September 1803 were no doubt old model, the old *habit longues*. A new *habit* made in 1802 had a lifespan of four years – would a colonel simply throw away brand-new clothing? It seems unlikely. Any *habit* made before 24 September 1803 would likewise not be expected to be taken out of use until 1806. Thus, the new *habits* would come into use as clothing needed replacing. Of course, we must remember that what was worn was all at the colonel's discretion: each was free to do as they pleased to a certain extent. The 1801 *modèle habit de cuirass* was single-breasted, closed to the waist with ten buttons, had long pockets to the short tails and three buttoned cuff flaps. The *surtout* was cut in the same manner, but with no pockets to the tails, and we assume it was entirely blue.

For some regiments it is likely that this '*habit*' was introduced fairly quickly, as the inspection returns for the 3ᵉ *Cuirassiers* mention that the regiment was still not quite completely clothed in the *habit* of the new model, implying that the distribution of the new *habit* had at least started. By *habit* we actually mean the *surtout*, as Ian Smith shrewdly observes that Preval's orders concerning the adjutant's cane show that the single-breasted *habit* must have been that used in this regiment, as Preval dictates that the cane was to be secured to the third button of the *habit* and NOT the third button on the left *revers* of the *habit*.[5] Yet when we look at the archive sources for his regiment, it is clear the regiment used both the *habit de cuirass* and the *habit à revers*.

To try to understand what actually happened, we have to rely on two sources of evidence:

Clothing the *Cuirassiers* 1801–05   9

Corporal – brigadier – *habit de cuirass* of the 12ᵉ *Cuirassiers*. This type of garment had been adopted in 1803 and was used throughout the course of the Empire period.

1. Textual references. i.e., inspection returns.
2. Eyewitness artists' observations, by this I mean artists like Hoffmann, Zimmerman, Weiland, who drew what they observed, and not sources like Martinet, who used a pro-forma engraving that was coloured to suit the regiment shown.

We now discuss the archive sources as they exist to inform us about the *habit* of the *cuirassiers*:

1ᵉ *Cuirassiers*

Created on 10 October 1801, when the regiment was reviewed on 7 April 1802 it had 452 *habits*, of which 181 had been made since 1800.[6] These were without a shadow of a doubt *habits longues*. When reviewed again 12 July 1803, 411 *habits* were in use, all being made since 1802. These were beyond reasonable doubt *habits de cuirass*.[7] Inspected on 26 July 1805, the regiment had a mix of *habits* and *surtouts* in use. The *habits* were described as 'cut short'.[8]

2ᵉ *Cuirassiers*

Becoming the 2ᵉ *Cavalerie-cuirassiers* on 12 October 1802, the regiment was reviewed on 8 August 1803, when it had 356 brand-new *habits* in use, all issued since the review of 30 January 1802. No doubt these were *habits à revers*.[9] The 1804 inspection report merely states that the clothing was entirely new, and one might conclude that this refers to the new model of *habit* as described in 1803.[10] However, interestingly, and to contradict this, the inspection report of 1805 observes that some of the *habits* worn in this regiment were still of the old model (i.e., long-tailed cavalry *habits*, with *revers*). Perhaps, to make an

10 Napoleon's Heavy Cavalry

instant and lasting impression, the colonel had everyone clothed identically in the new model for the 1804 inspection, but he retained the old *habits*, which were then simply continued in use as required.[11]

3ᵉ *Cuirassiers*

Inspected on 28 August 1803, the general reported that the clothing of the regiment was good but incomplete: '*Tenue bonne, solide, fois exacte, pas trop de recherche.*' In other words, it was well made, sewn in good cloth, but the master tailor needed to look more closely at the *An X* regulations. Overall, the clothing was 'good but still not all of the new model'. This must be the *An X* regulation as the *An XII* did not exist at this date. We do know that the regiment was to receive 625 new *habits*, *surtouts* and *gilets*, 601 stable coats and stable trousers, 625 pairs of *culottes de peau*, *chapeaux*, helmets, *bonnets de police*, waistbelts of the new model with slings, new model *porte-manteaux* and pairs of boots.[12]

In essence, the regiment was to receive its '*cuirassier* start-up kit' by the time of the next inspection. Inspected again on 23 September 1804, the regiment still had no *cuirasses*, and the clothing had 'much greater uniformity'. Of the 625 new *habits* authorised, 417 old *habits* were in use, and 195 had been issued since August 1803, despite the authorisation for 250 being given the previous year. These 195 new *habits* were authorised before the implementation of the decree introducing the *Cuirassiers habit*, so clearly were the old *cavalerie* model, along with the other *habits*. In addition, nine *caissons* of new model sabres were at Compiègne awaiting delivery. Furthermore, 352 *surtouts* were in use in good condition and 136 needed to be disposed of, while 232 had been issued new since 1803, less than the official allowance of 250.[13] By the time of the of the next inspection on 30 July 1805, since 1804, 84 new *habits* had been made, bringing the total up to 488. All of these must have been the old model. Furthermore, 224 new *surtouts* had been made, bringing the total up to 527 in existence, of which 477 were in good condition and 50 needed to be replaced. In total 232 new *surtouts* had been made up to 1804 and a further 224 since 1804, some 456 examples of new-model *surtouts*, which are arguably the *habit de cuirass* of 1803. Of the *habits*, 195 were made new before the September decree, so must be the *cavalerie* model, with a further 84 of these made since 1804.[14]

We know nothing about the dress of the trumpeters from period iconography, other than assuming reversed colours. Archive documents tell us that on 18 August 1802 we find 46fr 80 spent on embroidered silver numbers for the tails of the *sous-officiers habits*, 29fr 16 on *chapeau* pompoms for the *sapeurs*, 213fr 30 on lace for the *housse*, 42fr on *sous-officiers'* lace and importantly 36fr on livery for the trumpeters.[15] We assume this was the 1791 lace, applied in the manner of that regulation on blue *habits*.

4ᵉ *Cuirassiers*

Reviewed on 2 July 1803, the inspector noted that the clothing was bad and was in the process of being changed, 'especially the cut of the *habits*'. At the time of the review 395 *habits* were in use, all bar 98 dating from before 6 October 1801 and thus were *habit longues.*[16] The inspection reports for the regiment of October 1804 refers to the '*habit-veste ou habit court*', i.e., short-cut *habit*. Every single one of the 441 *habits* in use had been made after July 1803. Presumably these were the new *habit de cuirass*, which were worn alongside 582 *surtouts*, virtually all of which were long tailed and pre-dated July 1803.[17] On 5 October 1805, the inspector noted the clothing, despite being well, had been sewn from low-grade materials and liberties had been taken in the cut: presumably the *habits* did not match the regulations in some way or another. A total of 527 *habits* were in use and 109 *surtouts*. Some 210 *habits* had been made since 1804, 175 of which remained unused in stores.[18]

5ᵉ *Cuirassiers*

Inspected on 13 August 1803, General Canclaux noted, rather unsurprisingly, that the regiment's clothing did not conform to the new model of *cuirassiers*, and were to wear their *surtouts*, we assume in lieu of the *cavalerie habits*.[19] Inspected on 23 September 1804, the officer conducting the inspection noted that the *surtouts* and equipment were of the model authorised for *cuirassiers*. Therefore, the regiment beyond reasonable doubt had *habit à revers*, and was dressed in old *cavalerie surtouts*, it seems, with possibly the tails lopped off.[20]

The 1805 inspection report (27 July 1805) states that '*la coupe des habits du 5e n'etait pas conforme a celle du modèle envoye par le Ministre.*' i.e., they were not made according to the example supplied by the Ministry of War. This is most interesting for two reasons: it proves that the 1803 regulation concerning the cut of the new *habit* wasn't always strictly observed, and it also confirms that this regiment had been sent an actual example of the new 1803 *habit*, to use as a model to copy. Our conclusion is that for the practical reasons of wearing a *cuirass* on horseback, the regiment used the *cavalerie habit* with the tails cropped off, and that the new short *habits* had *revers*, based on the amount of red cloth listed as having been used since the last inspection in 1804. Up to the 1803 inspection, 54m 23 of scarlet broadcloth had been used to make 59 *habits* and 93 *surtouts*, up to 1805 inspection a mere 2m 25 had been used in the production of thirteen *habits* and 5 *surtouts* – a tiny amount in comparison to the 406m 72 of scarlet broadcloth. Yet we also note that on 26 July 1805, the day before the inspection, 463 brand-new *habits de cuirass* had been delivered but were not distributed. We also note that the vast majority of the 544 *surtouts*, 426, needed repair and just two new *surtouts* had been made.[21] A second report of 27 July notes that the cut of the *habits* did not conform to the model, the stable trousers and stable coats were all in bad condition and the *culottes de peau* were in need of repair or total replacement.[22]

6ᵉ *Cuirassiers*

Inspected on 10 May 1803, the regiment was dressed as *cavalerie* in long-tailed *habits* and *chapeaux*.[23] When inspected on 11 October 1805, the regiment was still wearing old

12   Napoleon's Heavy Cavalry

habits but cut short.[24] By the time of the 1807 inspection 1,087 *habits* had been made and issued and just 164 *surtouts*.[25]

7ᵉ *Cuirassiers*

Reviewed on 1 October 1804, the regiment was wearing '*habits-vestes*' but they had been made of low-grade materials. The *surtouts* all needed replacing. Every one of the 4,345 *habits-vestes* had been issued after 23 September 1802.[26] When inspected on 19 October 1805, the regiment was dressed entirely in new *habits-vestes* and some of the *cuirasses* were of poor construction.[27] Arguably these were *habits de cuirass*.

8ᵉ *Cuirassiers*

The inspection report of October 1803 states that this regiment was still awaiting an example of the new model of *habit* before making its own.[28] That is quite remarkable as the regiment had been waiting for such an item for two years! This item it seems never arrived as when inspected 12 October 1805 we note that 318 *habits* were in use, all bar 65 dating from before 1803, and were in use alongside 497 *surtouts*: clearly for the 640 men under arms, a mix-and-match approach of clothing was used.[29] We assume these were old *cavalerie* items with the tails cropped down. Following the review of 12 October 1805, 919 *habits* and 603 *surtouts* were made.[30] The former were, we assume, *habits de cuirass*.[31]

9ᵉ *Cuirassiers*

Inspected on 17 June 1803, in use were 534 *habits* and 504 *surtouts*, the bulk of which were made before 9 January 1802.[32] At the time of the inspection of 21 October 1804, the inspector reports that the clothing did not conform to regulations. In use were 541 *habits courtes*, alongside 541 *habits longues* and 457 *surtouts* that were to be phased out from use. When reviewed on 5 August 1805, the inspector noted that 548 *habits courtes* were in use, alongside 538 *habits longues* and 27 *surtouts*. The *habits courtes* are no doubt *habits de cuirass*. The trumpeters, it seems, had *surtouts*, so too adjutants. Presumably the old *cavalerie habits* were worn for dismounted duties, and by 1805 were four years old, being made during 1801.[33]

10ᵉ *Cuirassiers*

Inspected on 28 July 1805, the 619 men under arms were wearing 451 *habits-vestes* and 651 *surtouts*. Clearly some men had two *surtouts*, and not every man had a *habit-veste*. Interestingly, only 584 helmets were in use and 546 *cuirasses*. Men must have been wearing *surtouts* under the *cuirass*, and some clearly had helmets but no armour. Of interest, 610 *chapeaux* were in service. The regiment must have presented a far from uniform look.[34]

11ᵉ *Cuirassiers*

Inspected on 15 October 1803, 446 *habits* were in use, 74 being made before January 1802. The inspector noted 494 *surtouts* in use that were in 'passable' condition, the *habits* being in 'good condition'.[35] When reviewed on 26 September 1804, 450 new *habits* had been made since 1803. These are likely to be the *habits de cuirass*. This is, however, our assessment and not fact.[36] Reviewed again on 20 July 1805, the 588 men under arms were wearing 454 *habits*, all bar 1 having existed since the previous review, and 493 *surtouts*, 490 of which were brand new. Clearly, clothing was a mix and match affair![37]

12ᵉ *Cuirassiers*

The 16 October 1804 inspection report states that this regiment '*portait en grande partie un habit à revers, a pans raccourcis*', by which I assume that the regiment had simply modernised its old cavalry *habits* by shortening and re-cutting the tails. However, elsewhere the inspector noted 'the clothing entirely conformed to the models and instructions sent by his excellency the Ministry of War'. We noted 486 *habits* had been made since the 1803 review, bringing the total in use up to 498, and 589 *surtouts* were in use by the 594 men under arms. One oddity shown up in this inspection was that the regiment used 18m of chestnut brown broadcloth and 21m 10 of grey broadcloth in the production of clothing. Regimental archives note the presence of 231 pairs of gaiters: were they made from grey broadcloth? Possibly. The chestnut brown may have been destined for legwear.[38]

Moving forward to the time of the next review, the regiment still had *habits à revers* and *surtouts* on 8 August 1805 as 512 *habits* existed, 54 being made since the previous review, and 612 *surtouts*, 105 of which were new. The inspector commented the regiments dress entirely conformed to regulation, so proof positive that the short-tailed *habit à revers* and *surtout* were considered regulation at this date.[39]

Comment

With the conversion of *cuirassiers* in 1803 and formation of the Lancers, a system of sealed patterns was adopted. Each regiment received from the War Ministry an example of each item of uniform for the master tailors of the regiment to copy. This was an integral part of the Bardin regulation. Rather than hoping that the master workmen would interpret the text correctly, between February and September 1812 the War Ministry produced hundreds of 'sealed patterns' of every item of uniform and equipment, which were then distributed to every regiment of the army. In this way there could be no mistakes in how an item looked.

This was a pragmatic and common-sense approach to regulating the dress of the army. For us, however, with no access to the sealed patterns, we are left wondering what elements of Bardin were altered or deleted as part of the sealed pattern process. When we consult regimental inspections in 1814 and 1815, we find sealed patterns, literally

14 Napoleon's Heavy Cavalry

items '*de modelle*' in regimental stores. The use of sealed patterns was a radical departure in how the French army had regulated its clothing. Colonels no longer had freedom of expression in how the written word was interpreted. Here was a centralised system, originating from the War Ministry. Henceforth any ambiguities about how an item of clothing or equipment was to look no longer existed – at the time of an inspection, the sealed pattern would be taken from the stores, against which all items in use and stores would be compared. Any item showing variations from the sealed pattern would be amended or scrapped, at least in theory.

This was a radical departure in quality control of uniforms and equipment. Yet it is incredible that despite it being such an important change to the way in which quality and uniformity of clothing was detailed, to date no author has ever commented upon the change! Perhaps this is because the system has been deduced by back engineering the process starting at regimental level by reading the inspection returns, which to date have never been used to assess the appearance of the army of 1799–1815, or indeed other periods, as the study has relied for too long on museum objects and a study of 'pretty pictures' and not the written word. However, once one has read comments about the issuing of model items to copy, and found model items in the depots, one can quickly create a system of official checks and balances based upon the British Army sealed pattern system. We cannot, however, state with certainty if colonels chose to follow the sealed patterns, of course. The system became an integral part of Bardin. At the end of the empire, for example, the 1^e *Cuirassiers'* depot had a sealed pattern trumpeters' *habit*.[40] The 4^e *cuirassiers* in 1815 records a *habit de veterinarian* and *chapeau de modelle*, one *gilet de modelle, capotes de modelle, habit de modelle* as well as *banderole de giberne* and waist belts all '*de modelle*'.[41]

Yet this was only part of the story. Colonels may have chosen not to follow the sealed pattern, and certainly when it came to rapid changes in regulation, such as the *manteaux*, many regiments having already produced hundreds of the item, only to find they were now non regulation, kept the old model items in use in the interests of cost-effectiveness and practicality.

Judging by the 1805 inspections, it seems that the 5e, 6e, 8e and 12e used the old *cavalerie habits*, with the tails cropped down and mixed and matched with newly made *habits à revers* with short tails. The 9e still had long-tailed *cavalerie habits*, which they certainly still had by the middle years of the empire, while the 7e seem to have had them as we shall see and the 3e used the *habit à revers* side by side with the *surtout*. Thus, the archive paperwork is overwhelming that the *habit de cuirass* was in use by more than half of all regiments by the time the army marched to Austerlitz, and that the *habit à revers* existed beyond reasonable doubt in just four regiments, crucially before the July 1806 decree! Therefore, no decree was needed to introduce this garment into use. The September 1803 decree, as we said before, was ambiguous, and the term *habit* refers to both the *habit de cuirass* and the *habit à revers*. Most regiments took a pragmatic approach and simply lopped the tails of *habits* and *surtouts*. For only the 1e *Cuirassiers* do we have solid proof that they adopted the *habit de cuirass* thanks to *Chef de Brigade* Margaron's correspondence with General Berthier.

Stable Coats and Waistcoats

What of the stable coats (*gilets d'ecurie*) mentioned in July 1803? Under the 1791 regulations, they were cut from tricot, and were double breasted, being closed with two rows of ten small regimental buttons, were lined in white *cadis* (serge) and had a stand and fall collar.[42] The stable coat of the *grenadiers à cheval* in 1799 matched this description[43] – alas we do not know what form the stable coat took at this period, 1803, as by January 1808 it was single breasted.[44] The 1806 and 1809 pattern stable coat was double breasted.[45]

A colonel who had issued brand new *surtouts* would not cut them up to make them into stable coats – thus the *surtout* would have remained in use, alongside the *habit de cuirass* and the *habit à revers*! Certainly, regiments did have stable coats, but as to their appearance we cannot say. Some were no doubt made from cut up *surtouts*.

Under the *habit de cuirass*, *habit à revers* or *surtout* a *gilet* was worn. Made from white broadcloth, it was lined in serge. It had a low collar, and the front was closed by twelve small uniform buttons. A soldier was issued one of these garments a year, and must have become horribly stained with sweat.

Given the ambiguity of the exact details of what was worn, the truth of the matter seems to be that the old-fashioned *habits* were used side by side with the *habit de cuirass*, *surtouts* and stable coats. No one regiment was ever uniformly dressed in the *habit de cuirass* until 1814.

Cuirassiers were issued *culottes de peau* for parade dress, and stable trousers (*pantalons de treillis* or *pantalons d'ecurie*: same item with difference names) for dismounted duties and these could be worn over the *culottes*. The knee of the *culottes* was protected with a knee guard called a *manchette du botte*. For campaign use, the *culottes* became easily waterlogged, and the stiches rotted. Many regiments unofficially adopted ankle-length *pantalons* made from broadcloth reinforced on the inner leg with leather, as we shall see.

Facing Colours

Concerning the dress of the *cuirassiers*, the regulation of 24 September 1803 did not affect the distinguishing colours of the cavalry regiments now that they were *cuirassiers*; they remained the same as when laid down in the regulation of 1791; scarlet for regiments 1 to 6 and yellow (*jonquil*) for regiments 7 to 12.

However, on 1 October 1803, an amendment to this authorised the 1ᵉ to 4ᵉ to have scarlet facings, 7ᵉ to 9ᵉ yellow, and 10ᵉ to 12ᵉ rose.[46] When questioned about this change by the colonel of the 10ᵉ, the Minister for War in a letter dated 20 December 1803, stated that regimental facing colours were to remain as they were then, i.e., scarlet 1ᵉ to 6ᵉ, yellow 7ᵉ to 12ᵉ.[47]

Epaulettes

Formed under the decree of 10 October 1801, Article 13 of the Decree stipulates:

> The first company of the first squadron of each cavalry regiment, dragoons, chasseurs and hussars, will take the name of Elite Company. This company will be formed of men chosen in all Corps, conforming to the instructions which will be given by the Minister of War.[48]

The men were allowed bearskins and epaulettes as the equivalent of grenadiers in the infantry. To mark out the status of grenadiers, under the 1786 regulations, grenadiers were issued with red broadcloth shoulder straps piped white, the same shape and form as the straps for fusiliers. Red-fringed epaulettes were authorised 1 April 1791.[49] The regulations allowed for the scarlet broadcloth to make the shoulder boards and wool fringing in the same colour.[50]

Général d'Hautpoul signed the document for the *procès-verbal d'organisation* for the 8e *Cuirassiers* on *22 Floréal An X* (12 May 1802), which included the provision of an elite company.[51] On 15 May, Colonel Merlin, writing to the Minister of War, stated that the elite company was in the process of formation, and requested that it be distinguished by white *crinières* for the helmets.[52] Sometime later, on 22 June 1802, in response to Merlin's letter, the Minister of War pointed out that the *cuirassiers* were members of the elite corps and as such did not have to have the aforementioned distinguishing marks, and that the proposed marks were not authorised.[53]

In response to this edict, the elite companies of the 1e and 8e *cuirassiers* were abolished in July 1802, while those of the 2e, 3e, 4e *Cuirassiers* and 25e *Cavalerie* were abolished at the end of 1802. However, the elite companies remained in the 5e, 6e and 7e *Cuirassiers*, as well as the 19e and 23e *Cavalerie*, at the start of 1803 and last but not least the 9e *Cuirassiers* and 18e *Cavalerie* in the third quarter of 1803.[54]

Given the confusion about elite status upon conversion to *cuirassiers*, it is not surprising that we find in the archives a letter from the 9e *Cuirassiers Conseil d'Administration*, dated 8 December 1803, to the Minister of War. In the letter, the colonel demanded to know whether they should be able to wear plumes, and if so, in what colour, ditto the same question for epaulettes, and whether or not their symbol on *habits* and *housses* should be the grenade. Finally, if the answer is yes to all these questions, they demand funds to help pay for such items. The Minister for War replied in a letter dated 20 December 1803, and stated that as *cuirassiers* were elite every man was allowed scarlet-fringed epaulettes, grenade devices to the turnbacks and red plumes by all regiments, and it is probable that by 1805, all regiments had adopted these items.[55]

Unfortunately, not a single pair of epaulettes is listed in the inspection returns up to 1814 – we assume they were counted with the *habits*.

As well as epaulettes, some elite companies adopted bearskins. On 14 June 1803 the elite company of the 10e were wearing sixty bearskins.[56] The 11e had fifty-nine bearskins in use in October 1803.[57] On 4 June 1803 the 12e regiment had fifty-nine bearskins in service, but by October 1804 just twelve bearskins were in use with the trumpeters.[58]

Associated with the elite company were *sapeurs*. In July 1802, a War Ministry circular advised the regiments of mounted troops that it was the intention of the government to provide the elite companies, as well as with their normal armament, the following tools: the *sous-officiers* with bill-hooks, one third of the men with axes, a third with spades and a third with pick-axes. The corps were authorised to pass contracts for their purchase and the tools were actually distributed in some companies.[59] In August 1802 the 3e *cavalerie* bought *chapeaux* pompoms for the *sapeurs* and spent 51fr 20 repairing the bearskins of the *sapeurs* and 14fr 50 repairing the *sapeurs* tools.[60] How long the 3e had *sapeurs* is not known: conceivably they disappeared on conversion to *cuirassiers*.

Plumes

Since 1791, cavalry regiments had had black plumes with the top in the regiment's facing colour. On the march and on campaign a *houpette* was worn in the *chapeau* – it was cone-shaped, 3 pouces tall and 2 pouces in diameter. No colour was specified.[61] Under the 1801 regulation, plumes were made from cock feather mounted on whale bone, the portion covered in feather to be 21 pouces (roughly 28cm) with a shaft approximately 10cm long with no feathering to be fitted into the plume socket of the head gear. The allowance for plumes was 1fr 25. Plumes were not furnished by the government as part of the clothing *masse*, and came from regimental funds.[62] Unfortunately, plumes don't appear until the 1807 inspections.

Chapter 3

Armour and Helmets 1801–05

We can't write about the *cuirassiers* and not mention armour! There is no such thing as 1812 types or pattern *cuirass*. What exists, based on *cuirasses* recovered from battlefields, are early and late or first and second types. The first type has a central, vertical ridge along the breastplate, with a notably pointed bottom edge, and broad shoulders. Every known *cuirass* to have been recovered from the field of Essling and Wagram are of this type. Nearly every *cuirass* recovered from Waterloo has a rounded bottom edge, a 'pot belly' front plate and narrow shoulders. When this type came into use, we cannot say, but likely at the same time that the *carabiniers* took up armour. As ever, the new type would not be in full use until 1813 or 1814. Certainly, the later type required less steel than the earlier type and were quicker to make. The narrower shoulders both increased mobility of the arms and also required less steel: the first type of *cuirass* is very restrictive in the range of movement one has. Having worn and ridden in both the first and second types, the second allows greater range of movement in the arm, and also in the lower body. As with the so-called 1811-type helmet, no firm dating exists for *cuirasses*, and we can only make judgements based on archaeologically recovered items.

A *cuirass* was a hugely expensive item. The coke for the blacksmith's forge cost 1fr 50, the iron cost 13fr 30, the smith's time was charged at 3fr 90, the sixty-eight rivets cost 2fr 10, the *epaulières* (shoulder straps) less the broadcloth facing that the state supplied cost 4fr 40, slightly more than the finishing and polish of the front and back plate, which cost 4fr. In total a *cuirass* cost 44fr 22. *Carabinier* armour cost 63fr and had a major design issue: the copper sheeting was sweated onto the iron. To do so each plate was put in a bath of sulphuric acid, dried and then tinned and the sheet of copper pressed into the solder. The iron and copper reacted when exposed to damp, and the copper sheeting would become loose and fall off over time.

The *fraise* required 4m 56 of linen tape, the same amount of 10mm wide worsted *cul-de-dé* lace, and 2fr 25 of linen thonging to attach each *fraise* to the *cuirass*. *Cuirasses* were delivered in batches of 500, complete with *fraise* and *matelassure* (liner). The first design of *cuirass* was bullet proof, and tests were carried out on 11 June 1807 to assess this: a cavalry pistol at 18m had no effect, and a musket ball had no effect at 100m. In 1811, when a new design of *cuirass* was introduced, tests showed a musket ball at 100m would pass through the front plate and lodge against the back plate.[1]

The *cuirass* comprised a number of components. Obviously the front and back plates; they were connected by leather-backed copper scale *epaulières*. The plates were made from steel roughly 2.8mm thick and each plate weighed approximately 7.5kg. The front and back plates were buckled together by a waistbelt that was rivetted to the back plate and fasted at the centre front of the front plate. Inside the *cuirass* was the *matelassure*. Made from *treillis* (herringbone-weave hemp canvas – the same material was used to line the *housse*, *porte-manteaux* and also to make stable trousers). It was held in place by different methods:

1. The most common mode of attachment was to rivet the liner to the front or back plate. The decorative rivets around the armour literally held in the liner.
2. A linen ribbon was rivetted to the armour and the liner sewn to the ribbon.
3. A metal wire was wound around the rivets and the liner sewn to the wire.

In all three modes of attachment, the liner could not come out of the *cuirass*. One can only imagine how disgusting these became, and how easily they trapped moisture, rusting the inner face of the armour and one suspects going mouldy. The lining was interlined with horse hair, and the liner to the front plate held a pocket in which the soldier kept his *livret* (pay) book.

Trooper's *cuirass* complete with the padded liner of the second model. (*Photograph and collection of Bertrand Malvaux*)

20 Napoleon's Heavy Cavalry

Helmet and *cuirass* of the 1e *Cuirassiers* of the second model. (*Photograph and collection of Bertrand Malvaux*)

Officer of the 8e regiment of *Cavalerie* as they appeared in 1786. They had worn armour since the late seventeenth century.

Trooper of the 8e regiment of *Cavalerie* – we ignored the designation 7, this is an artist's error.

Attached around the arm openings of the *cuirass* was the *fraise* or *garnitures de cuirass*. The *fraise*, based on extant items, was made from scarlet broadcloth. It measured 60mm wide and 2m 60 long. The leading edge was bound over with white *cul-de-dé* lace. The lace is 10mm, and sewn to show a narrow 5mm strip. The trailing edge is sewn to the *matelassure*. Only 30mm of the *fraise* was to be visible outside the *cuirass* judging by ware marks.[2] The 1817 artillery manual states the *fraise* was to be 3 pouces (74mm) wide and 2 aune long (1 aune = 119cm), and that 2 aunes of broadcloth was needed to make fourteen pairs of *fraise*. No width is specified for the lace.[3]

The first issue of *cuirass* had a markedly 'pigeon-style' chest with a central ridge and pointed bottom edge to the front plate. The central ridge became rounded out with the so-called 1807 issue and the bottom edge became curved. No formal decrees exist for the *cuirass* until after the epoch.

Helmets

The helmet was a steel version of the dragoon helmet. The *turban* was made from leather and covered in bearskin – did this come from the elite companies' bearskin caps we wonder? – and the *bombe* (skull cap) was made from steel with a red brass *cimier* (crest) ornamented with a black horse hair *crinière* (main) and *houpette* (tuft). It was held in place by copper chinscales. The leather peak at the front could have brass binding to keep it in shape. The disadvantage of this model was the fact the *cimier* literally formed a gutter, which in wet weather allowed water to penetrate and not only wet the soldier's head, but caused rust to set in on the iron bolts and could cause the bindings that held the *crinière* in place to rot. Water could also flow under the breastplate, and soak the entire back. To overcome this defect, the soldiers plaited the *crinière* along the top of the *cimier*. In 1807 a new model was developed with a top plate to the *cimier* that prevented water running into its body. The sides of the *cimier* received elaborate stamped decoration, which made it more robust.

Trooper of the 1ᵉ *Cuirassiers* c.1805 by Hoffmann. The tails of the *habit* are cut very wide, and the way the pockets touch almost the bottom of the tails implies this is an older style of garment, with the tails cropped down.

The 8^e *Cavalerie* had been wearing helmets from 1801 and armour since the 1790s.

Helmets were not regulated officially until the Bardin regulation. They were produced according to regimental designs by the regiment by craftsmen who were employed by the regiment. The *cuirass* was government issued, like the weapons, but the helmet was not regulated and colonels were free to design a helmet however they felt best. At the end of the 1805–07 campaign, General Espagne reported to the War Ministry his observations about *cuirassier* helmets then in use: his opening remark was that the *cuirassier* helmets were useless as an item of equipment. He added that they were too heavy and too expensive. He commented furthermore that water ingress rotted the stiches that held the turban on, and the *cimier* was easily detached from the *bombe* with one or two sword blows, as the copper screws were insufficient to attach the *cimier*. Worse, he noted that without a top plate to the *cimier*, water ingress into the helmet resulted in the trooper getting a wet head, the *crinières* 'disintegrated' and the *bombe* rusted: for this reason, many helmets were only fit for scrap at the end of the campaigns, he noted. He added that the new helmet form should be designed to cover the soldier's neck properly, and this would at the same time get rid of the need to have both the *crinière* and the turban, thereby protecting the soldier's head much more effectively. Furthermore, he added that the men found the *crinière* to be tiring (my guess is that it presumably slowed down their refraction times in being able to turn their heads quickly during a melee, and on the march the *crinière* becomes a burden, particularly when wet). Overall, he concludes, the troopers would prefer to have something rather more solid and practical/useful. He recommended the adoption of 'an antique helmet made totally from iron in the minerva form'.[4] Such recommendations never came to fruition: we assume he was talking about a helmet akin to that of the *carabiniers*. It is interesting that the helmet from 1801 was always considered a liability!

Colonel of the 1^e *Cuirassiers* as he appeared in 1805.

Clearly the helmet had fundamental design issues from 'day one', and these flaws were not just restricted to the '1811' helmet, which is often regarded as 'useless' largely thanks to the writing of Lucien Rousselot.

Armour and Helmets 1801–05   23

The artist Nicholas Hoffmann shows us the 1e *Cuirassiers* (possibly the 3e) in review order in 1805. Firstly we see the junior officers of the regiment assembled behind the colonel. Secondly, we see the rear of a senior officer, and lastly, we see the rank and file drawn up in review order. Of note, the trumpeters are wearing *habits à revers* in reversed colours, no doubt worn at Austerlitz.

The 1811 design is notable that the *cimier* is devoid of its palm-leaf ornaments and of internal ribs that gave it a degree of solidity, and it no longer had anything more than the regimental number on the front plate. The peak lost its copper edging. Very few complete examples of this helmet exist. An example from the 7e regiment is kept at the Clermont-Ferrand Museum, while another can be found in the collection of the Musée de l'Empéri. Helmets of this type have been recovered from grave sites and battlefields in Russia, but this only means that this type were in use at that point. It is perfectly possible that these simplified helmets were made in 1809 after Essling and Wagram as locally produced replacement items: as no regulation for *cuirassier* helmets existed and no archive documents mention a new type of helmet, we can only demonstrate some of these types were used in Russia, and the simplified *cimier* leads directly to the Bardin

24 Napoleon's Heavy Cavalry

type, placing it in a chronology of sorts of Essling to Borodino, not necessarily meaning an 1811 date of adoption.

The '1811' and Bardin helmet comes in for heavy critique by modern-day writers, particularly concerning the *cimier*.

The thick casting of the front plate made getting a good soldered joint to the flanks difficult because of the heat exchange difference between the casting and stamped parts: on both the so-called '1811' and Bardin helmets the front plate was stamped, the edges were turned back, and being made from the same grade copper plate made soldering far easier. Under Bardin a spacing bar and rivet held the front plate on, making a far more robust design. Yet, at the end of 1814, a report by General Saint-German informs us that this headgear 'which had been good in principle had become so faulty that all haste should be made to change almost all the helmets presently in service', adding 'the absence of metal edging allowed the peak to lose its shape under the influence of rain and sun, the crest tuft was thin and the horsehair *crinière* quickly deteriorated'.[5] The complaints made in 1807 and at the end of 1814 are almost identical, yet Rousselot takes the 1814 complaint out of context. One recommendation made in 1814 was to fit a top plate to the helmet and a neck guard universally across all regiments rather than modifications carried out at regimental level, notably by the 3ᵉ *cuirassiers*.[6] Examination of helmets from 1814–15 reveals nearly all have non-regulation top plates fitted to the *cimier* to prevent water ingress! Of interest some pre-1811 examples do not have brass edging to the peak either, therefore a lot of the comments made about poor design are taken out of context. *Cuirassier* expert Ian Smith comments:

> The quality of the plain 1811 *cimiers* was just as good as the 1804 types *cimiers* with stamped gaudrons, etc.
>
> I can see no reason why this element of the helmet should have caused any complaints except that it was not a good looker.
>
> Throughout the period, all troopers' helmets had 4 spacers to keep the sides parallel, and to provide a measure of protection from sword blows. The spacers were actually solid iron bars, of 5 to 6mm in diameter.
>
> Officers' *cimiers* were invariably soldered instead.
>
> The 1811 visieres definitely lacked the brass jonc, which was a major issue for blows aimed in this direction. Most 1811 *cimiers* didn't have a brass top cover, so water would have poured onto the horsehair roots and into the helmet too. Earlier patterns lacked the top cover plate also, and they are not seen on officers' helmets or troopers' examples till very late on in the Empire, probably from 1813 onwards. By 1815, some troopers' helmets and most officers' examples had developed neck guards, inspired by those on the *carabiniers'* helmets.
>
> In form and profile, the '1811' helmets are very boxy, sitting on top of the head without any attempt to shape the turban over and around the ears of the wearer.
>
> Having examined two personally (that of the 7ᵉ at Emperi, and the one of the 4ᵉ at Les Invalides), I can see no reason why they should have been so heavily criticised for falling apart.[7]

I agree with his comments. There we have it folks, the '1811' and Bardin helmet was no better or no worse than earlier designs! The top plate was often added unofficially, and the 1811 type was as robust as earlier models. We suppose fault with the helmets lay not with the design, but in their manufacture. We know these helmets were used in the Russian campaign as helmet parts of this design for the 3ᵉ and 14ᵉ have been recovered from the site of the Battle of the Berezina: this suggests that when the 14ᵉ transferred from Dutch service, it adopted this design of helmet in French service, neatly dating this helmet's design to 1810, and its service life to 1812 and perhaps not later.

Getting Armour into Service

The process of transforming *cavalerie* regiments into armoured cavalry was long and slow. Production of armour and helmets took over eighteen months:

1ᵉ *Cuirassiers*

Inspected on 28 March 1802, the 1ᵉ *Cuirassiers* had not a single helmet or *cuirass*. The regiment received from the arsenal of Paris by the end of November 1802, 406 *cuirasses* and helmets, and a further 219 examples of each between December 1802 and February 1803. When inspected on 12 July 1803 the regiment had 625 *cuirasses* and helmets.[8]

2ᵉ *Cuirassiers*

Becoming the 2ᵉ *Cavalerie-cuirassiers* on 12 October 1802, the regiment was reviewed on 8 August 1803, when it had 300 helmets.[9] When reviewed on 7 October 1804, 552 helmets were in use and no armour.[10] Inspected on 8 August 1805, 588 helmets were in service and there were 625 *cuirasses* for 656 men under arms.[11]

3ᵉ *Cuirassiers*

Inspected on 12 January 1803, the regiment had 300 helmets – half the regiment had *chapeaux* and half had helmets. When inspected on 23 September 1804, the regiment still had no *cuirasses*, and 87 *chapeaux* were in use alongside 418 helmets. Given the 3ᵉ *Cuirassiers* still had no armour, we assume they wore the old *habit* for full dress, the *surtout* for undress, with the helmet for parade, and the *chapeau* for other duties? Men in the depot still had the old-pattern waistbelt and insufficient existed of the new type to give every man an example beyond the war squadrons.[12]

By the time of the of the next inspection on 30 July 1805 the regiment had 418 new helmets in use, and some 496 new-model waistbelts and *cuirasses*. It is interesting to note that the mobilised men in the war squadrons mustered 485 rank and file, of which 433 were mounted. Clearly some men still had *chapeaux* by this date.[13]

4ᵉ *Cuirassiers*

On 2 July 1803, the 4ᵉ *Cuirassiers* had no helmets and *cuirasses* in use.[14] When inspected some eighteen months later on 18 October 1804, the regiment had 480 helmets and *cuirasses* in use.[15]

5ᵉ *Cuirassiers*

Inspected in September 1804, the regiment had received 564 helmets and no *cuirasses*.[16] The next inspection return of 24 January 1805 reveals the regiment had 625 *cuirasses* and helmets, so clearly the regiment had had no armour for some time.[17]

6ᵉ *Cuirassiers*

General de Bourmont, whose actions in 1815 made him famous for being a traitor, inspected the regiment on 10 May 1803, when the regiment had no *cuirasses* or helmets. On 3 August 1803 when inspected by the First Consul, the regiment still had no armour and were dressed as *cavalerie*. On the next inspection of 15 October 1804, the regiment had 625 *cuirasses* and 491 helmets in service.[18] Inspected on 11 October 1805, the regiment had 974 *cuirasses*, some 357 coming from the arsenal at Plaisance.[19]

7ᵉ *Cuirassiers*

Inspected on 1 September 1803 the regiment had 598 *cuirasses* and helmets, and by 28 September a further 27 helmets and *cuirasses*, making a total of 625 sets in use.[20]

8ᵉ *Cuirassiers*

The first regiment to wear the *cuirass*, in May 1802 had 500 helmets and *cuirasses* in use. On 6 June 1803 the regiment had 500 *cuirasess* and 418 helmets.[21] The inspection return of 4 October 1804 reveals the regiment had in the depot 259 old *cuirasses* in bad condition, 65 to be replaced that had been 'used since the formation of the regiment in 1666' with a further 418 in use.[22] Clearly the men were wearing new helmets and armour dating from the middle decades of the eighteenth century. When inspected on 12 October 1805, 625 *cuirasses* existed for the 640 men under arms: clearly trumpeters were not armoured. We also note 266 *cuirasses* had been delivered 6 October 1804 and a further 259 had arrived on 1 January 1805.[23] Seemingly these *cuirasses* replaced the venerable eighteenth-century items. It is probably these were refurbished and became the so-called 1804 pattern for officers. On examining these *cuirasses*, they have a very distinctive and archaic look, straight from the English Civil War.

9ᵉ *Cuirassiers*

The regiment received 625 *cuirasses* and helmets on 28 May 1804. Of these, 85 sets were defective and returned to the arsenal for repairs and were replaced on 6 March 1805.[24]

10ᵉ *Cuirassiers*

When inspected on 28 July 1805, 584 helmets were in use and 546 *cuirasses*. Of interest, 610 *chapeaux* were in service. The regiment must have presented a far from uniform look, with some men in helmets and no armour. Notable was the presence of 552 plumes for the helmets.[25]

11ᵉ *Cuirassiers*

The regiment received 625 *cuirasses* and helmets on 21 March 1804.[26] However, when reviewed on 20 July 1805, the 588 men under arms wore 516 helmets and 588 *cuirasses*, which included the trumpeters and corporal-trumpeter. The men lacking helmets were in *chapeaux*, of which 610 existed![27]

12ᵉ *Cuirassiers*

The 16 October 1804 inspection report states the trumpeters were wearing 14 bearskins and 531 helmets were in service.[28] The regiment received 625 *cuirasses* on 12 November 1804.[29]

Getting armour and helmets made was a slow process. What we are not seeing is the tremendous learning curve the officers and men must have been on to learn to move in the armour, to use their sabre and to learn to ride. From practical experience as a rider for over thirty years riding for film and TV, compared to a fifteenth-century suit of armour, the weight of the *cuirass* is a major impact on the balance of the rider and how you move in the saddle. It is akin to a suit of mail for weight on the shoulders. The slightest loss of balance, and off you flop. When trotting or cantering, the *cuirass* bangs up and down on the shoulders, leaving deep bruising, and the *giberne* belt often departs company as it has nothing to hold it in place at the shoulder. The lack of freedom of movement when using a sabre is remarkable, and makes you very vulnerable under the arm. I suspect many troopers learned how to ride in the *cuirass* the hard way with lots of knocks, bruises and broken bones. The lack of manoeuvrability of the arms in the first type explains why with the second type, the shoulders of the *cuirass* are much narrower, and the arm cut-out is deeper – making you more vulnerable to under-arm wounds, but you can actually cross your arms and use your sabre better. Either way, in a melee, the *cuirassier* was at a disadvantage: the *cuirass* is uncomfortable and turning around in the saddle to attack an opponent to the rear or side is difficult or impossible, indeed a lot of the sabre manual is not possible with any degree of dexterity. Yes, a *cuirass* protects the rider from sword cuts, and has a psychological impact on attacker and defender, but how useful it was is open to debate. I doubt its cost outweighed the inconvenience to horse and man, and its impact on the performance on the trooper.

Chapter 4
Cuirassier Horse Equipment 1801–05

Despite the advice of the colonel of the 1ᵉ *Cavalerie*, since October 1801, *cuirassiers* had replaced the practical sheepskin *schabraque* with cloth *chaperons*. Yet, the changeover period took time. A new rectangular cloth *housse* and sheepskin *schabraque* made in 1800 had a lifespan of eight years, thus it is no surprise that some regiments used a mix of pre- and post-1801 items. *Schabraques* were still so common in 1807 that on 17 February Marshal Berthier issued a circular stating that no more new sheepskin *schabraques* were to be paid for, and that regiments were to replace the *schabraques* as soon as possible with cloth *chaperons*.[1] We wonder how many *schabraques* made brand new in 1806 lingered on? The 1807 circular should have clarified the situation, yet on 5 December 1811 a War Ministry circular ordered Inspectors of Review, when inspecting *Cuirassier* regiments, to tolerate *schabraques*.[2] Clearly many regiments had clung on to *schabraques*, which were officially part of the 1812 regulation.

Colonel of the 3ᵉ *Cuirassiers* in 1805. Of note is the leopard skin *schabraque*.

An idea of the mix-and-match approach to horse equipment comes from inspection returns:

1ᵉ *Cuirassiers*

In January 1808 the 1ᵉ *Cuirassiers* had 776 sheepskin half-*schabraques*, of which 533 had been delivered since July 1805 along with 558 surcingles. The depot had held sixteen of these in 1805. So clearly the regiment was using the *schabraque* and not regulation *chaperons*. In addition, 774 *housses* were in use.[3]

2ᵉ *Cuirassiers*

In 1805 the regiment had not a single pair of *chaperons*, it possessed in the depot 54 new *housses* and 11 half-*schabraques*. By 23 December 1807, some 401 *housses* had been made along with 403 half-*schabraques*.[4]

3ᵉ *Cuirassiers*

Inspected 23 September 1804, the regiment had no *chaperons* in use and the depot between 1803 and 1804 had issued 104 *schabraques*. Some 389 *housses* were in use along with 398 *schabraques*.[5] On 30 July 1805, 430 *housses* were in use along with 431 *schabraques*.[6]

5ᵉ *Cuirassiers*

Inspected on 13 August 1803, the regiment possessed 307 *housses* and 308 pairs of *chaperons*.[7] By 23 September 1804 the depot held 4 pairs of *chaperons*, 39 *schabraques* and not a single *housse*. In use were 389 *housses* needing repairs and 462 *schabraques*.[8] Clearly in the intervening year, *chaperons* had been discontinued in favour of the sheepskin *schabraque*.

6ᵉ *Cuirassiers*

Inspected on 11 October 1805, the regiment had 32 *schabraques* brand-new unissued in the depot, and not a single pair of *chaperons* in use or in the depot.[9] By the time of the 1807 inspection 789 *schabraques* had been made and issued.[10]

7ᵉ *Cuirassiers*

On 31 December 1807 the regiment had 740 *housses* in service, 220 sets of *chaperons* and 321 sheepskin *schabraques*, virtually all of which were brand new and received after 10 October 1805.[11]

8ᵉ *Cuirassiers*

Since the October 1805 inspection, the depot had taken in 200 new sheepskin half-*schabraques*, 150 new pairs of *chaperons* and 792 *housses*. Furthermore, 663 sheepskin half-*schabraques* were in use, 780 *housses* and 120 pairs of *chaperons*, all of which were new.[12]

9ᵉ *Cuirassiers*

In 1805 the regiment had brand new in the depot 129 *housses*, 3 *porte-manteaux* and 78 new half-*schabraques*. Between July 1805 and December 1807, the depot had made 500 *housses*, 186 pairs of *chaperons* and 515 half-*schabraques*. In use, the regiment had 703 *housses*, 182 pairs of *chaperons* and 638 half-*schabraques*.[13] Clearly a mix of half-*schabraques* and *chaperons* were in use: were *chaperons* reserved for *sous-officiers* and trumpeters?

11ᵉ *Cuirassiers*

Inspected at Colmar on 30 January 1808, the regiment had 783 *housses*, of which 381 had been made new since 1805. In addition, 773 half-*schabraques* were in use, 455 of which were new. Not a single pair of *chaperons* existed in the regiment in 1805 or 1808. We suppose the regiment never had them.[14]

12ᵉ *Cuirassiers*

The regiment had 400 pairs of *chaperons* and 400 *schabraques* in use at the time of the 18 October 1804 inspection. The inspector furthermore noted that the *porte-manteaux* were all of the old round model, and that the bridles for officers and men, did not have the chain head piece as detailed in the regulations.[15]

Colonel of the 10ᵉ *Cuirassiers* as he appeared in 1805.

Clearly the process of equipping the horses took time; and it is fair to suggest that a mix-and-match approach to horse equipment was a constant theme of the *cuirassiers* in both harness and clothing.

Chapter 5

Continuity and Change 1805–08

After the Battle of Austerlitz, the Grande Armée remained in Germany. In March 1806 Napoléon began reorganising his cavalry force and obtaining remounts and replacements. Officially no change was made to the clothing of the *cuirassiers*: given the ambiguity of the exact details of what was worn, the truth of the matter seems to be that the old-fashioned *habits à revers* had their tails cropped off and were used side-by-side with the *habits de cuirass* and the pre-existing *surtouts*, again with the tails cropped down. Because of the ambiguity over what was worn, in 1806 a new decree was issued. On 25 April 1806, a *cuirassier* was allowed 84fr 96 for his clothing.[1] However, three months later, another decree, of 6 July 1806, was issued that stated:

Trooper of the 7ᵉ *Cuirassiers* as he appeared in 1806.

> The clothing fund established as follows will be in place from 1 October and paid in two portions: the 1e is the clothing fund which will cover the expense of the construction of the *habits*, *vestes*, *gilets d'ecurie*, *surtouts*, *culottes de peau*, stable trousers, *caleçons*, *manteaux*, *porte-manteaux*, helmets, armour, waistbelt, *giberne*, *porte-giberne*, sword knot, gauntlets, boots and trumpets as well as the costs for repairs to clothing, equipment and harness as well as the purchase of epaulettes, lace for *sous-officiers*, plumes etc. and is fixed for *cuirassiers* at 67fr 10; the 2e is the fund for harnessing and shoeing, established at 20fr 08.[2]

Of note, stable coats (*gilets d'ecurie*) appear as separate garments, and were made from tricot and double breasted. Furthermore, compared to the decree of 25 April 1806, where the combined clothing fund had been established at 84fr 96, the new allowance was 87fr 18, or an increase of 2fr 22. Clearly, *cuirassiers*, as under the terms of the 1802 dress

32   Napoleon's Heavy Cavalry

regulations, still had a *habit* and a *surtout*. We can assume the *habit* had *revers*. This was certainly the case when we look at the 1806 tariff. One could assume that the increase was to pay for the garment, which was to cost 2fr 22. Indeed, this is the view taken by Rousselot and others. Yet it is deeply simplistic: the increase was for the stable coat which was now made from new cloth.

The July 1806 decree in essence confirmed what was already happening. Since 1802 *cuirassiers* had had both a *surtout* and a *habit*. The specification of the *cuirassiers'* clothing was as follows:[3]

Item	Cloth	1806 Specification
Habits	Blue broadcloth	1m 50
	Facing cloth	0m 23
	Facing colour serge	3m 26
	Linen for lining	0m 89
	Small buttons	22
	Large buttons	11
Surtouts	Blue broadcloth	1m 73
	Facing cloth	0m
	Facing colour serge	3m 26
	Linen for lining	0m 89
	Large buttons	8
	Small buttons	2
Vestes	White broadcloth	1m 09
	White serge	2m 52
	Linen for lining	0m 29
	Buttons	12
Manteaux	*Blanc picque de bleu*	5m 75
	Facing colour serge	1m 48
Housses et Chaperons	Blue broadcloth	0m 59
	White lace 0m 40 wide	5m 95

The *habit* had seven small buttons on each *rever*, three on each cuff and two at the shoulder. The eight large buttons were on the back, two in the small of the back and the others on the three-pointed pocket flaps. The *surtout* had no facing cloth allocated to it, so we assume it was wholly blue, without facing colour tail facing and lining. This makes a lot of sense, as the collar of the *habit* is concealed by the *fraise* of the *cuirass* and the gauntlets hide the cuffs – thus why pay for expensive cloth for features of the uniform that are concealed? The 1801 *modèle habit de cuirass* only appeared in service very slowly, as we noted earlier, and most colonels took a pragmatic line and adopted what clothing they already had: thus the decree merely confirmed what was already common practice.

Concerning the existence or not of the 1806 *habit*, I am indebted to Ian Smith for his notes and research on the subject:

Since 1801 *cuirassiers* had worn *habit à revers*. This example belonged to Squadron Commander Scherb of the 11ᵉ *Cuirassiers*. Officers wore these garments for 'walking out dress' with broadcloth knee breeches, silk stockings and buckled shoes. *Cuirassiers* wore these garments under the *cuirass*. We can easily imagine how sweat would stain very easily the yellow facings. (*Photo KM*)

I doubt that the so called 1806 *habit* was in universal use with all twelve *Cuirassier* regiments, if it existed.

Firstly, the regiments had not been based near or at their French depots since Autumn 1805, when the army departed northern France for the Austerlitz campaign, and didn't return until after Tilsit. Therefore, we must ask, how and when would the *Cuirassier* troopers receive this new 1806 *habit* between 1805 and 1807? I strongly suspect that there would be no way that regimental quartermasters would sanction 450 to 500 brand new *habits* being made, then taken from the magazine, loaded into wagons, and sent to Germany or Poland, just in case they were needed!

In my opinion, only a few regiments made and issued the 1806 *habits*, which were issued when the regiments returned to France after Tilsit. The reality of wearing a *cuirass* is that the heavy hemp/jute lining soaks up rust and sweat likes a sponge, which would then *very* easily transfer itself as a permanent stain on the red or yellow *revers* of the *habit* – hence the reason one sees both '*habits*' and '*surtouts*' listed in the same inspection return. The single-breasted *surtout* is simply that and the *habit* listed is the '*habit de cuirass*'.

Other colonels, recognising the expense of two garments per man, stuck to the single-breasted *habit*, which is termed either *habit* or *surtout* in the returns, depending on the adjutant's whim, I suspect, and the short-tailed *habit* as a brand new garment was only adopted during peacetime in 1808 to 1809 depending on the date of introduction of the *surtout* again. The *habit à revers*, the one used in formal, dismounted tenue, without the *cuirass*, is impossible to identify from inspection returns.

And in any case, their period of manufacture would not have been long, owing to the sanctioned introduction of the *habit-surtout* in 1809. I strongly suspect that the twelve *cuirassier* regiments simply wore the 1803 *habits* or the cut-down *Cavalerie habits* for the 1805, 1806 and 1807 campaigns – which is, after all, what they wore when they set out from the depot for Austerlitz.[4]

Exceptionally well-preserved troopers *cuirass* complete with padded line – the *matelassure* – and also the decorative edging – *fraise* or *garniture de curaiss*. The *fraise* is sewn to the *matelassure*, which in turn is rivetted into the *cuirass*. The *cuirass* came as a complete item with *matelassure* and *fraise*, and was issued by the artillery. Helmets were made at regimental level, armour was issued by the state.

It seems though that clothing was made locally in Germany, as we come to later, and the 10ᵉ *Cuirassiers*, acting on the decree of 12 May 1806, dispatched clothing and equipment to Germany from the depot, the transport cost being 45fr 90.[5]

1806 Reviews

A wide-ranging inspection of the twelve *cuirassier* regiments was carried out on 1 October 1806 to assess what clothing and equipment needs the regiments had for the following year. The 1st Division of *Cuirassiers*, comprising the 2ᵉ and 9ᵉ and 3ᵉ and 12ᵉ regiments, was reviewed by General Nansouty. He reported:

2ᵉ *Cuirassiers*

The men were wearing 183 *surtouts* in lieu of *habits* and have 197 *capotes* rather than *manteaux*. The clothing is overall very bad, it has not been replaced since the regiment left France. A goodly number of the *culottes de peau* and boots are life expired or needed repairs. The *capotes* are all entirely bad. The saddles and equipment for the men and horses received from Breslau is all bad. The horse equipment received from Potsdam is generally bad of different models.

3ᵉ *Cuirassiers*

The *sous-officiers* were short of seven *surtouts*. The regiment's clothing is not very good. The colonel must work on this. The regiment has received no new clothing since it left France, this is why it is all in a bad condition.

9ᵉ *Cuirassiers*

The *habits* are all very old, having been in service longer than the regulation duration and are all in bad condition. Fifty-one bad *habits* were supplied from Breslau. The helmets are in generally good condition, but nearly all need repairs. Sabres carried are all in bad condition, the sabres are all bad and the mountings are all deteriorated due to the rigours of war.

12ᵉ *Cuirassiers*

The regiment's clothing and equipment is not too bad a condition. The weapons are needing repairs. 20 horses have been re-formed. They have 85 pairs of *chaperons* and 651 *schabraques*.[6]

The 2nd Division comprised the 1ᵉ and 5ᵉ and 10ᵉ and 11ᵉ regiments commanded by General Saint-Sulpice. The inspector reported:

1ᵉ *Cuirassiers*

The *habits* are in good condition, but badly made – the collars are too tall and too large. The *manteaux* are of German manufacture and of bad quality. The breeches are not tall enough, the helmets are generally in bad condition, it is urgent to repair these. All items of grand equipment are in good condition as repairs have been made. The boots are made from bad-quality leather. The saddlery of the regiments is in as good a condition as manageable … The effects have been in use for too long at a time of war. It would be good to change the *retroussis* to broadcloth. The buff work is not regulation. The *schabraques* all need repair.

5ᵉ *Cuirassiers*

In the 5ᵉ *Cuirassiers*, the same observations are made. The *habits* are well cut and well sewn except the collars, which are too tall and large. The colonel, for the good of service, is to ensure that the tails of the *habits* are to be lined in broadcloth rather than serge, which has worn badly … the boots are made from low-grade leather, as are the knee guards.

10ᵉ *Cuirassiers*

The *habits* are all good, as are the stable coats, *bonnets de police* and *vestes*, but they were old, the regiment not having received any new items for a number of years. The *manteaux* are good in condition but the lining needs repairs in most cases. The regiment urgently need new *culottes de peau*. The vast majority of the *gibernes* and *banderoles* are not regulation, are very old and needed replacing. The *cuirasses* needed new leather work, new brass scales, new waistbelts – this will occasion a large expense. Many men need gauntlets.

11ᵉ *Cuirassiers*

Analogous observations to the 10ᵉ for the clothing, and comprising the lining to the *manteau*, the gauntlets, the shoulder straps to the *cuirass*. Many of the *gibernes* need to be replaced, many are not regulation. The regiment is missing many pairs of epaulettes. The men have *schabraques*, they are all bad.[7]

The 3rd Division comprised the 4ᵉ and 6ᵉ and 7ᵉ and 8ᵉ regiment commanded by General Espagne. The inspector reported that:

Clothing. All regiments have *habits*, *bonnets de police* and a *capote* or *manteaux*. There are missing in the 4ᵉ 589 *surtouts*, in the 6ᵉ 599 *surtouts*, in the 7ᵉ 621, there is no demand in the 8ᵉ. There are 537 *vestes* needed for the 6ᵉ, the others are complete. The 7ᵉ need 673 pairs of gauntlets, the other regiments have sufficient.

Equipment. All four regiments have no need for *gibernes* and *porte-gibernes*, none had indicated the need for *frais*, scabbards or sword knots.

Small Equipment. All four regiments indicate they have sufficient pairs of gaiters, black stocks, knee guards and musettes.

Harness. 2,264 men, 741 blankets, 2,146 *schabraques* in sheepskin, 65 pairs of *chaperons* are in use in the division, all with the 7ᵉ *Cuirassiers*.

4ᵉ *Cuirassiers*

The clothing of the regiment is to be replaced at the end of the current campaign. The broadcloth used to make the *habits* is very bad. The colour is in consequence also very bad, as is the cut and construction … the boots are very bad quality … a large number of *porte-manteaux* need new lace.

6ᵉ *Cuirassiers*

The clothing of the regiment is to be replaced at the end of the current campaign. The *manteaux* have been supplied from Potsdam, are blue and made from bad-quality cloth and need replacing, as do the stable coats and *porte-manteaux*. The *porte-manteaux* were supplied from Potsdam using the *modèle* supplied by the regiment, but they are not well made.

Continuity and Change 1805–08 37

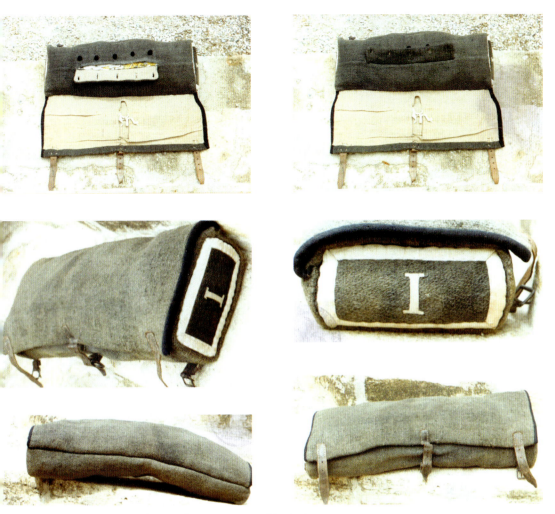

Exceptionally rare original trooper's *port-manteau* of the 1ᵉ *Cuirassiers*.

7ᵉ *Cuirassiers*

Many *habits* have been supplied from the magazine from Brunn and are not made according to the regulation. There are none for the *sous-officiers*, who instead wear *surtouts* ... the helmets are generally badly made.[8]

It seems that a mix of *habits de cuirass*, *habits à revers* and *surtouts* were in use side by side. Clearly the *cuirassiers* were in poor shape at the time of the reviews.

1807 Reviews

Following the Heilsberg and Friedland campaigns, all the regiments of *cuirassiers* were given a shake-down inspection. The returns from 1 July 1807 mention *habits* and *surtouts* often in use side by side in the same regiment:[9]

38   Napoleon's Heavy Cavalry

Regiment	Item	In Good Repair	In Need of Repair	To be Replaced	Total	Observations
1ᵉ Cuirassiers	Habits	320	104		678	For immediate use, the regiment needs 327 *gilets en drap*, 36 stable coats, 67 pairs of *culottes de peau*, 628 *bonnets de police* and 138 plumes to supplement the 493 plumes in use.
	Surtouts					
	Gilets en drap	281		20	301	
	Gilets d'ecurie	424	63	95	502	
2ᵉ Cuirassiers	Habits		254	408	662	472 *manteaux* in use, 197 *capotes*, 632 pairs of *culottes de peau*. The regiment has no stable trousers.
	Surtouts		183		183	
	Gilets en drap		151	509	660	
	Gilets d'ecurie		169	415	584	
3ᵉ Cuirassiers	Habits	336	184	142	662	For immediate needs, the regiment requires 12 *habits*, 326 *gilets*, 53 stable coats, plus 25 *manteaux*, 265 pairs of *culottes de peau* and 38 pairs of stable trousers.
	Surtouts	6	1		7	
	Gilets en drap	205	10	105	348	
	Gilets d'ecurie	329	166	124	619	
4ᵉ Cuirassiers	Habits	578	255	65	598	For immediate needs, 25 *habits*, 589 *surtouts*, 57 *gilets en drap*, 59 stable coats, 53 *manteaux*, 33 pairs of *culottes de peau*, 84 *bonnets de police* and 180 plumes. The regiment has no *gibernes* and belts.
	Surtouts	1	11	12	24	
	Gilets en drap	226	171	159	536	
	Gilets d'ecurie	214	176	164	554	
5ᵉ Cuirassiers	Habits	492	96		589	For immediate needs, the regiment requires 350 *gilets en drap*. 589 scarlet plumes are in service. The regiment has 589 pairs of stable trousers in use. The boots are falling apart and are made from weak leather, except the knee guards.
	Surtouts					
	Gilets en drap	194	44		239	
	Gilets d'ecurie	441	48	100	589	

Continuity and Change 1805–08   39

Regiment	Item	In Good Repair	In Need of Repair	To be Replaced	Total	Observations
6ᵉ *Cuirassiers*	*Habits*	175	263	141	579	For immediate use, the regiment needs 20 *habits*, 599 *surtouts*, 538 *gilets en drap*, 83 stable coats, 68 *manteaux*, 28 pairs of *culottes de peau*, 27 *bonnets de police* and 56 plumes. The *manteaux* are blue, which gives a very bad effect. The regiment has no *gibernes* and belts.
	Surtouts					
	Gilets en drap			62	62	
	Gilets d'ecurie	127	254	133	514	
7ᵉ *Cuirassiers*	*Habits*	231	385	80	696	For immediate needs, the regiment requires 621 *surtouts*, 53 stable coats, 8 *manteaux*, 19 pairs of *culottes de peau*, 18 *bonnets de police* and 35 plumes. The regiment has no *gibernes* and belts.
	Surtouts	9	30	25	64	
	Gilets en drap	300	285	100	685	
	Gilets d'ecurie	263	232	137	632	
8ᵉ *Cuirassiers*	*Habits*	487	100	345	622	For immediate needs, the regiment requires 16 *habits*, 120 *gilets*, 83 stable coats, 37 *manteaux*, 76 pairs of *culottes de peau*, 30 *bonnets de police* and 85 red plumes. The regiment has no *gibernes* and belts.
	Surtouts					
	Gilets en drap	158	201	149	508	
	Gilets d'ecurie	99	254	200	554	
9ᵉ *Cuirassiers*	*Habits*	333		427	760	In addition, the regiment has 766 *manteaux*, 765 pairs of *culottes de peau* and 777 *bonnets de police* in service.
	Surtouts					
	Gilets en drap	233		304	537	
	Gilets d'ecurie	256		468	724	
10ᵉ *Cuirassiers*	*Habits*	542		125	667	The regiment has 643 *manteaux* in service, 432 pairs of *culottes de peau*, 663 *bonnets de police* and 530 plumes. The *gibernes* are extremely old and are not regulation; they all need replacing.
	Surtouts					
	Gilets en drap	331		269	620	
	Gilets d'ecurie	651			651	

40 Napoleon's Heavy Cavalry

Regiment	Item	In Good Repair	In Need of Repair	To be Replaced	Total	Observations
11ᵉ *Cuirassiers*	*Habits*	484		210	694	The regiment has 689 *manteaux*, 449 pairs of *culottes de peau*, 696 *bonnets de police* and 688 plumes in service. Most men have no epaulettes.
	Surtouts					
	Gilets en drap	104		89	193	
	Gilets d'ecurie	678		18	689	
12ᵉ *Cuirassiers*	*Habits*	624	97	63	782	811 pairs of *culottes de peau* are in use, and 811 *manteaux*.
	Surtouts					
	Gilets en drap	403	31	324	728	
	Gilets d'ecurie	418	128	129	13	

It seems that the 2ᵉ, 4ᵉ, 7ᵉ, 8ᵉ, 9ᵉ, 10ᵉ and 12ᵉ wore *habit à revers*, the trumpeters in the 3ᵉ, 4ᵉ and 7ᵉ wore *surtout*s and the *sous-officiers* and trumpeters of the 2ᵉ had the luxury of both *surtouts* and a *habit à revers*! We assume the trumpeters' *surtouts* were in reversed colours. At the close of the campaign, the 4ᵉ were ordered to produce 589 *surtouts* and 15 *habits*, to give every man 1 of each garment, likewise the 6ᵉ had to produce 599 *surtouts* and 7ᵉ 621. Were these garments to replace the *habit à revers* or in addition to them? Of interest, not every regiment had a plume nor epaulettes. The 10ᵉ still had their old *cavalerie giberne*s in service.

Late empire helmet attributed to a major or lieutenant colonel of the 1ᵉ *Cuirassiers*. (*Private Collection, Belgium*)

Chapter 6
1808 Reviews

Following the victory at Friedland and Treaties of Tilsit, the army returned to barracks. Another wide-ranging shake-down inspection was made of the army once it was back in France over winter 1807. These inspections are our next point of reference for the dress of the *cuirassiers*.

First-issue *cuirassier* helmet with the solid cast front plate.

1ᵉ *Cuirassiers*

The 1ᵉ *Cuirassiers* were inspected at Lodi on 1 January 1808. The clothing and equipment in use were as follows:[1]

Item	In Good Repair	In Need of Repair	To be Written Off	Total	Total Made Since 26 July 1805	To be Replaced
Habits	869			869	898	
Surtouts	357			357	111	
Manteaux	812			812	526	
Gilets	507			507	806	

42 Napoleon's Heavy Cavalry

Item	In Good Repair	In Need of Repair	To be Written Off	Total	Total Made Since 26 July 1805	To be Replaced
Gilets d'ecurie	849			849	698	
Culottes de peau	238		600	838	1,043	
Pantalons d'ecurie	238		625	863	1,043	
Helmets	554		365	859	477	
Caleçons	397			397	397	
Bonnets de police	899			899	672	
Ceinturons	845			845	510	
Gibernes	503			503	400	
Porte-gibernes	503			503	400	
Porte-manteaux	812		85	897	802	
Boots	672		173	845	891	
Fraise for cuirass	365		322	687	365	
Saddles	597		221	818	597	
Housses	774			774	214	
Chaperons						
Schabraques	776			776	533	

Notably, the regiment had no cloth *chaperons* in use at all, all ranks had the sheepskin *schabraque*. The archive says nothing about the dress of the trumpeters.

2ᵉ *Cuirassiers*

The 2ᵉ *Cuirassiers* were inspected at Vitry-sur-Seine on 23 December 1807. The clothing and equipment in use were as follows:[2]

Item	In Good Repair	In Need of Repair	To be Written Off	Total	Total Made Since 20 June 1805	Comment
Habits	400	60	683	1,143	587	Of the 683 to be written off, 481 are in the magazine, with 628 *gilets* used during the last campaign.
Surtouts	225	28	628	881	259	
Manteaux	576	386	119	1,081	576	
Gilets	309	653	48	1,010	408	
Gilets d'ecurie	297	330	505	1,132	581	
Culottes de peau	172	251	1,264	1,687	1,086	
Pantalons d'ecurie	400	191	557	1,148	591	
Helmets	758	104	184	1,046	458	
Bonnets de police	376	386	501	1,263	668	
Ceinturons	952	30	67	1,029	668	
Gibernes	857			857	457	
Porte-gibernes	853			853	453	

Item	In Good Repair	In Need of Repair	To be Written Off	Total	Total Made Since 20 June 1805	Comment
Porte-manteaux	469	97	248	814	217	
Boots	484	478	255	1,217	684	
Saddles	665	256		921	465	
Housses	601	199	57	857	401	
Chaperons	None issued					
Schabraques	603		256	859	403	

Virtually all of the regiment's clothing was to be disposed of as life expired. The *habits* and *vestes* I strongly suspect were heavily stained by sweat and rust and thus were disposed of. Not a single *surtout* existed in the depot on 20 June 1805, with 253 being made between that date and December 1807.

3ᵉ *Cuirassiers*

Inspected on 20 December 1807, the following clothing and equipment was in use by men in the depot. The inspector was ignorant of the dress of the war squadrons:[3]

Item	In Good Repair	In Need of Repair	To be Written Off	Total	Total Made Since 1805	Comment
Habits	77		8	85	843	
Surtouts	28			28	71	
Manteaux	50			50	704	
Gilets	77			77	801	
Gilets d'ecurie	145		18	163	1,017	
Culottes de pcau	80		19	99	1,110	
Pantalons d'ecurie	140		38	178	1,116	
Helmets	57			57	553	
Bonnets de police	150		7	157	903	
Ceinturons	53			53	594	
Gibernes	53			53	454	
Porte-gibernes	53			53	454	
Porte-manteaux	50			50	532	
Boots	72			72	800	
Saddles	40		7	47	557	
Housses	40			40	646	
Chaperons	40			40	380	
Schabraques	The regiment has none					

The regiment used *chaperons*, it seems, and not the sheepskin *schabraque*. Of interest, the regiment was issued 470 carbines and *banderole-porte-carabines* on 13 January 1806 taken from the arsenal at Vienna. In addition, 96 *cuirasses* had been sent to the regiment from Strasbourg on 1 November 1806, 150 further examples from Paris on 13 June 1807, 38 further examples arrived from Mayence on 4 November 1807, with 140 additional *cuirasses* arriving on 2 December, 5 more on 5 December, and lastly 31 examples on 17 December. The ten trumpeters in the war squadrons were armoured.

4ᵉ *Cuirassiers*

Inspected on 30 December 1807, the following clothing and equipment in use were as follows:[4]

Item	In Good Repair	In Need of Repair	To be Written Off	Total	Total Made Since 1805	Comment
Habits	191			191	191	
Surtouts	27			27	27	
Manteaux	136			136	136	
Gilets	The regiment has none					
Gilets d'ecurie	203			203	203	
Culottes de peau	226			226	226	
Pantalons d'ecurie	226			226	226	
Helmets	191			191	191	
Bonnets de police	226			226	226	
Ceinturons	190			190	190	
Gibernes	The regiment has none					
Porte-gibernes						
Porte-manteaux	210			210	210	
Boots	157			157	157	
Saddles	84			84	84	
Housses	113			1,113	113	
Chaperons	79			79	79	
Schabraques	The regiment has none					

The regiment's *habits* clearly closed to the waist due to the lack of *gilets* to cover an expanse of shirt, and we assume were *habits de cuirass*. The *surtouts* seem to be for trumpeters and others. The sabre belts were all in 'terrible condition' according

Cuirassier trooper's helmet from the middle years of the empire. The front plate is now far more refined than earlier models.

Officer's helmet of the 1e *Cuirassiers* from the end of the 1st Empire. (*Musée de l'Empéri, Collections du Musée de l'Armée, Anciennes collections Jean et Raoul Brunon*)

to the inspector, who was incredulous that the regiment had no armour – yet 536 *cuirasses* had existed in summer 1807! – and asked where it was along with the *gibernes* and belts. One suspects a lot of the kit in use on returning to home was 'junked'. After Heilsberg the inspector noted the clothing had been worn since 1805, the cloth of the *habits* was terrible, the colour of them was described as bad: basically, everything was worn out and in desperate need of repair or replacement. Had the *cuirasses* gone off for repairs? Of note, the regiment still carried its old *cavalerie* sabres and not the new *cuirassier* type. The helmet turbans all needed replacing as they had rotted and the fur had fallen out; the *crinière* were rotten as well.[5]

5e *Cuirassiers*

Inspected on 4 December 1807, the first time since July 1807, the regiment had the following items in use:[6]

Item	In Good Repair	In Need of Repair	To be Written Off	Total	Total Made Since July 1805	Comment
Habits	442	134	311	887	982	The regiment has been on active service since 1805, it is generally in a good state and the 500 men that the depot has furnished in 1806 and 1807 are clothed and equipped from new upon departing from the depot.
Surtouts	198	474	224	896	672	
Manteaux	515	164	208	887	515	
Vestes	429	168	290	887	429	
Gilets d'ecurie	730	98	59	887	1,102	
Epaulettes	The regiment has none					
Culottes de peau	760		127	887	1,353	
Pantalons d'ecurie	449		438	887	796	
Helmets	788	98	1	887	505	
Bonnets de police	787		100	887	1,016	
Ceinturons	803	26	58	887	488	
Gibernes	677	114	96	887	479	
Porte-manteaux	759	85	43	887	663	

Since the inspection in July 1805, the regiment had made and received 1,132 new *habits*, of which 982 had been issued. Some 706 *surtouts* had been made, 533 *manteaux*, 460 *gilets* and 1,130 stable coats. Some 3,446m 32 of Imperial Blue broadcloth had been

46   Napoleon's Heavy Cavalry

used, 353m 90 of scarlet broadcloth, 2,652m 34 of white broadcloth, 5,538m 15 of scarlet serge and 3,128m 96 of white milled serge. But of which pattern were the new *habits*? The *habit* with *revers* of 1806 or the previous model? The lack of epaulettes is most surprising.

6ᵉ *Cuirassiers*

When inspected on 13 January 1808, the first time since 11 October 1805, the return reveals that the regiment had received 1,087 new *habits* and just 164 *surtouts*. The regiment had not taken part in the campaign of 1805 and was stationed in Italy, but had taken part in later campaigns. Indeed, 15 men on a foraging party had been taken prisoner on 3 February 1807, and 109 pistols and 84 sabres had been lost at Heilsberg on 10 June 1807, but not a single *cuirass*! Were these items recovered, where serviceable, off the dead? No *habits* or *surtouts* had been in stores in 1805. In the same period some 398 new *manteaux* had been made and issued, 149 new *vestes*, 1,099 new stable coats with 856 pairs of stable trousers, 40 *chapeaux*, 336 new helmets and 703 *bonnets de police*. Some 27m 17 of silver lace had been used for *sous-officiers'* rank stripes. The trumpeters of the regiment were issued 10 *cuirasses*, 61 were issued to the *sous-officiers*, which included the corporal trumpeter, and 856 to the rank and file. Of the *cuirasses*, a whopping 617 had arrived since October 1805, 357 being in service in October 1805, and had come from the arsenal at Plaisance. Furthermore, sixty-four Prussian *cuirasses* had been taken from the stores at Potsdam, were in use and were to be placed in the arsenal at Mantua.[7]

7ᵉ *Cuirassiers*

When inspected at Lodi on 31 December 1807 the clothing and equipment in use were as follows:[8]

Item	In Good Repair	In Need of Repair	To be Written Off	Total	Total Made Since 10 October 1805	Comment
Habits	21	70		91	1,030	
Surtouts	16			16	77	
Manteaux	20		68	88	629	
Vestes	The regiment has none				143	I am ignorant as to the war squadrons as all I have been able to review is the depot.
Gilets d'ecurie	40	15	10	65	728	
Epaulettes	20		72	92	680	
Culottes de peau	50		54	104	1,394	
Pantalons d'ecurie	27			27	412	
Chapeaux			4	4	82	
Helmets	52			52	350	
Plumes	20		17	37	564	
Bonnets de police	48		34	82	911	

Item	In Good Repair	In Need of Repair	To be Written Off	Total	Total Made Since 10 October 1805	Comment
Ceinturons	64			64	433	
Giberne plaques	60			60	467	
Porte-gibernes et gibernes	The regiment has none					
Porte-manteaux	20		71	91	802	

General Comte de Pully was very much an officer who adhered to regulations and was a stickler for enforcing them. Despite the printed pro-forma inspection report not listing epaulettes, plumes and spurs, he duly accounted for them. Of interest, the depot held a lot of *giberne plaques* but not a single *giberne* and belt – does this mean the regiment did not have these in use at the time? Seemingly so.

8ᵉ *Cuirassiers*

When inspected at Lodi on 1 January 1808 the clothing and equipment in use were as follows:[9]

Item	In Good Repair	In Need of Repair	To be Written Off	Total	Total Made Since 12 October 1805	To be Replaced
Habits	385	378	166	879	919	
Surtouts	61	152	276	489	603	
Manteaux	464	395		859	485	
Gilets	361	214	196	771	377	
Gilets d'ecurie	440	424		864	778	
Culottes de peau	376		283	659	1,126	
Pantalons d'ecurie	413			413	430	
Helmets	654	182	43	879	300	
Bonnets de police	450	465		915	1,226	
Ceinturons	729	119	34	882	369	
Gibernes						
Porte-gibernes	The regiment has none					
Musket slings						
Porte-manteaux	499	348	47	894	421	
Boots	400	275	153	828	744	
Saddles	444	335	19	798	429	
Housses	634	104	42	780	772	
Chaperons	120			120	120	
Schabraques	300	63	300	663	300	

48   Napoleon's Heavy Cavalry

Of comment, the regiment had no *gibernes* and no *giberne* belts, a situation seemingly since 1805, if not earlier, and one that would last, as we shall see, until 1812. The regiment was also using a mix of wool *schabraques* and broadcloth *chaperons*. The regiment mustered 890 sub-officers and men, we can see clearly that a mix of *surtouts* and *habits* were in use. Virtually every man had a *habit* issued. At the time of the 1805 inspection, 3 *habits* existed in the depot and 919 had been made and issued. The three in the depot had been repaired and issued. Therefore, these *habits* are all likely to be the *habit à revers*. Some 167 *surtouts* existed at the time of the 1805 inspection, with 609 being made since then. We also note 109 of the *surtouts* were repaired and reissued by 1808. A huge shortfall in *culottes de peau* is notable, with over 300 men lacking these, and the inspector noted the men were wearing grey *pantalons à cheval*. Stocks of materials in the depot included:

367m 43 blue broadcloth
107m 30 white broadcloth
0m scarlet broadcloth, although 135m had been used prior to 1 January 1808
469m 90 *blanc picque de bleu* broadcloth for *manteaux*
21m 40 yellow broadcloth
232m white serge
1,117m 43 yellow serge

The scarlet cloth was likely used to make the *fraise* for the *cuirass*, epaulettes and the festoon to the *schabraque*. This shows the latter items were not in the regiment's facing colour.

9ᵉ *Cuirassiers*

When inspected at Mayence on 14 December 1807 the clothing and equipment in use were as follows:[10]

Item	In Good Repair	In Need of Repair	To be Written Off	Total	Total Made Since 5 August 1805
Habits	840	142	7	989	874
Surtouts	1	5		6	6
Manteaux	627	246	57	930	619
Gilets	966	23		989	967
Gilets d'ecurie	266	200	63	529	810
Culottes de peau	989			989	2,387
Pantalons d'ecurie	64	252	20	336	714
Helmets	980			980	574
Bonnets de police	600		20	620	973
Ceinturons	942		47	989	600
Gibernes	839		60	899	563

Item	In Good Repair	In Need of Repair	To be Written Off	Total	Total Made Since 5 August 1805
Porte-gibernes	839		60	899	563
Porte-manteaux	492	245	252	989	541
Boots	476	180	273	929	1,005
Saddles	783			783	692
Housses	552	200	30	783	609
Chaperons	182			182	182
Schabraques	593		45	638	893

The inspecting general commented:

> The regiment has constantly been with the Grande Armée since the Austrian campaign. It has therefore been impossible to keep a record of the clothing and equipment in use on active service until the time of this inspection as well as the men entering the depot, some having good clothing and others mediocre.[11]

Compared to other regiments though, as we shall see, the clothing was overall in good condition despite the rigours of campaign. The regiment always seem to have worn *habits* as only six *surtout*s existed – were the *habits* the old 1803 type? Very likely. Not a single *surtout* existed in the depot in 1805, with just six being made between 1805 and 1807. Of the 1,206 *habits* made in the same period, 874 were issued and 336 were in the depot, brand-new unissued and 170 were held for disposal. Cloth in the depot comprised:[12]

> 0m 48 blue broadcloth, although 3,492m 05 had been used between 1805 and 1807
> 0m 20 *blanc picque de bleu* for *manteaux*, although 3,219m 75 had been used between 1805 and 1807
> 0m white broadcloth, although 1,079m 90 had been used between 1805 and 1807
> 0m scarlet broadcloth, although 87m 50 had been used between 1805 and 1807
> 11m 22 yellow broadcloth, some 357m 20 being used between 1805 and 1807
> 845m 98 yellow serge, with some 5,363m 50 being used between 1805 and 1807
> 13m 76 white serge, with 2,193m 52 being used between 1805 and 1807

Given the regiment was away from its depot, huge quantities of cloth had been employed in making clothing. The scarlet cloth again raises an interesting question. The 9ᵉ always had yellow facings, so was the scarlet destined, as with the 8ᵉ, for trumpeters or at some time unknown had the 8ᵉ and 9ᵉ adopted scarlet facings? More reasonable is the use of the scarlet cloth to make the *fraise* for the *cuirass*, which shows they were made in-house at regimental level.

In the fourth quarter of 1809, while garrisoned at Mayence, the regiment was totally redressed, no doubt into the new *habit-surtout* introduced that year. The regiment's master tailors bill for clothing the regiment was as follows:[13]

50   Napoleon's Heavy Cavalry

1 pair of gaiters. Total 4fr 90.
727 *habits* at 2fr 10 each. Total 1,599fr 40.
754 *vestes* at 1fr each. Total 754fr.
167 *manteaux* at 1fr 20 each. Total 200fr 40.
200 stable coats at 1fr 20 each. Total 240fr.
150 *bonnets de police* at 40 centimes each. Total 60fr.
19 pairs of stable trousers at 1fr 10 each. Total 20fr 90.
19 pairs of *surculottes* at 1fr 10 each. Total 20fr 90.
164 *housses* at 1fr 20 each. Total 196fr 40.
164 pairs of *chaperons* at 4fr each. Total 656fr.
35 *porte-manteaux* at 2fr 50 each. Total 87fr 50.

The master boot makers bill was as follows:[14]

32 pairs of boots at 32fr a pair. Total 736fr
60 pairs of boots at 23fr a pair. Total 1,580fr
201 pairs of *culottes de peau* at 11fr each. Total 2,211fr
Repairs to boots at 1fr a boot, total 34fr

Also bought was 1,191m of linen to line the *schabraques*, costing 1,568fr 52, 56m 20 of white linen for making underwear costing 59fr 16, 158m of *treillis* to line the *schabraques* costing 248fr 40, 12 saddles costing 81fr each and 150 pairs of stirrups with a total cost of 87fr 50.[15] Interestingly, a mix of *chaperons* and *schabraques* were in use.

Reviewed on 1 January 1810, the regiment had 804 *schabraques* and *housses* in use, 964 helmets, 937 waistbelts with plates and 937 copper grenades for the *gibernes*. Every man was armoured.[16] Contrary to myth and the Otto manuscript, no bearskins existed in 1805, 1807, 1809 or 1810.

10ᵉ *Cuirassiers*

Inspected 31 December 1807, the regiment had the following items of clothing and equipment in use:[17]

Item	In Good Repair	In Need of Repair	To be Written Off	Total	Total Made Since 1805
Habits	496	178	256	393	1,242
Surtouts	270	101	125	496	456
Manteaux	625	72	158	855	806
Gilets	554	154	224	932	1,053
Gilets d'ecurie	445	225	252	922	1,016
Culottes de peau	485	190	320	995	1,847
Caleçons	344	131	963	838	531

Item	In Good Repair	In Need of Repair	To be Written Off	Total	Total Made Since 1805
Pantalons d'ecurie	The regiment has none				
Chapeaux			45	45	102
Helmets	470	426	85	981	490
Gauntlets	540	165	179	884	773
Bonnets de police	520	237	157	914	619
Plumes	495	60	279	834	542
Ceinturons	615	170	175	960	418
Gibernes	462	225	201	888	506
Porte-gibernes	468	216	204	888	559
Sword knots	492	148	306	946	559
Porte-manteaux	505	168	240	913	603
Boots	620	125	224	969	866
Trumpets	8	3	2	13	12
Saddles	670	175	69	914	756
Housses	616	175	123	914	769
Chaperons	174			174	174
Schabraques	495	115	140	750	623

Stores returns notes the use of 137m 60 of black twill to make gaiters, of which 689 pairs existed along with 641 pairs of shoes for stable duties. We also note 201m 90 of madder red broadcloth had been used to make *fraise*, epaulette boards and the festoon for the *schabraque*. We note the 12 trumpeters were armoured and that 396 *cuirasses* had been delivered on 1 November 1807 from Mayence. The regiment was wearing grey *pantalons* reinforced with black leather for campaign dress and stable duties in imitation of the light cavalry.

11ᵉ *Cuirassiers*

Inspected at Colmar on 30 January 1808, the regiment had the following items of clothing and equipment in use:[18]

Item	In Good Repair	In Need of Repair	To be Written Off	Total	Total Made Since 4 August 1805
Habits	461		485	946	990
Plumes	758			758	
Epaulettes	400		546	946	
Surtouts	22			22	118
Manteaux	442	358		800	425
Gilets	455	164	313	932	591

52 Napoleon's Heavy Cavalry

Item	In Good Repair	In Need of Repair	To be Written Off	Total	Total Made Since 4 August 1805
Gilets d'ecurie	496	136	314	946	630
Culottes de peau	518		428	946	1,591
Pantalons d'ecurie	88	450	408	946	1,257
Helmets	354	590		944	536
Bonnets de police	84	417	445	946	391
Ceinturons	799	135		964	557
Gibernes	735	138		873	465
Porte-gibernes	735	138		873	528
Porte-manteaux	600	330		930	563
Boots	390	300	178	868	866
Saddles	543	200	45	788	497
Housses	504	199	80	783	381
Chaperons					
Schabraques	304	399	70	773	455

The returns are interesting. This is the only inspection report that clearly and specifically mentions plumes and epaulettes. It is also obvious the regiment had very few *surtouts*, and seemingly were of such low number as to make them for sub-officers, trumpeters or regimental workmen. The vast majority of the regiment's clothing in winter 1808 was in dire need of being replaced as it was life expired. The regiment solely used the sheepskin *schabraque* and the *demi-croupelin housses* rather than the cloth *chaperons*. All ranks wore *cuirasses*, eleven being issued to the trumpeters. Stocks of cloth and material in the depot comprised 29m 09 of blue broadcloth, 3,096m 75 being used prior to January 1808, and 814m 90 of white broadcloth cloth, some 839m 83 being used prior to the inspection. Not an inch of serge or any other broadcloth is recorded as being purchased between 1805 and 1808. We are left to wonder if this is a mistake, or did the regiment wear entirely blue *habits*? Again, at the time of the 1805 inspection, 10 *habits* were in stores, with 1,209 being made since the inspection. Of these, 990 were issued, and a further 173 *habits* were repaired, leaving 3 brand-new *habits* in the depot, 10 needing to be repaired and 43 to be disposed of.

Concerning the *surtouts*, 209 existed in 1805 and 814 were made, a total of 1,023 examples, of which 1,011 were issued. A further 8,936 *surtouts* had been repaired by the depot. At the time of the 1808 inspection, 12 were in the depot, 1 was brand new but unissued, 5 needed repairs and 6 were to be disposed of, 118 *surtouts* had been issued, and 893 had been repaired. Clearly, the *surtouts*, with nearly 900 needing to be repaired, were clearly 'worn to death' by the regiment and in far higher numbers than the *habit*, leaving only 22 actually in use. Therefore, can we suggest that the *surtouts* were worn on the 1805, 1806 campaigns, and the *habit* introduced for service after 1806? Clearly by January 1808, the regiment was entirely dressed in *habits* rather than *surtouts* – but with no facing colour cloth – were both the *habits* and *surtouts* the same garment, i.e., single breasted and entirely blue?

12ᵉ *Cuirassiers*

Inspected on 6 January 1808, the regiment had the following items of clothing and equipment in use:[19]

Item	In Good Repair	In Need of Repair	To be Written Off	Total	Total Made Since 1805
Habits	953		3	956	953
Surtouts	208		13	221	243
Manteaux	855			855	710
Gilets	873		165	1,038	1,174
Gilets d'ecurie	461	80		541	673
Culottes de peau	510		342	852	1,478
Pantalons d'ecurie	537			537	1,282
Helmets	880	80	20	980	530
Bonnets de police	499			499	730
Ceinturons	976			976	591
Gibernes	955			955	657
Porte-gibernes	962			962	646
Porte-manteaux	833			833	672
Boots	669			669	877
Saddles	811			811	614
Housses	833			833	646
Chaperons	200			200	200
Schabraques	631			631	439

Trooper's first-model *cuirass*. (*Photograph and collection of Bertrand Malvaux*)

54 Napoleon's Heavy Cavalry

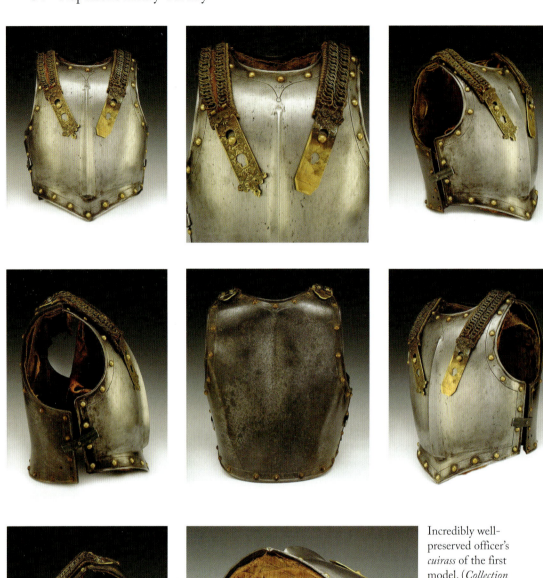

Incredibly well-preserved officer's *cuirass* of the first model. (*Collection and photograph of Bertrand Malvaux*)

Stores held chestnut brown and grey broadcloth, and reported the use of 283m 60 of scarlet broadcloth for making the *fraise*, epaulette boards and *schabraque* festoon. Also noted was the use of 6m of yellow tricot, which was used to make *porte-manteaux*, and in theory the *schabraque* festoon, presumably in this case for trumpeters. Also issued were 710 shirts, 762 black stocks, 817 pair of woollen knee socks, 1,101 pairs of shoes and 748 pairs of black gaiters. Of note, the trumpeters were not armoured, but were issued pistols and sabres.

Conclusion

As with the summer 1807 reviews, regiments had both *surtouts* and *habits* in use. Sadly, we cannot ascertain if a *habit* is a *habit de cuiras* or *habit à revers*. Regiments retained both garments side by side:

1ᵉ *Cuirassiers*: 869 *habits* and 357 *surtouts*.[20]
2ᵉ *Cuirassiers*: 1,143 *habits* and 881 *surtouts*.[21]
3ᵉ *Cuirassiers*: 898 *habits* and 111 *surtouts*.[22]
4ᵉ *Cuirassiers*: 191 *habits* and 27 *surtouts*. 679 *habits* made since August 1805, 118 *surtout*s made since 1805.[23]
5ᵉ *Cuirassiers*: 887 *habits* and 896 *surtouts*.[24]
6ᵉ *Cuirassiers*: 1,087 new *habits* and 164 *surtouts*.[25]
7ᵉ *Cuirassiers*: 1,030 *habits* and 77 *surtouts*.[26]
8ᵉ *Cuirassiers*: 879 *habits* and 489 *surtouts*.[27]
9ᵉ *Cuirassiers*: 989 *habits* and 6 *surtouts*.[28]
10ᵉ *Cuirassiers*: 930 *habits* and 456 *surtouts*.[29]
11ᵉ *Cuirassiers*: 946 *habits* and 22 *surtouts*.[30]
12ᵉ *Cuirassiers*: 956 *habits* and 221 *surtouts*.[31]

Given the mix-and-match approach of garments, in all bar the 2ᵉ and 5ᵉ *Cuirassiers* possibly, what we are looking at is the majority of regiments used *habits de cuiras* and *surtouts* side by side. The 2ᵉ regiment used far more scarlet cloth than the other regiments, thus the unit seems to have had *habit à revers*, which we know it did use in 1805 – therefore more of the same had obviously been made.[32] The 11ᵉ had no *surtouts* whatsoever earlier in 1807, so the appearance of twenty-two such garments make us suppose that these were for trumpeters, as is the case with the 9ᵉ. We also note, contrary to what the Otto series manuscript shows, no bearskins existed for trumpeters.

What is clear is that a lot of clothing was replaced in Germany at the end of the 1807 campaign: the *cuirasses* had been supplied from Potsdam and Breslau and the boots, *culottes de peau* and clothing was all condemned out of hand as being badly made, made from low-grade materials and not according exactly to regulations. Clearly between summer 1807 and returning to the home depots, regiments had received a new allocation of clothing.[33]

Chapter 7
1812 Campaign Preparations

Alas, we know nothing more until after Wagram. Reviewed in September 1810 by General Nansouty, he remarked that the, 4ᵉ, 6ᵉ, 7ᵉ and 8ᵉ should adopt sheepskin *pantalons* and not *culottes*, should wear *Suvarov* boots rather than traditional long boots, and on campaign adopt grey broadcloth *surculottes*, worn inside the boot. Nansouty argued that the long-tailed *surtouts* and *habits* were to be replaced with short-tailed garments with immediate effect – the long tails being totally incompatible with mounted service. Furthermore, he noted the regiments were 'plagued' with overtly heavy sabres, adjutants were wearing the distinctions of a captain, *sous-officiers* were likewise wearing epaulettes almost indistinguishable from captains' epaulettes and they had also abandoned wearing the stock for large kerchiefs and habitually wore the shirt collars *rabattu* i.e., thrown up to show above the collar and kerchief! Nansouty

Drawn by Sauerweid, we see a trooper of the 6ᵉ *Cuirassiers* sometime in 1805. He retains the round *porte-manteau*, and has a grenade badge to his *giberne*.

argued all these infringements of regulations should not happen.[1] Clearly, in these four regiments we have to imagine a very different look to the one we imagine *cuirassiers* to have had! The whim of the colonel or divisional commander was self-evident in October 1810 and more so in 1811.

Based on Nansouty's critique, the *habit à revers* was officially supressed on 11 March 1811.[2] In its place, a new *habit-surtout* was adopted: it had a single row of ten buttons to the front, and two large buttons in the small of the back, it was cut slightly longer in front than the previous design and had much shorter tails, which barely covered the soldier's rump based on period iconography.[3] These new garments were to be brought into use from 1 October 1811.[4] Why was this? Every regiment was inspected on 1 October, when the regiments' clothing needs for the following year was established for new garments and replacements; however, by October 1811, regiments were in Germany, hundreds of

This portrait of a squadron commander of the 10ᵉ *Cuirassiers* perhaps reflects the confusion over the design of the *habit*. Our officer was born on 13 September 1759, engaged aged 19 as a soldier, and was promoted to squadron commander on 7 September 1799. Awarded the Coveted Cross of the Legion of Honour on 15 June 1804, he was promoted to major on 25 May 1807. This portrait therefore dates from 1804–07. Is this the *habit de cuirass* of 1803? (*Private collection France*)

miles away from home, and the inspections that assessed what was needed for the year 1812 were not carried out until November 1811 into early 1812. Without a shadow of a doubt, it is unlikely any made it into the field with the war squadrons. An original example is preserved in the Musée de l'Empéri for an officer of the 7ᵉ. It may have been worn in 1812, or perhaps in 1813. This meant that at least four regulation garments were in use side by side!

On 1 May 1811 Nansouty reviewed the 2ᵉ Cuirassiers. He noted the regiment had 35 *habits à revers* to be disposed of and 211 *surtouts* needing repairs; the 3ᵉ *Cuirassiers* he reported had 323 *habits à revers* that needed replacing, 2 *surtouts* and 243 stable coats; the 9ᵉ was missing 102 *cuirasses* and 74 *housses*. The 12ᵉ *cuirassiers* were in 'the worst condition imaginable' Nansouty noted, 'no money has been expended on clothing since the 1809 campaign'. He noted 14 *habits*, 408 *vestes*, 55 pairs of *culottes de peau*, 516 stable coats, 144 *bonnets de police*, 103 *manteaux* and 37 helmets were '*hors de service*'. He also reported that 82 *porte-manteaux*, 221 *fraise*, 74 bridles, 100 *housses*, 36 *schabraques* and 137 saddle blankets were all expired. Nansouty reported that for the 717 other ranks, just 612 fit horses were with the regiment, with 105 being needed immediately. Even at times of peace and plenty, the mounted arm suffered from lack of funds to procure new equipment.

As part of the build-up to the Russian campaign, the *cuirassiers* underwent a root and branch shake-down inspection. The 1ᵉ *Cuirassiers* were reviewed 13 November 1811 by

58   Napoleon's Heavy Cavalry

General Nansouty. He reported that the new *habits* were made of a poor-quality cloth, and the old *habits* were of a blue that was almost violet in shade. The *culottes de peau* needed replacing within six months and were overall fairly bad. Nansouty also added that: 'the *Eperons* (spurs) are ridiculously long and the *schabraques* of a terrible cut', and remarkably the '*schabraques* were made from black sheepskin, which gave a very bad look to the regiment'.[5] The 1[e] must have looked remarkable with sombre black sheepskins! Certainly, the regiment would have looked totally unique – this was demonstrably the point the colonel was making!

Nansouty inspected the 5[e] and 8[e] at Cologne on 24 November 1811:

5[e] *Cuirassiers*
This regiment has got a lot of old horses; a lot of them are bad, several are mediocre and many were in bad health when they arrived; they are getting better.

This regiment has only received 32 remounts this year; there are 266 horses missing for the count to be good (900). Out of the 266, 128 have already been negotiated but it is possible they will not arrive quickly and that with such a number, some of them may be refused when they come before the sellers. At the depot, the corps has 200, complete, good-quality teams according to the account that I have been given. There are still 66 horses missing from them to be up to strength.

Clothing is mediocre, the clothes are badly made, the collars are much too big and not uniform; orders have been given for the collars to be reduced in size and each man to have the same collar instead of the enormous silk or muslin cravats or little horse hair and wool pads they put around their necks to fill out their oversized collars. Half the *habits* are bad, the leather *culottes* are reasonably good, the boots are smoothed, the spurs are much too long and without rowels, the cartridge box is of a special type and too small; they are decorated with a crowned 'N' on the flap; the *vestes* are of poor quality and several are unwearable; the *porte-manteaux* are bad as are the cloaks; the *schabraques* are generally bad and greatly in need of repair and replacing. The saddlework needs repairing, and the breastplates are bad, the stable coats in the form of a jacket [i.e. single breasted] are bad. The sabres are in reasonable condition; there is only one pistol per man, and not everybody has one.

8e *Cuirassiers*
Half of the clothing is new, the rest is getting worn, although it is only two years old … the collars of the *habits* are much too big. A *l'écuyère* boots, many of which are too tightly fitting at the knee. Cloaks are too small and badly cut; several helmet turbans are bad, visors in bad condition and of different shapes; the cartridge box belts are of light cavalry style. The weapons are in good condition, some scabbards are bad although they are the latest model. The breastplate straps [*épaulières*] of the regiment are made of black leather whereas in all other regiments they are covered in copper scales … The *housses* are very small and hardly cover the flanks of the horse.[6]

The 5ᵉ must have appeared rather odd with light cavalry *giberne*s with crowned 'N' *giberne* plates, and it seems they did use the July 1803 decree stable coat. The 8ᵉ with black leather *épaulières* to the *cuirass* must have also been distinctive, and they again used the light cavalry *giberne* and belt. Despite having been out of action since summer 1809, the clothing was in bad condition, yet the 5ᵉ and 8ᵉ were in better shape than the 4ᵉ, which was given a shake-down in Hamburg on 25 January 1812:

Uniform. I had expected it to be bad not through any fault in the officers' and soldiers' goodwill, but because of the sorry state that all sections of the regiment are in. I noticed that the whole regiment had *surtouts* instead of *habits-vestes*; being unaware of any order on this subject, I do not know which is considered as the uniform. What is certain is that two thirds of the *cuirassier* regiments are wearing *habits-vestes* and the other is wearing the *surtout*. This point could do with clearing up, so as to bring uniformity into this part of the uniform.

The *surtouts* are quite good, but the cut is bad.

Vestes: There are only 247 in good condition, 530 are missing.

Stable coats: This regiment wears its old *surtouts*, which are all threadbare. It is true that the squadron commander has been informed that they were going to receive this article of clothing very shortly for the years 1810 and 1811.

Leather *culotte*: All the *cuirassiers* have them, but at least half of them are in bad condition.

Boots: Boots are generally in reasonably good condition.

Helmets: This regiment's helmets are in the worst condition imaginable, all the turbans have to be replaced, they are awful. Likewise, for the visors, which need totally replacement; a total overhaul of this item is needed, only the *bombe* and *cimier* are capable of being used.

Breastplates: These are generally in good condition, but they are in great need of being repaired such as being reshaped, necessitating great expense; all the rivets need to be removed and replaced. Moreover, some of the waistbelts need replacing as they are too short or worn; the shoulder straps also need repairing.

Sabres: Two thirds of the scabbards are made from iron, the rest from leather; some metal scabbards have even been lined in leather.

Waistbelts: These are generally bad and about a quarter of them cannot be slung over the shoulder.

Gibernes: One thing that surprised me was to see the regiment without *gibernes* and nothing to hold their cartridges. The squadron commander told me that they had never been issued. The shoulder belt had been used to repair the sword belts; heavens knows what has happened to the actual *gibernes*!

Saddles: These are in reasonably good condition.

Schabraque: These are all bad.

Porte-manteaux: There are only 777 for the whole regiment and 400 of them need throwing out.

Manteaux: Of 776, there are only 300 good ones, 376 mediocre and 100 that needed to be destroyed.[7]

Even at times of 'peace and plenty', the 4ᵉ looked shabby and had kit long past its best in use. Regimental records show that between 1804 and 1808 just 191 *gibernes* and belts had been made, and all had been lost by December 1807.[8] Indeed, as far back as spring 1808, General Comte de Pully noted that the regiment's leather work was 'exceptionally bad'.[9] Clearly the 4ᵉ was in terrible shape clothing wise for four years prior to the review!

The 1812 inspection also raises the old issue of what *cuirassiers* actually wore as a regimental coat. The 4ᵉ clearly wore long-tailed *surtouts*, different to the short-tailed garments that doubled up as *gilets d'ecurie*. The inspecting general, however, notes that the bulk of *cuirassier* regiments were wearing short *habits* as opposed to the *surtout*. Arguably therefore, *cuirassiers* wore the *habit* with revers from 1803 through to the Battle of Borodino. Les Gupil notes that in 1809 when the new *habit-surtout* came into use, the old short *surtouts* were to become new *gilets d'ecurie* for summer use. Clearly, this is what the 4ᵉ were doing.[10]

The *surtout* had a service life of three years, and colonels would not simply convert them into stable coats until the *surtout* were unusable, or had been replaced. Clearly the *habit de cuirass* and *surtout* were still worn side-by-side right up to the Russian campaign.

Trooper of the 10ᵉ *Cuirassiers* c.1806. (*Collection KM*)

Troopers and trumpeters of an unknown *cuirassier* regiment in 1805, thought to be the 10ᵉ. (*Collection KM*)

The mounted arm was by far the most costly and difficult to get ready for war. Not only had thousands of horses to be purchased, but also saddles and harness. To aid this process, remount depots were established in the Confederation of the Rhine, the whole process being overseen by General Bourcier. However, the process was far from simple, as we shall see. After undergoing basic training, once equipped, detachments of dismounted men then marched or travelled by post to Hanover to be mounted and receive the rest of their equipment. However, some detachments were dispatched only with their stable clothing.[11] Others arrived at the dépôt before their harness and saddle.[12] A detachment of thirteen men from the 10e *Cuirassiers* had arrived at the dépôt on 22 February 1812 wearing nothing but their canvas stable trousers and coats, a *bonnet de police* and shoes. The rest of their uniform, arms and equipment had not arrived at the dépôt. The same was true with a detachment of men from 12e *Cuirassiers*, who had nothing but their regimental boots and were still wearing civilian clothes.[13] Interestingly, as part of the build-up to the Russian campaign, the 10e replaced its costly *culotte de peau* with grey broadcloth *pantalons* with the inner leg reinforced with black leather: we find 760 pairs costing 10,640fr were purchased in 1812, 154fr was spent buying 11 pairs in 1813 and a single pair was obtained in 1814 for 14fr.[14] Clearly not every man had these at the close of the Empire, and we suppose they were restricted to *sous-officiers*.

To conclude, the so-called 1809–10 *habit-surtout*, made from 1811, was merely the 1802 *surtout* with slight changes to cut. The bulk of regiments were already decked out in *surtouts*, so it made sense to keep making 'more of the same' and stop once and for all the production of *habits à revers* and the *habit de cuirass*. Arguably this is what the 1804 decree had sought to do, and yet no standardisation in the dress of the *cuirassiers* would be achieved until 1813–14.

Cuirassiers wore rigid long riding boots: regimental orders from the 3^e, tells us they were worn only immediately prior to mounting, and were removed as soon as parade was finished. At other times men wore shoes. From 1814 the men wore boots like a modern a dressage boot, made from softer leather that finished below knee. These boots had been recommended in 1810 as superior to the boots then in use.

Chapter 8

Bardin Regulations

Perhaps the most famous of all French army uniform regulations are the so-called Bardin or 1812 regulations. Neither name is correct. Bardin was the secretary of the committee that wrote the regulations, and the regulations were written in 1811 for implementation by February 1813. Be that as it may, what the army wore was a permanent issue for the War Administration in terms of its cut, the durability of its construction and above all else its cost.[1] The Bardin regulation stated the following for the dress of *cuirassiers*. The text was heavily edited in April 1813:

Section 3. *Cuirassiers*
Art 1. Clothing
984. Composition of the Clothing
The clothing of the *sous-officiers* and *cuirassiers* will comprise a *habit veste*, a *gilet* in white broadcloth with no sleeves, a *gilets d'ecurie*, a pair of *culottes de peau* [remainder illegible] to the prescribed general dispositions No. 297.

985. *Habit Veste*
The *habit veste* is made from blue broadcloth closed in front with a row of buttons of the colour indicated in table of uniforms No. 1017, exactly the same as those of the *carabiniers* [see No. 778]. The tails will carry grenades cut from cloth the same colour as the *habit*. The epaulettes are the same as those worn by the grenadiers and the brides are cut from broadcloth the same colour as the *habit* body. The *habit* is garnished with 10 large buttons and 8 small.

986. *Gilet*
The *gilet* is cut from white broadcloth and is the same model as used by the *carabiniers'* white broadcloth and will conform to the model, viz. No. 301.[2]

This is where things get confusing. Bardin describes for the *carabiniers* a *surtout*, with no pockets on the tails. The front closed by eight large buttons, two at the small of the back. The cuffs clearly had three buttons to the flaps, and two small buttons appeared at the shoulder. This is logically the *surtout* as outlined under the October 1801 decree.

However, the tariff accompanying the regulations issued in 1813 to *cuirassier* regiments makes use of seventeen large buttons, i.e., nine to the front and eight on the back: two at the small of the back and three on each pocket, and is describing the *habit de cuirass*! It states that the *habit* required 1m 35 of blue broadcloth, 0m 24 of facing cloth for piping and cuffs, 1m 03 of facing colour serge, 1m 44 for lining the upper body, sleeves and pockets, seventeen large buttons, eight small, and three hooks and eyes. Labour cost 2fr 45 and the complete garment came in at 26fr 01. The *manteau* was the most costly item, needing 5m 33 of broadcloth, and cost 54fr 82, compared to 13fr 96 for a helmet, 21fr for the boots and 3fr 50 for the epaulettes. Less the *cuirass*, a trooper cost 392fr 50 to equip.[3] This is surely the *habit de cuirass*. From the tariff we see that front of the *habit* was cut a little lower to allow for the additional ninth button compared to the eight buttons on the *surtout*. Even in the printed form of the decree, not a word is uttered about the form of the cuffs or tail pockets, but we assume from the number of buttons issued that the cuffs had flaps closed by three small buttons.[4]

Clearly the original decree of Bardin confirmed the then current design of *habit* in use, i.e., the *surtout*. At some stage later came the choice to use the *habit de cuirass* as the sole garment. When this change occurred we cannot say: April 1813 or actually in 1812?

The epaulette brides were piped in the regiment's facing colour. Variation in colour to the cuff facings, piping and collar designated regimental identity:[5]

1^e to 3^e: Scarlet
4^e to 6^e: Aurore
7^e to 9^e: Yellow
10^e to 12^e: Rose
13^e and 14^e: Wine Lees

Far from clarifying things, Bardin regulation is confusing, and at times contradictory! Given the confused nature of the decree, we suspect that regiments simply continued to make the *habits de cuirass* and *surtouts* of both types, all confusingly recorded in 1814 as *habits*!

The published clothing tariff for the *cuirassiers* was as follows:[6]

Item	Cloth	1811	1812
Surtouts	Blue broadcloth	1m 65	1m 43
	Facing cloth	0m 12	0m 25
	Facing colour serge	1m 75	1m 03
	Linen for lining	1m 41	1m 45
	Large buttons	12	17
	Small buttons	6	8
Vestes	White broadcloth	1m 09	0m 66
	White serge	2m 52	
	Linen for lining	0m 29	0m 70
	Buttons	12	10
Surculottes	*Gris-beige* broadcloth		0m 93
	Linen		0m 30
	Bone buttons		24

64 Napoleon's Heavy Cavalry

Item	Cloth	1811	1812
Stable coat	Blue broadcloth	1m 19	
	Blue tricot		1m 81
	Linen	1m 34	1m 30
	Small buttons	24	16
Bonnets de police	Blue broadcloth	0m 25	0m 28
	Facing colour broadcloth	0m 02	0m 2
	Linen	0m 12	0m 21
Manteaux	Blanc picque de bleu broadcloth	4m 75	5m 35
	Facing colour serge	1m 48	1m 47
	Treillis		0m 05
Housse et Chaperons	Blue broadcloth	0m 59	
	White lace 0m 40 wide	5m 95	
Porte-manteaux	Blue tricot	1m 34	1m 34
	Treillis	1m 73	1m 73
	White lace 0m 22 wide	1m 34	1m 34

The confusing nature of the various decrees meant that colonels were literally free to 'pick and choose' which garments their regiments wore, as nothing was codified into a single, easy to understand collection of orders. Certainly, a new *habit à revers* made in 1810 would be in use until 1812, and likewise a *surtout* made in 1811 would be in use until 1813. As regiments marched to war in 1811, they left behind depots heaving with clothing. On 3 October 1811 every regiment was ordered to prepare 'clothing reserve', anticipating the needs for 1812: 200 *habits*, *surtout*s, stable coats, *culottes de peau* etc. were to be made.[7] Therefore a colonel no doubt simply ordered 'more of the same'. These garments were pressed into use in winter 1812 to clothe men flooding into the depots to make up the substantial losses of the Russian campaign.[8] All that was to change. Or was it? The Bardin regulation came into operation for the *cuirassiers*, along with the army as a whole from 1 October 1812, when each regiment received from the War Ministry an example of each item of uniform for the master tailors of the regiment to copy, along with a written copy of the regulation.[9] Under the pretext of the decree, *cuirassiers* received a new helmet with bear pelt turban: the turban was to be 101mm tall, and rather than a plume, the helmet was to be decorated with a pompom. *Cuirassiers* also gained Imperial Livery and also a light cavalry carbine and belt.[10] Sheepskin half-*schabraques* were to be adopted, but the War Ministry allowed the cloth *chaperons* to be used until 'life expired'.[11]

Officers

When we look at the section of Bardin relating to officers of *cuirassiers*, we find that:[12]

> 1007. Clothing of the officers
> The clothing of the officers of *cuirassiers* will conform to the general dispositions No. 419 and 418, and their uniform to No. 1017. Their *manteau* will be in blue broadcloth. Their *habit* for service will be cut short and in *tenue de societie* they will wear the *habit long* conforming to decree No. [left blank].[13]

This section of the decree clearly gave officers two *habits*, one the same as the other ranks with short tails, and allowed a *habit* with long tails – as no formal decree was listed dictating the form this garment was to take, we assume officers had great latitude in the *habit* they wore as the regulations merely says it was to be 'cut long'. When we refer to No. 419, we read that officers were also allowed a *frac*. The *frac* had no pockets to the rear and instead had pockets fitted into the pleat, which makes us understand the pockets were '*à la soubise*' rather than the large three-pointed flap. We also find in this section of the decree that *cuirassier* officers did not use black sheepskin *schabraques*: this is clearly a myth by wargamers and artists and is not based in historical fact. The campaign *schabraque* was made from blue broadcloth, decorated with blue lace, and rather than a sheepskin half-*schabraque* used cloth *chaperons*.[14]

It is no surprise, therefore, to find portraits of officers wearing *habits-vestes* with *revers* in regimental facing colour as this is implied by this portion of the decree. Yet the plates accompanying the Bardin regulations consistently show officers in service dress with long-tailed *habits*, which is clearly fantasy on the part of the artists. This further goes to show that we cannot trust the plate section of the regulations to any great degree when it shows costumed figures.

Towards Bardin Mark 2

On 10 April 1813, the Bardin decree of February 1812 was comprehensively rewritten. For the heavy cavalry and dragoons a new pattern of *manteau* was adopted, this time with sleeves and the front fastening with a single row of cloth-covered buttons.[15]

When the Bourbon monarchy was restored to power in 1814, they inherited a bankrupt and demoralised country, fatigued after almost twenty-five years of fighting. The army was ill-equipped and under-strength. Some regiments were little more than a battalion or squadron strong. The army was to be consolidated around a hard-core nucleus of veterans.

The Royal Ordonnance of 12 May 1814 disbanded the Imperial army.[16] All three arms were culled, and only the senior regiments of cavalry and infantry were to be taken into the new Royal army. The Royal Ordonnance furthermore decreed that only the senior regiments of cavalry and infantry were to be taken into the new Royal army. The cavalry was reduced from 110 regiments to 56. The 13ᵉ and 14ᵉ regiments of *Cuirassiers* were disbanded.[17]

66   Napoleon's Heavy Cavalry

The time of peace following the 1st Restoration allowed shake-down inspections of the army to be made, and serious consideration given to new uniform regulations. To do so a committee of senior cavalry officers was convened, overseen by General of Division Comte de Saint-Germain.

The first issue raised by the committee was quality control and standard of workmanship and materials used. The committee agreed that the use of private contractors to clothe and equip the army was a total failure: low-grade workmanship using 'cheap substandard materials' was harmful to the army, and the contractors had been able to inflate prices to maximise their profit, and had put many regiments into debt. Hence forward, everything would be made in the regimental workshops using regulated materials. In order to ensure standards were met, inspectors of review would inspect the materials and quality of workmanship rather than colonels.

About the dress of the *carabiniers* and *cuirassiers*, the committee found fault. The *habit* was 'so short as to be little more than a sleeved waistcoat' and in future it was to be cut so the bottom edge 'extended 3 fingers' below the bottom edge of the *cuirass* and was to cover the waistband of the breeches. Experience had shown that wearing a *gilet* beneath the *habit* was 'hot and very uncomfortable', and the lining in the back of the *habit* had often been removed. Henceforward the *gilet* was to be dispensed with. To ensure that the bottom of the shirt was not exposed, the committee ordered that the legwear was to be cut higher. About the legwear, the committee raised several points: 'It is proposed that the *culottes de peau* be withdrawn from service, as they are too expensive, difficult to ride in and mount up when wet, and take much too long to dry when in the field/on campaign and are impossible to keep clean, and are altogether a mad item of clothing. Instead of *culottes de peau,* they are to be replaced by *pantalons en drap*, i.e., broadcloth. The General Comte de Saint-Germain proposes that for the heavy cavalry white broadcloth riding trousers should be worn on parade, with long grey trousers for campaign use, to be worn outside the new model of boots, which should no longer have a knee piece.' The knee guards – *manchette du botte* – were to be suppressed, and the money saved from their production carried over to produce the *pantalons en drap.*

The committee felt the long heavy cavalry boot was altogether a bad design, and instead a long riding boot finishing below the knee was to be introduced to be 'the same as those used by the Saxon cavalry'. These were stiff riding boots that came just above the knee, as had been proposed in 1801 as with the *manteaux-capote*!

Cuirassier helmets were next on the agenda. Comte de Saint-Germain felt that the helmets were not solid as they could be to protect the head from sword blows, and looked 'inelegant', preferring the form of the *carabinier* helmet. The inspections of summer 1814 revealed different models of helmet were in use and of differing qualities. In the 3[e] *Cuirassiers*, Colonel Saint Croix advised the committee that he had added a top plate to the *cimier* in brass for both aesthetic, defensive and practical purposes, as well as a short leather peak to the rear of the helmet, to rain prevent water from soaking the collar and back of the soldier's tunic. Such an addition to the helmet would not cost much and would meet with the inspector general's approval for use by the arm as a whole. Saint

Croix noted that the *crinière* often rotted and shed its hair because of damp problems: taxidermy does not like getting wet. On examining original helmets, in one case the *crinière* is cut from a section of horse's mane – complete with skin and fur from the neck – or a strip of hair and skin cut from a horse's tail. The resulting hair and skin was left in a bucket of salt for six weeks before being sewn to a carrying length of leather and fixed to a helmet. Therefore, one can easily see why the hair fell out, and Saint Croix wanted to keep the *crinière* dry and to prevent the soldier's head getting wet, and rusting the top of the helmet. The committee also noted that a longer turban that formed a small neck guard, with cut-outs for the ears, was acceptable to the overall design and 'look' of the helmet and afforded more protection.

Cuirassiers and *carabiniers* were to lose their carbines – many never had them – and *gibernes*, as had been proposed way back in 1801. And, just as proposed by Margaron in 1801, *cuirassiers* were to have just one pistol, and the empty pistol holster was to be adapted to carry tools to clean the pistol in the bottom part of the holster. Fitting into the top was to be a circular wooden cartridge block with eight rounds of ammunition, which was 'considered sufficient, as without a carbine, and possessing just one pistol, the *Cuirassiers* are not expected to use up very much ammunition when in action'.

Next up the committee ordered that for the heavy cavalry, the *manteau*, which had formally been folded on the *porte-manteau*, was now to be carried at the front of the saddle. The broadcloth *housse* was to be abolished, and sheepskin *schabraque* like the light cavalry used, which totally covered the saddle and saddle blanket, was to be adopted, along with the round *porte-manteau*. The last point the committee made was to officially authorise 'pockets to be made in the sheepskins to access the pistols': this is a very common-sense idea as it is on practical experience almost impossible to get to the pistols under the sheepskin! The committee's recommendations were signed off on 12 January 1815 by Comte Victor Latour-Maubourg.[18]

This was codified in the decree of 8 February 1815. The regulations were framed in the Bardin regulation of 1812. It was the first time that the army had had a chance to be totally re-equipped with new-pattern clothing and equipment, although some regiments clung onto the old-style *habits* and other idiosyncrasies. A huge reclothing programme began in spring 1815. The decree of 23 April 1814 ordered that all Imperial iconography was to be removed from use. Trumpeters were to be dressed in blue; their *habits* adorned with the King's Livery. *Fleur-de-lys* were to replace grenades, eagles or other devices on uniforms. The decree also outlined that any clothing not made to the regulation of 1812 was to be replaced forthwith, and new facing colours were to be adopted by the *cuirassiers*.[19]

Any chance of rolling out the new regulation came to a juddering halt with Napoléon's return. How far the changeover was completed in rolling out new boots, *schabraques* etc. we can only judge, but the changes were enshrined in the 1817 regulations.

Chapter 9

Regulations in Practice 1812–15

How far were the regulations followed? Did the Bardin regulation exist? What follows is a detailed review of the *cuirassiers* from 1805 to 1815. This is the sum total of archive sources available on the subject.

1e *Cuirassiers*

Reviewed on 31 May 1813, the 3e, 4e and 5e *escadron* mustered 5 sergeant majors, 18 sergeants, 5 *fourriers*, 29 corporals, 10 trumpeters and 203 *cuirassiers*. There were 270 other ranks with just 45 horses. The inspector noted that the *dépôt* had taken in 216 new conscripts: 104 from the infantry *dépôt*, 73 from the national guard, 30 from the *gendarmerie* and 90 were conscripts of the class of 1814. The regiment had passed a contract to buy 205 horses from a horse dealer in Belgium, and had secured 12 horses from the 6e *artillerie à cheval* and 10 from the 7e *chevau-légers-lanciers*. The men in the *dépôt* had no clothing, and the workmen were waiting for deliveries of cloth and other materials. The regiment was missing 201 *mousquetons*, 116 sabres and 141 pairs of pistols. The major reported he was waiting for the delivery of the men's equipment, boots, helmet and armour from Paris.[1] The regiment had just two squadrons in the field, and men were

Martinet offers us three figures from the 1^e *Cuirassiers* c.1810. The trooper, it seems, has a black or dark grey *schabraque*. The trumpeter has a sky-blue uniform, which cannot be traced in the regimental archive, and lastly, we have an officer of the regiment.

Regulations in Practice 1812–15

Eyewitness drawing of a trooper of the 1ᵉ *Cuirassiers* in 1812. Of note is the black sheepskin *schabraque*: months before the drawing was made General Nansouty commented in November 1811 that '… the *housse* and *schabraques* of are of a terrible cut. The *schabraques* themselves are made from black sheepskin, which give a very bad look to the regiment.' Clearly our eye-witness artist had indeed witnessed the 1ᵉ *Cuirassiers* first hand to get the colour of the *schabraque* correct.

Trooper of the 1ᵉ *Cuirassiers* by Martinet in a print published at the end of the 1st Empire. Of note is the black sheepskin *schabraque*. Seemingly the regiment used these from 1812 – if not earlier – through to disbandment judging by this image and archive documents.

Reconstruction of a trumpeter of the 1ᵉ *Cuirassiers*, 1808–10. At the time of the inspection on 1 June 1807 and when reviewed at Lodi on 1 January 1808, the trumpeters were armoured. According to the journal of an inhabitant of Luneburg, the 1ᵉ *Cuirassiers* arrived in that town on 9 September, 1808, and had a band:

> The 1st regiment of *Cuirassiers*, numbered 500 remarkable men, arrived here at midday from Luchow. They also had a band which was more harmonious than that of the 5th. Only the trumpeters did not have a new uniform. Likewise, they used yellow leather for their waistbelt, *culottes* and gloves. They were dressed in dark blue had a white horsehair crest on their helmets, and white epaulettes.

Does this imply the use of a trooper's *habit*? Very likely indeed. The white-maned helmets for 1ᵉ *Cuirassiers*, were it seems, those made for the elite company in 1802. The buff-coloured leather work is a reference we have not been able to verify. Not a single piece of archive evidence supports this diary entry, but it is hard to dispute these observations.

We present here a number of contemporary or just post-epoch images of the trumpeters. Up first is Martinet's print showing a sky-blue and scarlet-clad trumpeter. Trumpeters wore scarlet *habits* faced dark blue in 1805, presumably a parade garment, and it seems they also had an undress coat. In the 24th series of *Uniforms of the 1st Empire* published by Commandant Boucquoy, the painter Benigni has shown a portrait, a trumpeter in marching order, about 1805–06. He wears a scarlet *surtout* with round collar and cuffs, and tail facings of dark blue, and which fastens down the centre of his chest with a single row of nine buttons. The lace that edges his collar and cuffs, his epaulettes and trumpet cord, are all white. His chapeau, no doubt retained from the old cavalry regiment, is worn 'fore and aft' and is decorated with a white cockade loop. The plume has a blacked, oiled linen cover. His harness is of the regulation pattern and includes blue *chaperons* laced with white. The image is taken from a period engraving by Zix.

We know the trumpeters were armoured, and we present our reconstruction of a trumpeter in scarlet so dressed presumably as worn in the 1805 campaign and by 1811. Our second reconstruction is based on notes by Rousselot, presumably taken from Martinet and a water colour by Major Jolly, which we also present, of a wounded trumpeter. Lastly, a scarlet *surtout* is again shown in the painting 'Battle of the Moskova'. Here General Lejeune depicts a group of trumpeters galloping on the flank of a regiment of *Cuirassiers*, which precedes the *carabinier* brigade. It is probably the 1^e, who were in the same division as the *Carabiniers*. These trumpeters' all-red *surtouts* are devoid of all lacing and only have white epaulettes, and remarkably they wear a white colpack with red bag and plume. However, as the figures are not more than 25mm tall, and are in the very back of the image, we cannot place too much reliability on this image, certainly no archive paperwork exists to confirm the use of colpacks. Reversed colours make logical sense, yet the differences between Martinet, Jolly and Lejeune ask more questions than they resolve.

tied down uselessly in the *dépôt* for want of horses and clothing. Alas, we know nothing else, but the report does show that obtaining men to rebuild the shattered Grande Armée was far easier than finding horses, and above all in getting kit made for them! A shortage of materials was a huge problem that affected the army until after Waterloo was lost.

At the end of the 1814 campaign, the 1ᵉ *Cuirassiers'* clothing was in bad condition:[2]

Item	Good Condition	Need Repairs	To be Replaced	Need Replacing	Short Fall	
Habits	102	82	31	17	36	
Habits de trompette	6	2				
Vestes blanche	87	10	54	3	122	The clothing of the squadron that recently returned from Hamburg is included in the figures.
Gilets d'ecurie	82	41	59		94	
Pantalons de treillis	7		3	0	266	
Bonnets de police	121	29	26	21	79	
Surculottes gris	36	8	52	11	169	
Culottes de peau	113	12	27		124	
Manteaux	29	16	20		40	
Capote manteaux	130	41	0	0		
Porte-manteaux	132	49	28	17	50	
Helmets	194	53		8	21	
Garnitures de cuirass	170	38	13	1	54	

The bulk of clothing either needed repairs or to be replaced. The *garniture de cuirass*, otherwise known as *fraise*, was the red edging with white lace that was fitted into the edge of the front and back plate. The men were issued as items of *petit equipment*, 580 shirts, 185 black stocks, 350 white stocks, 344 pairs of linen stockings, 185 pairs of shoes, 155 pairs of black tricot gaiters, 142 combs, 183 grease brushes and boxers of grease, 143 clothes beaters and 325 cotton night caps. Cloth in the *dépôt* comprised 9m 04 white broadcloth, 21m 46 scarlet broadcloth, 4m 40 silver lace and 0m 30 worsted lace. We find the *dépôt* had sufficient items to replace the worn-out clothing. Items in the 1ᵉ *Cuirassiers'* magazine on 1 July 1814 were:[3]

	Habits de cuirassier	*Habits de trompette*	*Gilets de drap*	*Gilets d'ecurie*	*Pantalons de treillis*	*Bonnets de police*	*Surculottes gris*	*Culottes de peau*	*Manteaux*	Helmets	Pairs of Epaulettes	*Bretelles*	*Garnitures de cuirass*	*Plumes*
New	232	1	348	43	32	308	469	19	308	387	429	170	92	0
Repair	90	0	0	19	16	0	0	0	32	88	0	0	68	0
Hors de service	0	0	0	0	0	0	2	58	0	27	88	0	160	0
Total	322	1	348	62	48	308	471	77	340	502	517	170	320	0

Senior officer of the 1ᵉ *Cuirassiers* c.1810 by Vernet. Of interest, the *schabraque* is of almost identical form of that shown by Hoffmann. In Vernet's second image the officer has the expected *chaperons*.

Also, in the *dépôt* were 3 shirts, 28 brushes for cleaning copper, 37 black stocks, 23 wooden button sticks, 66 pairs of linen stockings, 1 pair of shoes, 9 pairs of black tricot gaiters as well 9 pairs of spurs, 6 *epinglettes* – vent pricks, 69 screwdrivers, 25 *trousses* – a soldier's housewife containing needles, thread, cloth, razor, soap etc., 14 nose bags, 14 musettes, 6 scarlet plumes and 24lb of wax for the *giberne*! General Exelmans, who conducted the inspection, noted that the regiment's dress was 'passable', but added that the clothing was 'expertly stitched', and noted that sufficient stocks existed in the *dépôt* to clothe all the men.[4]

Reconstruction of a trumpeter of the 1ᵉ *Cuirassiers*, 1813–14. We know the trumpeters at the disbandment were decked out in Imperial Livery and were not armoured.

The regiment ceased to exist on 2 July 1814 when the remaining 187 men of the 1ᵉ were merged with almost 600 Royalist volunteers who filled out the ranks of the newly raised *Cuirassiers du Roi*!

2ᵉ *Cuirassiers*

Reviewed on 24 November 1810, the regiment mustered 37 officers with 86 horses and 860 other ranks with 682 horses. The men were wearing 622 *habits*, 832 *surtouts* – clearly some men had both a *habit* AND a *surtout* – 613 white *vestes*, 643 pairs of *culottes de peau*, 731 pairs of stable trousers, 683 stable coats, 860 *manteaux* with 68 in stores, and 860 helmets. Interestingly, for 860 men, just 794 *gibernes* and belts were issued: presumably the senior *sous-officiers* and trumpeters lacked these items. A total of 830 sabre belts were in use for 849 sabres, which were decorated with 711 sword knots! A total of 730 pairs of gauntlets were in use, 830 pairs of boots, 858 pairs of grenadier's epaulettes and 814 *cuirasses*. We assume the trumpeters were not armoured. What is remarkable for a regiment on a peacetime footing is the amount of missing kit. To bring the regiment up to a strength of 956 other ranks, and to replace worn-out kit and to provide kit for new entrants, the inspector authorised the production of 343 *habits*, 133 *surtouts*, 535 white *vestes*, 322 pairs *of culottes de peau*, 234 pairs of stable trousers, 232 stable coats, 117 *bonnets de police*, 105 *manteaux*, 105 *cuirasses*, 110 *gibernes*, 105 sabre belts, 85 pairs of epaulettes, 116 sabres and 81 *cuirasses*.[5] Remarkably, just as detailed in the 1806 decree, men had both a *habit à revers* for duties when the *cuirass* was not needed and a *surtout* to be worn under armour! So yes, in the 2e at least men had both garments in use side by side.

Re-formed after the Russian campaign, a report from June 1813 lays bare the issues the regiment faced in clothing and equipping the men. The *dépôt* held 91 horses, of which 26 out of an expected 72 horses had come from the 7e *chevau-légers-lanciers* and were either sick or wounded and no longer fit for future service. It was 'impossible', said the major, to speed up the delivery of cloth from the manufacturers so that the regiment's tailors could proceed with making clothing. In addition, 918 helmets had been ordered from manufacturers in Paris.[6] A few days later, the major reported that 186 helmets had been completed and were ready for delivery. He added that thanks to the hard work of the *dépôt* work men, the *dépôt* would be able to issue 937 sets of grand equipment by the

Trooper of the 2[e] *Cuirassier* by Martinet. The first image of a trooper with *chaperons* must date to the early years of the Empire as when inspected on 23 December 1807, the regiment only used white sheepskin *schabraques*. The second image clearly dates from 1808 to 1815, likewise the officer.

74　Napoleon's Heavy Cavalry

end of the month, but only 88 saddles were available for service and a further 40 would be available by 1 August. For immediate issue the *dépôt* held 100 *habits* and contracts had been passed for the production of 869 *habits*, which were to be delivered by 31 August. Finally, he noted that the *dépôt* held 2,572m blue tricot and 4,400m broadcloth for *manteaux* along with 144 sabres, 204 *cuirasses*, 150 *gibernes* with belts, 150 sabre belts, 150 *porte-mousquetons* and 250 sword knots.[7]

We know nothing else until the regiment was reviewed at the start of October 1814, when the men had the following items of clothing and equipment:[8]

Item	In Good Repair	In Need of Repair	Need Replacing	Total	Items Missing
Habits de cuirassier	159	64	7	230	0
Habits de trompette	0	10	0	10	4
Gilets en drap blanc	216	22	2	240	0
Gilets d'ecurie	109	63	111	283	0
Culottes de peau	144	0	109	253	0
Surculottes en drap gris	139	4	142	285	0
Pantalons in wool	249	0	5	254	0
Stable trousers	0	0	0	0	214
Manteaux	234	13	2	249	0
Bonnets de police	195	0	4	199	15
Scarlet epaulettes	227	0	3	230	0
Helmets	218	32	0	250	0
Crinières for helmets	218	32	0	250	0
Braces	141	54	55	250	0
Boots and spurs	137	107	0	244	0
Waistbelts	245	1	0	246	0
Gibernes et porte-gibernes	192	0	0	192	22
Sword knots	216	0	0	216	0
Porte-manteaux	134	11	1	146	68
Banderole-porte-mousquetons	0	0	0	0	0
Bayonets	0	0	0	0	0
Trumpets	14	0	0	14	0
Gauntlets	230	19	0	258	0
Garnitures de cuirass	160	11	0	171	43
Sabres	247	2	0	249	0
Pistols	148	14	0	162	521
Carbines	0	0	0	0	0
Cuirasses	154	71	0	225	0
Shirts	572				
Black stocks	223				

Regulations in Practice 1812–15   75

Item	In Good Repair	In Need of Repair	Need Replacing	Total	Items Missing
Wool socks	252				
Pairs of shoes	227				
Black gaiters	5				
Ration bags	177				

The trumpeters' *habits* to be replaced without a shadow of a doubt were green with Imperial Livery. The broadcloth *pantalons* were also made from grey-brown broadcloth like the *surculotte*, but had the inner seat reinforced with black leather. These are very much non-regulation items, but are shown by contemporary artist Sauerweid. Stocks of cloth in the *dépôt* in 1814 were as follows:[9]

0m 7 beige broadcloth
9m 93 blue broadcloth
0m 42 white broadcloth
150m 34 scarlet broadcloth
0m green broadcloth
149m 38 *blanc picque de bleu* broadcloth
0m white serge
25m 98 blue tricot
1,346m linen for lining
4,695m linen for underpants

Trumpeter of the 2[e] *Cuirassier* by Rousselot dating from *c.*1805, and a second image that he dates to 1810. We are ignorant of his source. (*Collection KM*)

We present three reconstructions of the 2ᵉ. Up first is a trumpeter of the 2ᵉ *Cuirassiers* in 1813 to 1814 and during the 100 days. In October 1815, the regiment held 3m 27 of green broadcloth for trumpeters' habits and 30m of Imperial Livery. No trumpeters' lace existed in 1814, but ten trumpeters' *habits* in need of repair did exist. These we assume were green with Imperial Livery. No green cloth or Imperial Livery existed in 1814, so the green broadcloth and livery was clearly purchased in 1815.

Secondly is a trumpeter of the 2ᵉ *Cuirassiers* during the 1st Restoration. Becoming the *Cuirassiers du Reine*, the regiment decked out its trumpeters in Royalist Livery. Last is a trooper of the *Cuirassiers du Reine* as they appeared during the 1st Restoration and 100 days when they served at Waterloo as the 2ᵉ *Cuirassiers*.

The *dépôt* was bursting at the seams with clothing and equipment. Brand new items included 246 *capotes* – are these *capote manteaux* or literally infantry-style *capotes*?, 136 *cuirassier habits*, 366 pairs of grenadier epaulettes, 344 white *vestes*, 393 *gilets d'ecurie*, 27 pairs of grey broadcloth *pantalons* with black leather reinforcement, 15 pairs of stable trousers, 7 helmets, 149 sets of braces, 368 waistbelts, 410 *gibernes*, 424 *giberne* belts, 402 *porte-manteaux*, 213 *cuirasses* and 21 trumpets. Needing repairs were 70 *capotes*, 11 *habits*, 120 pairs of *culottes de peau*, 246 helmets, 64 waistbelts, 54 *gibernes*, 24 *giberne* belts, 66 *porte-manteaux*, 149 *cuirasses*, 115 pairs of boots and 166 *banderole-porte-mousquetons*. To be written off were 71 old-regulation *manteaux*, as well as 21 helmets, 148 waistbelts, 43 *gibernes*, 98 *giberne* belts, 84 *porte-manteaux* and 10 pairs of boots. The regiment had no musketoons, the *banderole-porte-mousquetons* may well be the self-same items as in the *dépôt* in summer 1813 and never issued. No lace or green broadcloth existed for the trumpeters. Had these items, along with the *habits*, been hurriedly taken from use and chucked in a corner of the *dépôt*? Very likely indeed.[10]

We know nothing more about the dress of the regiment until it was disbanded in December 1815, when the *dépôt* held the following amounts of cloth:[11]

130m 8 blue broadcloth
149m 38 *blanc picque de bleu* broadcloth
80m 68 scarlet broadcloth
329m 23 beige broadcloth
3m 27 green broadcloth

86m 52 scarlet serge
363m 13 linen for linings
396m lace for *garnitures de cuirass*
30m 60 trumpeters' lace

As Waterloo was being fought the *dépôt* was busy making new clothing. Some 2m 70 of green broadcloth had been cut out to make trumpeters' *habits*, which we assume were to be adorned with the trumpeters' lace in store, which was therefore Imperial Livery. *Habits* for troopers were also being made. The regiment's major notes that 43m 36 of blue broadcloth, 4m 56 of scarlet broadcloth, 31m 12 of scarlet serge and 26m of linen had been cut out for the production of *habits*. Clearly, Imperial Livery was used during the 100 days, which we suppose was taken up to replace blue *habits* with Royalist Livery: as the '*Cuirassiers du Reine*' or Queen's Own *Cuirassiers*, it is very likely the regiment had Royalist Livery during the 1st Restoration. The magazine held the following items of clothing and equipment:[12]

Item	In Magazine	In Service	Total	Observations
Habits de cuirassier	32	120	152	26 needing repairs
Gilets en drap blanc	125	91	216	
Gilets d'ecurie		77	77	
Culottes de peau		103	103	
Stable trousers	75	43	148	
Bonnets de police		82	82	
Manteaux	220	110	330	Plus 74 of the new model
Grey wool *surculottes*		75	75	
Helmets	191	135	326	191 needing repairs
Braces		74	74	
Scarlet-fringed epaulettes	141	116	257	
Waistbelts	404	129	533	
Waistbelt plates	344	129	473	
Gibernes	665	100	765	
Porte-gibernes	382	100	482	
Sword knots	108	127	235	
Porte-manteaux	297	118	415	
Gauntlets	70	100	170	
Pairs of boots	39	74	113	
Garnitures de cuirass	99	87	156	
Trumpets	1	6	7	
Banderole-porte-mousquetons	166		166	

Trooper of what maybe the 2ᵉ *cuirassiers*, or even the 4ᵉ depicted somtime in spring 1808 from the Otto manuscript. The 21 designation is unexplainable, unless this item was from the 21ᵉ Cavalerie, but would be the wrong shape: we are left perplexed by the image.

For the 166 *banderole-porte-mousquetons*, all of which were in the *dépôt*, we note the regiment had 58 *mousqueton*s in stores, and 24 were in use, making 82 in total. How these 24 firearms were carried we can only guess at: permanently carried from the saddle? Yet just 23 *bottes de carabine* were in use with 74 in the *dépôt*. Were the firearms carried over the shoulder of the *cuirassier* or shoved under the top flap of the *porte-manteaux*, or were all bar one simply permanently carried off the saddle? The 24 *mousquetons* were issued 24 bayonets with 18 scabbards. For the 127 men, 119 sabres were in use, 58 pistols and remarkably just 89 *cuirasses*, a further 217 being in stores. The *dépôt* also held 97 *housses* and 179 *schabraques*, with 104 *housses* being recorded as in use and 29 further examples were in stores waiting to be disposed of. Just 100 *schabraques* were in use by the 127 men under arms who were still mounted.[13]

3ᵉ *Cuirassiers*

The archive of the 3ᵉ *Cuirassiers* after 1807 is very sporadic in what it says about clothing. We know almost nothing from May 1811. The men of the 3ᵉ *Cuirassiers* had the following items in October 1814:[14]

Item	In Service, but due to Expire in the Next Year	In Need of Repair	To be Replaced in the Next Year	To be Replaced	Items Missing	Observations
Habits with epaulettes	164	22	8	28	51	
Habits de trompette						
Gilets en drap blanc	100	11	17	37	126	
Gilets d'ecurie	88	2			147	
Stable trousers	111				126	
Culottes de peau	182		23		55	
Surculottes	136			15	100	
Helmets	233			5	4	
Bonnets de police	99		52	41	148	
Capotes	160			2	77	
Gauntlets	203			8	34	

The following items of equipment were in use:[15]

Item	In Service, but due to Expire in the Next Year	In Need of Repair	To be Replaced in the Next Year	To be Replaced	Items Missing	Observations
Gibernes	213					
Porte-gibernes	213					
Waistbelts	226					
Porte-manteaux	243		4	1		
Sword knots	226					
Pairs of boots and spurs	155	37	17		36	
Trumpets	8					
Waistbelt plates	226					

The regiment on 3 October 1814 had in service 218 sabres in good condition and 6 needing repairs, 331 pistols, with 18 needing repairs, and 196 *cuirasses*. Not a single carbine was in use, contrary to expectations. Armament in the magazine was as follows:[16]

Item	Good Condition	To Be Repaired	To be Replaced	Observations
Carabines	125			
Sabres		35	28	
Pistols	55	28	21	
Bayonets	125	50		
Bayonet scabbards	125	20		
Garnitures de cuirass	125	89		
Cuirasses		132	8	

In the regiment's magazine were the following items:[17]

Item	New	To be Repaired	To be Replaced	Observations
Vestes en drap blanc	12		6	
Habits de cuirassier	4		7	
Habits de trompette				
Gilets d'ecurie				
Gilets d'ecurie de trompette			Nil	
Surculottes				
Culottes de peau			16	
Manteaux	1		70	
Bonnets de police			Nil	
Garnitures de cuirass	22		38	
Waistbelts	262		84	

Item	New	To be Repaired	To be Replaced	Observations
Gibernes	318		100	
Porte-gibernes	350	50	50	
Garnitures de cuirass			10	
Sword knots		20	30	
Porte-manteaux			17	
Pairs of boots			80	
Cuirassier helmets	22		38	
Waistbelt plates	262			
Adjutants' epaulettes			Nil	
Cuirassier epaulettes	83		6	

Martinet presents for us two figures from the regiment. Up first, a trooper as they appeared from 1807 through to disbandment. Reviewed in summer 1807, the regiment had 668 *habits* in use. Of these, 336 were in good condition, 184 needed repairs and the remainder were unfit for further service. They were worn with 348 white waistcoats, of which 10 needed repairs and 105 were unfit for further use. The inspecting officer noted the men were wearing a mix of *habits à revers* and *habits de cuirass*. The regiment's archive tells us that between July 1805 and December 1807, 836 new *habits* had been made, 834 being issued, 9 more had been repaired and 8 were to be written off. Furthermore, 71 new *surtouts* had been made and issued for NCOs and trumpeters, along with 704 *manteaux*, while 32 existing *manteaux* had been repaired, 28 were in stores and 4 were in store waiting to be repaired. Furthermore, 801 white *gilets*, 1,017 stable coats and 1,100 pairs of stable trousers had been made and issued. Secondly, an officer in parade dress.

The regiment's archive presents for us these tentative reconstructions of the trumpeters. Up first is a trumpeter dressed in blue in armour. We know from the regimental accounts that trumpeters had blue *habits* with lace: the pattern and colour of the lace or where it was worn is not known.

Secondly, when reviewed in summer 1807, the trumpeters of the 3e were issued seven *surtouts*. Our image is based on notes by Rousselot housed in the library of the Musée de l'Armée. The reconstruction is tentative and not fact as the point of inspiration for Rousselot's notes is not known.

Thirdly is our reconstruction of a trumpeter based on the regiment's archive for the period 1813 to 1814. In summer 1814 *habits de trompette* were listed in the inspection as being burned: clearly these were green with Imperial Livery as in August 1814 the regiment had 51m of trumpeters' lace, which was again burned.

Fourthly is a trumpeter reconstructed from the regiment's paper archive for the 1st Restoration period. At the time of disbandment in December 1815 the magazine held 5m of trumpeters' lace and 614m 37 of trumpeters' livery. Presumably the larger quantity was Imperial Livery that had never been used and the 5m of lace was all that was left from making Royalist Livery clothing.

Lastly is a reconstruction of a trumpeter of the 3^e *Cuirassiers* during the 100 days. The regiment's paper archive shows every man was armoured. It also records no specific trumpeters' clothing existed, and we therefore show the trumpeters wearing the same overall uniform as a trooper. The regiment also records that a total of 278 *habits*, 76 *vestes*, 373 *gilets d'ecurie*, 75 pairs of stable trousers, 320 pairs of broadcloth *pantalons*, 217 pairs of *culottes de peau*, 322 *manteaux*, 348 *bonnets de police*, 256 helmets and 253 pairs of epaulettes were lost at Waterloo in the retreat – an incredible loss of clothing and equipment. Assuming 1 man lost equalled 1 *habit*, then 278 men were lost in the campaign! Clearly, *vestes* were only issued to *sous-officiers*, corporals and trumpeters. Every man wore the non-regulation broadcloth *pantalons* rather than the hot and cumbersome *culottes de peau*. Indeed, 465 pairs of *pantalons* in grey broadcloth with black leather reinforcement to the inner seat had been made and issued in April to September 1815.

82   Napoleon's Heavy Cavalry

Also in the magazine were 633 shirts, 207 black stocks, 373 pairs of woollen stockings, 221 pairs of shoes, 182 pairs of black gaiters and 26 musket worms. In addition, were 5m of Imperial Livery for the trumpeters, 193m 59 of white worsted lace 40mm wide for the *housses*, and 211m 16 of white worsted lace 30mm wide for the *porte-manteaux*. Other items in the magazine included 16m 95 of white broadcloth, 249m 67 of blue broadcloth, 713m 91 of *blanc picque de bleu* broadcloth for *manteaux* and 15m 15 of scarlet broadcloth. Also included, was 59m 66 of white milled serge, 91m 47 of scarlet serge, 36m 09 blue tricot and 166m 17 of grey broadcloth for *surculottes*, 588m 61 of linen for lining clothing and 11m 91 of canvas for lining the *housses*.[18]

Moving on to after Waterloo, the *dépôt* held 108m 50 white broadcloth for the front and collars of *vestes*, 440m 61 *blanc picque de bleu* broadcloth, 88m 72 blue broadcloth, 22m 65 scarlet broadcloth, 186m 96 grey broadcloth, 181m 97 white tricot for lining and making the back of *vestes*, 60m 13 *treillis*, 18m 34 scarlet serge, 48m 66 lace for *porte-manteaux*, and 3 sets of trumpet cords. Clothing in the *dépôt* comprised 15 *habits*, 134 white *vestes*, 86 *gilets d'ecurie*, 37 pairs of stable trousers, 53 pairs of *culottes de peau*, 143 *manteaux*, 24 *bonnets de police*, 108 helmets, 4 pairs of epaulettes and 6 trumpets.

The regiment's archive tells us that issued to the regiment from 1 April 1815 to when it was disbanded in September 1815 were 413 *habits de cuirassier*, 107 *vestes*, 373 *gilets d'ecurie*, 75 pairs of stable trousers, 465 pairs of *pantalons* in grey broadcloth with black leather reinforcement to the inner seat, 265 pairs of *culottes de peau*, 331 *manteaux*, 448 *bonnets de police*, 265 helmets and 334 pairs of epaulettes. The regiment also records that a total of 278 *habits*, 76 *vestes*, 373 *gilets d'ecurie*, 75 pairs of stable trousers, 320 pairs of broadcloth *pantalons*, 217 pairs of *culottes de peau*, 322 *manteaux*, 348 *bonnets de police*, 256 helmets and 253 pairs of epaulettes were lost at Waterloo in the retreat – an incredible loss of clothing and equipment. Assuming one man lost equalled one *habit*, then 278 men were lost in the campaign! Clearly, *vestes* were only issued to *sous-officiers*, corporals, and trumpeters. Every man wore the non-regulation broadcloth *pantalons* rather than the hot and cumbersome *culottes de peau*.

We note no trumpeters' *habits* are listed as lost or existing, therefore the trumpeters were dressed as the rank and file, perhaps with just a white *crinière* to the helmet. Yet the time of disbandment in December 1815 the magazine held 5m of trumpeters' lace and 614m 37 of trumpeters' livery. Was this Royalist Livery or more Imperial Livery? Given exactly the same amount of Imperial Livery existed in 1815 as a year earlier, we assume therefore that the unused lace was Royalist Livery.[19]

4ᵉ *Cuirassiers*

As with most regiments of *cuirassiers* we have a huge gap in knowledge from 1808 onwards as to what the regiment was wearing. Reviewed in summer 1814, the men were wearing:[20]

Item	In Service, but due to Expire in the Next Year	In Need of Repair	To be Replaced in the Next Year	To be Replaced	Items Missing	Observations
Habits–vestes	146	4		63	13	
Gilet en drap blanc	144			18	54	
Gilets d'ecurie	84	24		61	40	
Culottes de peau	17		178		31	
Pantalons de treillis	24		142		14	
Surculottes	28		154	5	29	
Helmets	144	67			4	
Bonnets de police	209		4		3	
Adjutants' epaulettes			2			
Cuirassier epaulettes	192				11	
Pompoms and plumes	149			2	45	
Capote en Manteaux	107	2		30	17	
Braces					216	
Fraise	167				31	
Waistbelts	205	3			8	
Gibernes and belts	165				12	
Sword knots	206				10	
Gauntlets	156	1	2	9	48	
Pairs of boots and Spurs	90	41		41	44	
Trumpets	8				5	
Sabres	206					
Pistols	132	7				
Cuirasses	115	71				

The *dépôt* held in August 1814 the following stocks of materials:[21]

147m 45 blue broadcloth
0m 85 white broadcloth
0m 10 aurore broadcloth
0m 85 *garance* broadcloth
1m 95 green broadcloth
1m 34 blue tricot
0m 21 *garance* serge

Clothing in the *dépôt* included 30 *habits de cuirassier*, 24 *gilets*, 1 *veste d'ecurie de modèle*, 6 *bonnets de police*, 100 *manteaux*, 38 pairs of *surculottes*, 2 pairs of stable trousers, 32 pompoms, 193 helmets and 11 pairs of *culottes de peau*. One oddity is that the 4e had 213 pairs of wrist gloves in use and as well as gauntlets. Cloth purchased in 1814 was as follows:[22]

84 Napoleon's Heavy Cavalry

Martinet offers five images of the regiment. Up first, a print of a trooper of the 4ᵉ *Cuirassiers* in idealised circumstances. The regiment's inspection returns present the reality behind such images, to which our main text testifies. Martinet then gives us a trooper with a sheepskin *schabraque* and scarlet facings, and the same image but with aurore, and this dates to 1813 to 1815. Martinet also gives us an officer and a trumpeter sometime before 1812. At the time of the 1807 inspection, the trumpeters had 24 *surtouts*, we assume with reversed colours in use: 1 was in good condition, 11 needed repairs and 12 were life expired. We assume, therefore, that the clothing for the trumpeters was replaced in the course of 1808. We are ignorant as to how they were dressed after this point sadly. We do know that in 1805 and 1808 they were armoured.

61m 53 blue broadcloth
61m 72 white broadcloth
66m 82 aurore broadcloth
43m 25 *garance* broadcloth
266m 23 *blanc picquer de bleu*
2,158m 94 beige broadcloth
2m 18 *bleu picquer de blanc* broadcloth
491m 17 blue tricot
1,080m 69 linen
662m 79 *treillis*
276m 71 aurore serge
55m *lie de vin* serge[23]
25m rose serge[24]
15m 24 silver lace 27mm wide for *sous-officiers*
209m 64 lace for *porte-manteaux*, 40mm wide worsted *cul-de-dé*
260m 10 trumpeters' lace
52m 80 corporals' lace, 27mm wide worsted *cul-de-dé*
270m 20 12mm wide worsted *cul-de-dé* to edge the *fraise*

From the cloth list, the *garance* broadcloth must surely have been destined to make *cuirass fraise*, the aurore milled serge lined the *habits*, as well as lined the *manteaux*, and also made the festoon on the *schabraques*. The *lie de vin* and rose serge was not used until 1815 – every inch being used in the production of garments, no doubt repairing the clothing of the men from the former 13ᵉ *Cuirassiers*, who were taken into the 4ᵉ. This shows that the regiment would have presented a most bizarre appearance on the field of Waterloo, with men wearing two different uniforms in the same regiment! The *bleu picquer de blanc* broadcloth would have been a lighter shade of Imperial Blue – this cloth was the regulation fabric for veterinarians' *habits*, of which two such garments were made, who were also issued *chapeaux*.

The trumpeters' lace was clearly new Royalist issue. Indeed, we note in 1814, seventeen brand new trumpeters' *habits* were made, adorned with Royalist Livery. Yet we know from the presence of green broadcloth that trumpeters had worn green *habits* with Imperial Livery in 1811–14. In the course of 1814, nine *habits de modèle* were obtained for a *cuirassier*, corporal, sergeant, *fourrier*, sergeant major, farrier, trumpeter, trumpet corporal and trumpet major. Prior to 1814, the regiment had 'not acted upon the decree of February 1812 concerning the dispositions of clothing and equipment', so we presume that beyond the trumpeters all the clothing was 'old model'. Also received in 1814 were two *capote en manteaux de modèle* as well as one *gilet de modèle*. However, the *dépôt* did hold in August 1814 one waistbelt and one *giberne de modèle*. The regimental archive attests to the following items of clothing being made in 1814:[25]

Year	Cuirassier habits		Trumpeters' habits		Gilets		Stable coats		Epaulettes		Bonnets de police		Manteaux		Surculottex		Stable trousers	
	Made	Issued	Made	Issued	Made	Issued	Made	Issued	Made	Issued	Made	Issued	Made	Issued	Made	Issued	Made	Issued
In Magazine 6 August 1814	30				24		1				6		100		38		2	
1814	125	155	17	17	125	149	137	238	123	123	59	65	65	165	231	269	359	361
1815	376	306	8	4	275	271	417	372	488	290	412	411	386	238	329	359	244	244
Total	531	461	25	24	424	420	655	560	611	413	477	476	551	405	598	598	605	605
In Dépôt 21 December 1815		70		4		4		95		98		1		148				

The regiment had 306 pairs of *culottes de peau* made in 1814 and 414 in 1815, of which 317 were issued in 1814, and 249 in 1815, leaving 165 in the *dépôt*. The cloth used in the same period was as follows:[26]

Year	Broadcloth															
	Blue		White		Aurore		Garance for fraise		Blanc picque de bleu		Beige		Green		Bleu picque de blanc	
	Bought	Issued	Bought	Issued	Bought	Issued	Bought	Issued	Bought	Issued	Bought	Issued	Made	Issued	Made	Issued
In Magazine 6 August 1814	147m 45		0m 85		0m 10		0m 85				0m 11		1m95			
1814	61m 53	208m 98	61m 72	62m 57	66m 82	66m 83	43m 25	43m	266m 23	225m 73	215m 94	216m 50			2m18	2m18
1815	685m 76	449m 20	203m	129m	113m 98	74m 86		0m 30	1,905m 25	1,128m 75	445m 30	306m 93	5m42			
Total	894m 74	658m 18	265m 57	191m 51	180m 81	141m 69	44m 10	43m 30	2,131m 47	1,354m 48	661m 36	522m 98	7m37	1m95	2m18	2m18
In *Dépôt* 21 December 1815		236m 56		74m		39m 12		0m 80		126m 79		138m 38		5m42		

We present several reconstructions based on the regiment's paper archive. Firstly, we present a reconstruction of a trooper of the 4e *Cuirassiers*. The regiment was issued pompoms for the helmet rather than plumes. Prior to August 1814, 32 remained in the stores. Later that year 198 more pompoms were acquired, and in 1815, a further 615, making 845 altogether. A total of 230 pompoms were issued as new in 1814, and a further 359 were issued as new in 1815, making 589 altogether.

Secondly, a trumpeter in 1805–13 wearing armour. Thirdly, a trumpeter in 1813 to 1814. At the time of the August 1814 review, 1m 95 of green broadcloth was in stores, showing the trumpeters had worn Imperial Livery. We also note that the regiment had scarlet plumes for trumpeters and NCOs. Trumpeters lacked armour in summer 1814.

Fourthly, a reconstruction of a trumpeter during the 1st Restoration. We know from the regiment's archive that the unit purchased between 1 September 1814 and 1 April 1815 260m 10 of Royalist Livery for trumpeters. All of this was used to make 17 new *habits*, which were blue as we show here. The helmet is copied from a depiction of the regiment by Vernet.

Lastly, a tentative reconstruction of a trumpeter of the 4e *Cuirassiers* during the 100 days. The regiment's archive tells us that after 1 April 1815, 61m of Imperial Livery was purchased but never used and that eight trumpeters' *habits* were made, of which only four were issued. We can be sure that seven were blue, as only 5m 42 of green broadcloth was purchased, of which 1m 95 was used to make one trumpeter's *habit*, which never gained Imperial Livery. Clearly, blue *habits* were worn by the trumpeters at Waterloo. How they differed from troopers' garments we cannot say. We also know the trumpeters were armoured at Waterloo.

For the regiment's facing colour, aurore broadcloth was in good supply in the stores, with 66m 92 being acquired and used in 1814. This material was used to face and line the tails of the *habits* as well as the partial linings to the *manteaux*. In addition, a further 113m 98 was acquired in 1815, of which 74m 86 was used during that same year. The *habits* were definitely lined with serge, with 276m 71 being acquired after August 1814 and it was used later that same year. A further 451m 14 was acquired in 1815, of which 298m 70 was used. Hence, 575m of aurore serge was used in just ten months (August 1814 to June 1815), which seems a huge amount. Clearly it was used to line *habits* and the *manteaux*.

The list of small stores is fascinating: we find 2 black stocks with 189 *rabats*, 8 pairs of black gaiters, 5 pairs of *manchette du botte*, 45 pairs of grey gaiters, 19 pairs of epaulettes, 37 complete *trousses*, 13 brushes for cleaning copper, 39 boxes of grease, 25 *habit* brushes and 3 shoe brushes. Contrary to the Bardin regulations, the regiment used the old-style *manteaux*, specifically described as such in their 1814 inspection report, undertaken on 6 August. There were two '*capotes de modèle*' in the stores, again specifically and carefully listed as such but never copied as the regiment produced 65 new *manteaux* in 1814 and a further 386 in 1815. The troopers were clothed almost as new for the 100 days campaign, with the following returns from the stores: 30 brand new *habits de cuirassier* existed in the stores prior to August 1814, and 125 were made later that year, in the autumn, and 155 were issued, as new. In 1815, 376 *habits de cuirassier* were made, of which 306 were issued, as new.

Vernet presents for us three images of the regiment from the 1st Restoration. Firstly, a trumpeter and trooper in 1814. Of note, the trooper carries a carbine. When inspected in August 1814, 115 *gibernes* were in store. Then 50 more with belts were acquired in late 1814, and 724 more in 1815, making a total of 889. A total of 443 *gibernes* were issued for the 100 days campaign, leaving 446 still in the stores, unissued, when the regiment was disbanded. In total 411 *banderole-porte-mousquetons* existed in 1814, and, according to the paperwork, all 411 were used in 1815. I suspect that this means the remainder were cut up to make and repair *gibernes* and waistbelts, especially when considering that the regiment had models for both these two items in the stores. The regiment had, when inspected in August 1814, a total of 161 *mousquetons*, but no further examples were acquired after August 1814, and no mention is made of them in 1815. Clearly, Vernet captures one of the 161 men so armed before they lost their firearm.

Second is a group of troopers witnessed by Carl Vernet. The ankle-length grey overalls are most interesting, as in theory these closed at the knee! Lastly is the colonel of the 4[e] *Cuirassiers* in parade dress with dismounted trooper, as observed by Carl Vernet during the 1st Restoration.

90   Napoleon's Heavy Cavalry

Equipment wise, the regiment had, when inspected in August 1814, a total of 161 *mousquetons*, not a single *banderole-porte-mousqueton* was issued, and no further examples were acquired after August 1814, and none in 1815. The stores return records that all 161 *mousquetons* were issued in 1814. There is no record of them in 1815.

When inspected in August 1814 there were 115 *gibernes*, then 50 more were acquired in late 1814. In total 411 *banderole-porte-mousquetons* existed in 1814 in the *dépôt*, and, according to the paperwork, all 411 were used in 1815. I suspect that this means the remainder of the 161 issued were cut up to make and repair *giberne* belts and waistbelts, especially when considering that the regiment had models for both these two items in the stores.

The regiment was issued pompoms for the helmet rather than plumes: in 1814, 198 pompoms were acquired, and in 1815 a further 615, making 845 altogether. A total of 230 pompoms were issued as new in 1814, and a further 359 were issued as new in 1815, making 589 altogether. We also note four *houpettes* were purchased and issued in 1814.[27]

5ᵉ *Cuirassiers*

We know nothing about the dress of the regiment until it was reviewed in late summer 1814.[28]

Item	In Service, but due to Expire in the Next Year	In Need of Repair	To be Replaced in the Next Year	To be Replaced	Items Missing	Observations
Habits	63	58	25	74	136	
Gilets en drap blanc	27		10	1	318	
Gilets d'ecurie	80	17	36	30	193	
Bonnets de police	65	6	37	22	226	
Manteaux	133	21	20	8	174	
Culottes de peau	18		338			
Stable trousers			356			
Surculottes	108	2	246			
Helmets	191	152	13			
Epaulettes	63	58	25	74	136	

The *surculottes*, the inspector noted, were actually grey broadcloth *pantalons* with black leather reinforcement, which cost 5fr 50, of which 650 pairs had been purchased in the second quarter of 1813. The regiment also records that in 1813, 62 *surtouts* for the *sous-officiers* had been provided, the material and tailoring cost being 1,734fr 8, which were in addition to the *habits-vestes* of the *sous-officiers*, who still wore their hair powdered and in a que. The *surtouts* were a tolerated expense as they employed grooms to care for their horse, and thus their allowance for a stable coat was used to pay for the *surtout*. The *sous-officiers* also had two pairs of boots: rigid and highly polished *botté forte* and also

Martinet presents two troopers of the 5ᵉ *Cuirassiers*. The first image must date to *c.*1805 as when reviewed on 13 August 1803 the regiment possessed 306 sets of *chaperons* and *housses*, but by the time the regiment was reviewed in summer 1807 every man had sheepskin *schabraques*.

Second is a trooper from the 1st Restoration with a very vivid hue of aurore to the uniform. The 5ᵉ *Cuirassiers* were *d'Angoulême* and not *Berry*, contrary to Martinet.

the semi-soft *botte à l'écuyère* used by the men.[29] Much of the clothing was worn out, and furthermore, there was also actually a shortfall in many items. The men were short of 136 *habits*, and indeed the vast majority of the regiment's clothing is listed as *hors de service*, i.e., to be replaced, simply because of its age, so clearly resupply for this regiment had been something of an issue during the 1813 and 1814 campaigns, which implies that the clothing had been made in 1812 or earlier and was likely not to be Bardin regulation. For example, of the *culottes de peau*, some 338 pairs out of 356 pairs in total were too old to be serviceable, as were all 356 pairs of stable trousers.

The following items of equipment were in use:[30]

92 Napoleon's Heavy Cavalry

Item	In Service, but due to Expire in the Next Year	In Need of Repair	To be Replaced in the Next Year	To be Replaced	Items Missing	Observations
Waistbelts	314	10		5	25	
Gibernes	255				26	
Porte-gibernes	255				26	
Sword knots	293			2	59	
Pairs of boots	41	31	66	17	199	
Pairs of spurs	149		2	1	202	
Pairs of gauntlets	160	4	9	3	180	

We wonder what the men were wearing as footwear given the lack of boots? Were they wearing shoes and *surculottes*? For fact every 1 of the 356 men on parade had pairs of shoes. They also possessed between them 712 shirts, 63 pairs of linen *pantalons*, 336 black stocks, 347 white stocks, 356 pairs of linen socks, 796 pairs of woollen stockings, and 213 pairs of black gaiters. Armament was as follows:[31]

Item	Good Condition	To be Repaired	To be Replaced	Observations
Carabines		Nil		
Sabres	315	11		
Pistols	155	12	1	
Bayonets		Nil		
Cuirasses	166	65		

In the regiment's magazine were the following items:[32]

Item	New	To be Repaired	To be Replaced	Total
Habits			Nil	
Epaulettes				
Gilets				
Gilets d'ecurie				
Bonnets de police				
Manteaux			25	25
Culottes de peau			Nil	
Stable trousers				
Surculottes				
Helmets	87	111	40	238
Waistbelts	30		40	70
Gibernes	67		50	117
Porte-gibernes	87		40	127
Sword knots	20			20

Regulations in Practice 1812–15

Item	New	To be Repaired	To be Replaced	Total
Pars of spurs	25			25
Pairs of gauntlets		Nil		
Banderole-porte-mousquetons	140			140
Porte-manteaux	36		60	96

Trooper of the 5ᵉ *Cuirassiers* by Zimmermann dating from 1808. Of interest is the cut-out 5 on the *giberne*, and light cavalry-style belts. Yet, when reviewed at Cologne on 24 November 1811, general Nansouty commented 'the cartridge box is of a special type and too small; they are decorated with a crowned "N" on the flap'. Seemingly an N had replaced a 5!

There were 159 fusils – muskets – listed in use, although the inspector's observation states that they all came from the squadron that had been at Hamburg. Related to this, there were 140 brand new *banderole-porte-mousquetons* in the magazines. No other examples had been issued. This might well indicate that the Hamburg squadron had in fact acquired infantry muskets, otherwise they would have been issued with *banderole-porte-mousquetons*. Unusually, the regiment had 378 pairs of brand-new wrist gloves in the magazine. Quite a luxury and an expense for a line regiment, when the regulations stipulated gauntlets only, two pairs of gloves being rather extravagant. None appear to have been issued.

In addition, 26 men were without a *giberne*, and a total of 255 men out of 281 had 1. Again, a little odd, as there were 67 brand new ones in the magazine, so we wonder why these had not been issued. This regiment had 77 pairs of *manchettes* in the magazine, but in 1814 none were issued. Also in store were 175 shirts, 13 black stocks, 271 pairs of linen ankle socks, 57 pairs of woollen stockings, 114 additional pairs of shoes, 39 pairs of black gaiters, 90 *sacs à distribution* – the ration bag that was over 4ft long and 2ft wide – 193 buckles for the stock and 73 kitchen jackets made in linen: these items were used by the Garde Imperiale for men detailed to cook for their mess. We assume this 'slop kit' was issued to save the men getting their stable clothes dirty in the kitchens. The use of these garments in the 5ᵉ *Cuirassiers* at that time was unique.

The dress of the trumpeters and band are noted by an eyewitness. A diarist informs us that the 5e *Cuirassiers*, which arrived at Luneburg in February 1808 and left on 1 September 1808, had had some of its trumpeters transformed into horn players and trombonists. The trumpeters had all received new light-blue uniforms, but the musicians had, in addition, received white coats and white grenadier bearskins. These items were for parade only:

> The 5e regiment of French *Cuirassiers* which had arrived in February passed through here at 8 hours in the morning. The officers had obtained new horses from here. Some of the trumpeters had been converted into horn players and trombonists, while others had been changed into musicians … they had received new light-blue *habits*, and the musicians had white *habits* and white bearskins. This must be considered their 'state uniform'. The troopers and officers until recent times had waistbelts, *culotte* and gauntlets from yellow hide. Some officers now used white leather. The trumpeters and musicians numbered 19, the troopers 500.

The Martinet plate is perhaps as close as we will get to the dress of the trumpeters, who we know were armoured, at least on campaign, according to the regiment's archive. Our remaining images are by Rousselot taken from the Marckolsheim manuscript and need to be considered a 'best guess'

rather than hard, solid fact. The first shows a musician, the second a bandmaster and a trumpeter, purporting to show the uniform worn at Wagram. We have no clue as to the sources he used, and we cannot verify any aspect of this uniform from regimental archives. It may be total fiction. (*Collection KM*)

We present a study of reconstructions of the 4ᵉ *Cuirassiers* at the end of the Empire.

First is a trumpeter in 1812 based on Rousselot's notes. We know they were armoured from the regiment's paper archive.

Secondly is a trooper during the period 1813 to 1814 reconstructed from the paper archive. In summer 1814 the unit's *surculottes*, the inspector noted, were actually grey broadcloth *pantalons* with black leather reinforcement which cost 5fr 50, of which 650 pairs had been purchased in the second quarter of 1813. Unusually, the regiment had 378 pairs of brand-new wrist gloves in the magazine. Quite a luxury and an expense for a line regiment, when the regulations stipulated gauntlets only, two pairs of gloves being rather extravagant. None appear to have been issued.

Lastly is a tentative reconstruction of a trumpeter of the 5ᵉ *Cuirassiers* in 1813 to 1815. Nothing is said in the regiment's archive about trumpeters: we assume they were dressed as rank and file by the end of the Empire.

The regiment stores held scarce amounts of material, 38m 45 of aurore serge, and 1,337m 76 of blue tricot. We know nothing at all about the dress of the trumpeters.[33] The regiment's epaulettes may not have been standard grenadier models. The regiment's archive reports in 1810 that worsted tassels for the *bonnets de police*, 100 pairs of grenadiers' epaulettes and '*garnitures* for the epaulettes' were purchased for 1,481fr 61, all of which were classed as 'illegal expenses' by the inspector. Clearly the epaulettes cost far more than allowed for and perhaps had silver fringing and lace sewn on to scarlet epaulettes for the *sous-officiers*? The regiment also purchased ten brand new trumpets during the restoration, and the regimental wagon was repaired for 17fr 50.

No paperwork for the disbandment of the regiment in 1815 can be located at the time of writing, but the regiment records that 1,636fr 33 was spent repairing *habits*. A very small sum indeed, so we suspect the regiment was rather shabby at Waterloo.[34]

96   Napoleon's Heavy Cavalry

6ᵉ *Cuirassiers*

The paper archive of the 6ᵉ *Cuirassiers* is minimal for how the regiment was dressed. The sole document is from 1814, when clothing and equipment of the regiment in October that year was as follows:[35]

Item	In Service, but due to Expire in the Next Year	In Need of Repair	To be Replaced in the Next Year	To be Replaced	Items Missing	Observations
Habits de cuirassier	154					
Habits de trompette	Nil					
Gilets de drap blanc	154					
Gilets d'ecurie	81	4		69		
Bonnets de police	154					
Manteaux	154					
Culottes de peau	58		54	20		
Stable trousers	103		4		48	
Surculottes	84	5	1	49	22	
Helmets	154					
Epaulettes	154					

The following items of equipment were in use:[36]

Item	In Service, but due to Expire in the Next Year	In Need of Repair	To be Replaced in the Next Year	To be Replaced	Items Missing	Observations
Waistbelts	136	18				
Gibernes	146	8		1		
Porte-gibernes	146	8				
Sword knots	145				9	
Pairs of boots	112	37				
Pairs of spurs	149					
Pairs of gauntlets	128				21	

Armament comprised 154 sabres, 130 pistols, 149 *cuirassiers* and 148 *garnitures de cuirass*. In the regiment's magazine were the following items:[37]

Item	New	To be Repaired	To be Replaced	Observations
Habits	145	14	58	
Epaulettes	512	14	58	
Gilets de drap blanc	105	5	369	
Gilets d'ecurie		4	48	

Regulations in Practice 1812–15

Item	New	To be Repaired	To be Replaced	Observations
Bonnets de police	9		54	
Culottes de peau	15			
Stable trousers	1			
Helmets	54	140	31	
Waistbelts	60	8	47	
Gibernes	87	45	15	
Porte-gibernes	13	45	15	
Pairs of boots			40	
Banderole-porte-mousquetons		71		
Mousquetons	30	52		
Sabres		108	16	
Pistols	43	72		
Cuirasses	115	91	3	
Garnitures de cuirass	40	10	30	

Of interest, the regiment had no musketoons issued, these were all in the regiment's magazine: thirty were in good condition and fifty-two needed repairs. We note in stores

Martinet gives two troopers of the 6ᵉ *Cuirassiers*; firstly as they appeared c.1805 and from 1812 through to disbandment in 1815.

were 41 *bottes de mousqueton* and 1 *bottes de carabine*, 108 sabres needing repairs and 16 to be disposed of, 43 pistols in good condition, 115 *cuirasses* in the same condition, with 91 needing repairs and 3 to be written off.[38]

The regiment was disbanded on 21 November 1815. The *dépôt* held 93m 10 blue broadcloth, 56m white broadcloth, 1,044m 75 *blanc picque de bleu* broadcloth, 23m 82 aurore broadcloth, 76m 36 *gris-beige* broadcloth, 590m 43 *bleu de roi* tricot, and 27m 45 aurore serge. We also find 260 pistols, 360 sabres, 395 *cuirass*, 308 pairs of *garnitures de cuirass dit fraise* and 57 *mousquetons* with bayonets, yet not a single belt to carry them existed. Clothing and equipment in stores in December were as follows:[39]

Reconstruction of a trooper of the 6ᵉ *Cuirassiers* from the regiment's paper archive dated summer 1814.

Item	New	Good Condition	In Need of Repair	Total
Habits			58	58
Pair of epaulettes	20		72	92
Gilets sans manche			1	1
Bonnets de police			68	68
Surculottes				
Plumes			100	100
Manteaux		90	17	1,047
Helmets	159	100	118	377
Waistbelts and plates	72	100	96	268
Gibernes	169	170	91	430
Porte-gibernes	140	120	61	321
Trumpets			5	5
Gauntlets	33		187	220
Pairs of boots	12		175	187
Pairs of spurs with straps			122	122
Porte-manteaux		50	46	96

Not an inch of green broadcloth or Imperial Livery existed – presumably trumpeters wore the same clothing as the rank and file. Allowed to be carried away by the men at disbandment were 149 *habits* with epaulettes, 146 *gilets*, 149 *gilets d'ecurie*, 149 *bonnets de police*, 149 pairs of *culottes de peau* and *surculottes*, 146 pairs of stable trousers, 149 *porte-manteaux*, 7 *manteaux*, 6 pairs of boots and 6 horses with harness! During the 100 days the regiment obtained the following materials to carry out repairs to clothing then in use:[40]

Regulations in Practice 1812–15 99

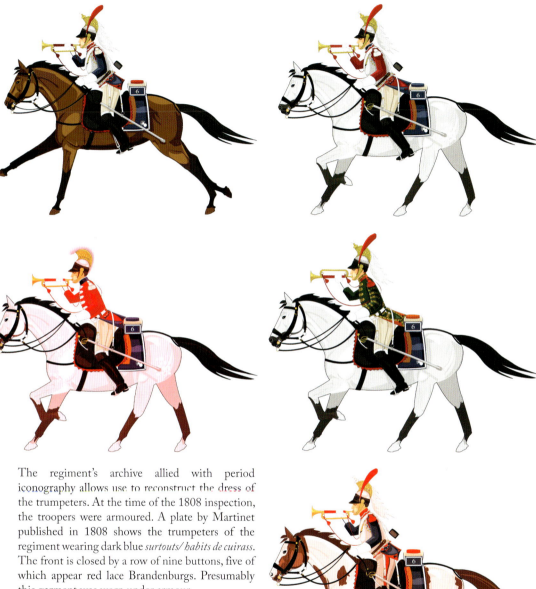

The regiment's archive allied with period iconography allows use to reconstruct the dress of the trumpeters. At the time of the 1808 inspection, the troopers were armoured. A plate by Martinet published in 1808 shows the trumpeters of the regiment wearing dark blue *surtouts/ habits de cuirass*. The front is closed by a row of nine buttons, five of which appear red lace Brandenburgs. Presumably this garment was worn under armour.

Secondly is a reconstruction of a trumpeter of the 6ᵉ *Cuirassiers* in 1809 from Rousselot's notes, as is our third image.

Fourthly is a speculative reconstruction of a trumpeter in 1814. At the time of the summer review, *habits de trompette* are listed, but all had been burnt: clearly these had been green with Imperial Livery. Lastly is a tentative reconstruction of a trumpeter during the 1st Restoration through to disbandment in 1815. No trumpeters' clothing is recorded in 1815, from this we assume that trumpeters were dressed as rank and file and were armoured. We may be wrong in what we show for clothing.

100   Napoleon's Heavy Cavalry

24m 30 blue broadcloth costing 255fr 15
23m 30 grey broadcloth costing 215fr 52
13m 30 blue tricot costing 70fr 09
30m of linen costing 50fr 50
35 dozen large buttons costing 9fr 80
40 dozen small buttons costing 9fr 60

The purchase of materials was small and limited perhaps due to lack of funds. We cannot say anything about the dress of trumpeters. We could assume a lot of things, but we won't, as any suggestion cannot be verified by primary documentation.

7ᵉ *Cuirassiers*

As with the majority of *cuirassier* regiments, the paper archive of the 7ᵉ is almost devoid of details about how it was dressed. The 7ᵉ *Cuirassiers* had the following items of clothing and equipment in August 1814:[41]

Item	In Good Repair	In Need of Repair	Need Replacing	Total	Items Missing
Habits	213	78	16	307	135
Gilets en drap blanc	213	78	16	307	135
Gilets d'ecurie	158	50	65	273	169
Culottes de peau	284	13	1	298	144
Surculottes en drap beige	60	16	12	88	354
Stable trousers	248	2	0	250	192
Manteaux ou capotes	241	31	6	278	164
Bonnets de police	198	39	62	299	143
Scarlet epaulettes	258	21	15	294	147
Helmets	252	17	1	270	172
Boots and spurs	134	66	12	212	230
Waistbelts	293	8	0	301	141
Gibernes et porte-gibernes	248	0	0	248	194
Sword knots	288	2	0	290	152
Porte-manteaux	223	71	20	314	128
Banderole-porte-carabines	0	0	0	0	442
Bayonets	0	0	0	0	442
Trumpets	17	0	0	17	0
Gauntlets	280	13	2	295	227
Garnitures de cuirass	238	0	0	238	204
Sabres	203	3	0	206	236
Pistols	182	4	1	187	255

Item	In Good Repair	In Need of Repair	Need Replacing	Total	Items Missing
Cuirasses	238	23	0	261	181
Shirts	804	0	0	804	0
Linen overalls	228	0	0	228	214
Black stock	285	0	0	285	157
White stock	593	0	0	593	0
Wool socks	369	0	0	369	73
Pairs of shoes	272	0	0	272	170
Black gaiters	232	0	0	232	210
Grey gaiters	219	0	0	219	223
Ration bags	1	0	0	1	441

Martinet presents three figures from the 7e *Cuirassiers*. First is a trooper *c.*1805, then a trooper *c.*1812, and lastly a trumpeter *c.*1810 by Martinet. Of note is the presence of sky-blue lace, white lace with sky-blue piping to the collar, or white lace and no piping. Which we wonder is the most reliable?

102   Napoleon's Heavy Cavalry

The gaiters were presumably for foot and barrack duties, along with the shoes. The *dépôt* held virtually nothing in terms of materials: 79m 36 of yellow serge and 23m 65 of *treillis*. Yet we find in stores, brand new and ready to be issued: 39 *vestes*, 30 *gilets d'ecurie*, 78 *bonnets de police*, 61 *manteaux*, 359 *manteaux-capote*, 65 pairs of *surculottes*, 140 pairs of stable trousers, 315 helmets and 69 pairs of epaulettes. Equipment included 134 *porte-manteaux*, 368 pairs of gauntlets, 30 *gibernes*, 30 *porte-gibernes*, 46 *banderole-porte-mousquetons* – with a further 187 needing repairs – and 342 sword knots. We also find in the *dépôt* 166 *mousquetons*, 39 sabres in good condition, 16 sabres needing repairs and 7 to be written off, 19 pairs of pistols, 102 *cuirasses* needing repairs and 21 brand new *fraise* accompanied by 33 to be disposed of. To be written off were 163 *habits*, 110 *gilets d'ecurie*, 23 *bonnets de police*, 73 *manteaux*, 34 *manteaux-capote*, 49 helmets and 56 pairs of epaulettes. The inspector commented that the regiment had not adopted the clothing rules of 7 February 1812 introducing Bardin regulation: yet we see here the regiment had both old- and new-pattern *manteaux*, so clearly some Bardin kit was in use; we assume the comment must refer to the *habits* in use. The regiment was ordered to alter the cut of the clothing to suit the regulation – were the men in *habit à revers*? It's not impossible that they were. The inspector also noted that the circular of 23 April 1814 that was to remove Imperial iconography had not been acted upon. The colonel was ordered to dress the trumpeters in blue and to remove forthwith the green trumpeters' clothing, as well as to replace the grenades on the *gibernes* and the tails of the *habits* with *fleur-de-lys*.[42]

The 7e *Cuirassiers* had the following items of clothing and equipment in December 1815:[43]

Item	New	Good Condition	In Need of Repair	Need Replacing	Total
Habits	28			70	98
Vestes en drap blanc de modèle	1				1
Gilets d'ecurie	14			75	89
Bonnets de police	6				6
Manteaux	50	91		6	147
Porte-manteaux				40	40
Surculottes en drap gris de modèle 1 *pair*		There are none			
Culottes de peau	330	31			361
Stable trousers		There are none			
Helmets	110	247		120	477
Crinières	113	257		80	450
Pairs of boots	20	114			134
Waistbelts		154		42	196
Gibernes	205	126			286
Porte-gibernes	159	127			286
Banderole-porte-mousquetons	0	0	0	0	0
Trumpets		5		3	8

Regulations in Practice 1812–15   103

Item	New	Good Condition	In Need of Repair	Need Replacing	Total
Gauntlets	85	17			102
Pair of grenadier's epaulettes	18				18
Sword knots	113	216			329

Cloth in the *dépôt* comprised:[44]

58m 21 blue broadcloth
39m 70 white broadcloth for *vestes*
21m 50 *blanc picquer de bleu* for *manteaux*
17m 85 yellow broadcloth
211m 93 *gris-beige* tricot for *surculottes*
186m 30 blue tricot for *porte-manteaux*
46m 40 yellow serge
341m 29 linen for lining
60 dozen and 5 large buttons
151 dozen and 6 small buttons
184 dozen bone buttons

Portrait of Francois-Joseph Offenstein *c.*1806, Colonel of the 7ᵉ *Cuirassiers.* (*Photograph and collection of Bertrand Malvaux*)

Of interest when we look at the equipment list, we find 278 *porte-crosse* in stores: these were used to carry dragoon muskets from the saddle. Remarkably we also find 322 *porte-cannon* and *botte-de-mousquetons*, which are the leather straps to carry the light cavalry carbine. We note, that at the time of disbandment, 48 men were still under arms with saddles and harness, every man being issued the *porte-crosse*, yet just 12 *mousquetons* existed! We also note the regiment possessed 221 sabres, 13 pairs of pistols, 234 *cuirasses* with 195 *fraise*. We also note a *veste* and pair of *surculottes de modèle*, which did not exist in 1814, which shows by Waterloo that the regiment had either changed over to Bardin, or was in the process of doing so. The presence of the *veste* is intriguing: when we look at the clothing the men took away with them at discharge, the 168 all had a *habit* and not one had a *veste*! Were these ever made? Wearing a *veste* under a *habit de cuirass* with armour over is very hot, and one can easily

Officer of the 7ᵉ *Cuirassiers c.*1812 by Weiland. (*Collection KM*)

We present reconstructions of the regiment based on its paper archive and the notes of Rousselot. Up first, a trump
in 1808. The report of October 1805 informs us that in the regiment there were as many *cuirasses* as there were mou
men, trumpeters included. This was also the case in 1807, when on 31 December General Comte de Pully recorded
trumpeters' *cuirasses*. The *surtout* and white epaulettes are taken from Martinet.

Secondly, this image can be found among the papers of Rousselot. A yellow *surtout* with Imperial Blue facing
perfectly acceptable as dress of the trumpeters. Indeed, at the time of the summer 1807 inspection, trumpeters and s
officiers were dressed in *surtouts*. Rousselot suggests this image is from 1812–13, as he shows both *culottes de peau*
surculottes.

Up third is a trumpeter in 1813–14 reconstructed from the regiment's paper archive. In summer 1814 the inspe
noted that the circular of 23 April 1814, which was to remove Imperial iconography, had not been acted upon. The col
was ordered to dress the trumpeters in blue and to remove forthwith the green trumpeters' clothing as well as to replace
grenades on the *gibernes* and the tails of the *habits* with *fleur-de-lys*. Fourthly, a trumpeter of the 7ᵉ *Cuirassiers* during
1st Restoration based on the regiment's paper archive. Lastly, a tentative reconstruction of a trumpeter of the 7ᵉ *Cuiras*
as they appeared during the 100 days. We have no clear indications of how trumpeters were dressed in 1815. We ass
they were dressed as rank and file, who we also show.

Regulations in Practice 1812–15   105

imagine the colonel removing *vestes* from use to stop the men overheating. No man had had a pair of *surculottes* either, despite cloth for their manufacture being in stock: the men clearly only had one pair of legwear, *culottes de peau* as no stable trousers existed either!

8ᵉ *Cuirassiers*

Between 1808 and 1814 we know almost nothing about the dress of the regiment. In October 1814, the regiment's magazine had very few bolts of cloth, holding just 4m 22 of blue broadcloth, 0m 95 of yellow milled serge, 0m 57 of blue tricot and 103m 76 of linen. Items of clothing in use in October 1814 were:[45]

Item	In Good Repair	In Need of Repair	Need Replacing	Items Missing
Habits and epaulettes	130	48	3	4
Gilets manches	132	10		42
Gilets d'ecurie	106	9	3	1
Culottes de peau	175			5
Capotes	164	10	1	6
Surculottes	58	12	9	104
Pantalons de treillis	87		2	50
Bonnets de police	176	1	2	8
Pairs of gauntlets	172			7
Helmets	170			
Waistbelts	173			7
Waistbelt plates	173			7
Gibernes	111			
Porte-gibernes	111			
Pairs of boots	100	34		46
Porte-manteaux	175	3		5
Trumpets	12			3
Sword knots	172			8

The men were also wearing 854 shirts between them, 82 pairs of *manchette du botte* – proof the men were wearing breeches and not *pantalons*, 288 black stocks, 576 white stocks, 317 pairs of woollen stockings, 69 pairs of linen ankle socks, 288 pairs of shoes and black tricot gaiters, 232 *epoussettes* (cleaning cloths), 288 pairs of wrist gloves, 288 *trousses* and 288 sets of brushes – *habit*, whitening, button, copper. Clearly whitening was applied with a brush. Two sets of gloves were quite a luxury. Stocks of cloth in the *dépôt* comprised 4m 22 yellow broadcloth, 0m 95 yellow milled serge, 0m 57 blue tricot, 67m of lace for *porte-manteaux* and 0m 95 *treillis*. Not an inch of green broadcloth or Imperial Livery existed; we suppose the trumpeters wore the same uniform as the rank and file. Of interest, the *dépôt* held 68 brand new '*gilets-manche*', i.e., sleeved *gilets* like the infantry, strictly non-regulation, and also 24 brand new *gilets d'ecurie*, as well as 153 brand

Trooper of the 9ᵉ *Cuirassiers* by Otto. Despite the title of the image, we can be sure it is not the 9ᵉ, and very likely to be the 7ᵉ. If the image dates to 1807, then we know at the time the 9ᵉ *Cuirassiers* had a *giberne* for every man who needed one: inspected in summer 1807, the 7ᵉ *Cuirassiers* had not a single *giberne* or belt. Inspected again at Lodi on 31 December 1807, the 7ᵉ *Cuirassiers* had no *gibernes* and belts. Given the similar in uniform, we can be confident that the Otto manuscript is showing the 7ᵉ, otherwise the omission of *giberne* belts from the 9ᵉ is totally unexplainable!

The sumptuous helmet of Colonel Dubois of the 7ᵉ *Cuirassiers* dating from the last years of the Empire. (*Private collection*)

new *manteaux-capote*. Equipment held included 120 *banderole-porte-mousquetons* in need of repair, of which the *dépôt* held 79 carbines in good condition and 26 needing repairs; none were issued. Likewise, no *porte-mousquetons* were in use. In stores were a further 81 shirts, 4 *sacs à distribution*, 15 *habit* brushes, 14 whitening brushes, 8 button brushes, 139 grease brushes and 10 pairs of *manchette du botte*. About the clothing, the inspector noted that the items issued in 1813 into the first quarter of 1814 was very 'particular' and ordered that all the *habits* had to be all exchanged for new pattern, which were to be 'cut short'. We cannot be sure which garment they were wearing, but either way, the regiment's *habits* were long tailed in 1814.[46]

We know nothing else until after Waterloo. On 5 December 1815, the regiment had the following items in use and in the *dépôt*:[47]

This slightly post-epoch image shows a trumpeter of the 7ᵉ wearing Imperial Livery. The regiment's archive does support such a uniform being worn.

Martinet gives three images of the regiment: a trooper *c.*1805, a trooper *c.*1813 and accompanied by an officer of the same date. The absence of a *giberne* dates the image to up to 1813. Yet we know this is not based on eyewitness observations as the regiment had black leather shoulder straps to the *cuirass*.

108   Napoleon's Heavy Cavalry

Item	In Magazine	In Use	Total
Habits	22	154	176
Vestes en drap blanc	237	17	309
Culottes de peau	92	147	239
Stable trousers	17	73	90
Bonnets de police	1	150	151
Gilets d'ecurie	8	120	128
Surculottes		98	98
Manteaux	72	159	231
Waistbelts	254	177	431
Gibernes	293	121	419
Porte–gibernes	298	121	419
Banderole-porte-carabines	75	2	77
Sword knots	208	173	381
Porte–manteaux	162	149	311
Pairs of boots with spurs	2	139	141
Pairs of gloves	242	140	382
Trumpets	1	4	5
Helmets	335	177	512
Plumes	165	77	242
Pairs of epaulettes	83	151	234

Stocks of cloth and materials comprised:[48]

> 120m 67 blue broadcloth
> 50m white broadcloth
> 346m 50 *blanc picquer de bleu* broadcloth
> 72m 93 *gris-beige* broadcloth
> 32m 92 yellow broadcloth
> 136m 99 yellow serge
> 136m 12 blue serge
> 602m 90 linen for lining
> 303m 7 *treillis*
> 225 dozen large tin buttons
> 344 dozen small buttons
> 300 dozen bone buttons
> 133 sets of hooks and eyes
> 163m 48 lace 24mm wide

As with other regiments of *cuirassiers*, not an inch of green cloth existed and not an inch of Imperial Livery. In 1814 the regiment had *gilets-manche*, by 1815 the regiment had *vestes* without sleeves. We wonder if these sleeved *gilet*s were ever worn under the *habit*? We note that 25 *bottes de carabine* were issued, and 2 *banderole-porte-carabines*, for 51 *mousquetons*! How were these carried we wonder? Certainly not slung across the shoulder on the musket sling as practical experience shows it is impossible to do so when wearing a *cuirass*. For 177 men remaining under arms at the time of disbandment, 177 sabres were issued, yet just 142 *cuirasses* with 138 *fraise*. Clearly some men had lost their armour on campaign, and others their *fraise*. We also note 1[e] company had plumes, 77 being in use, and only 152 men had a pair of epaulettes: presumably some men had lost these as 154 *habits*

Trumpeter of the 8[e] *Cuirassiers* in 1812–14. An identical helmet can be found in the collection of Vincent Bourgeot.

were issued, or were 2 *habits* for trumpeters and they had some other form of shoulder decoration? Insufficient *culottes de peau* and *surculottes* were issued for a man to have a pair of both, it was a case of either or. Likewise, some men only had their stable dress. In stores we find 7 pairs of black tricot gaiters, 11 pairs of *manchette du botte*, 99 black stocks, and 38 pairs of woollen stockings. Not a single pair of underwear existed in 1814 or 1815, so we can only assume the men used their shirt tails as a loincloth.[49]

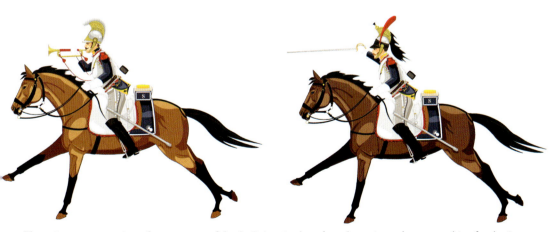

Tentative reconstruction of a trumpeter of the 8[e] *Cuirassiers* based on the regiment's paper archive for the 1st Restoration and 100 days period. As with other regiments of *Cuirassiers*, not an inch of green cloth existed and not an inch of Imperial Livery either in 1814 or 1815, so I assume they were dressed as troopers. If not, reversed colours would be possible. We also show a trooper of the regiment from the end of the Empire.

Trooper of the 9ᵉ *Cuirassiers* by Martinet. The first image can be dated to *c*.1808. The 9ᵉ *Cuirassiers* were inspected at Mayence on 14 December 1807, when the regiment had 182 pairs of *chaperons* in use – as Martinet shows – and 893 sheepskin *schabraques*. Martinet is wrong in showing no *giberne*: the regiment had 889 of these in use that day, as they had 6 months earlier on 1 June. Martinet shows a red festoon to the *schabraque*: the regimental archive reports 87m 50 of scarlet broadcloth had been used in 1805 to 1807. Was this used to make the festoon? Presumably so. The second image dates from 1812–14, again the absence of a *giberne* is an error.

9ᵉ *Cuirassiers*

As with all the heavy cavalry, the regiment had been destroyed in the Russian campaign. The regiment had left behind 75 men in the *dépôt* in summer 1812: they became the cadre for the regiment raised in new year 1813. The 4ᵉ *escadron Bis* was raised on 28 February 1813 and mustered one officer, two sergeant majors, eight sergeants, two *fourriers*, 16 corporals and not a single *cuirassier*! Just two horses were allocated for training the recruits. The 9ᵉ and 10ᵉ companies were missing 49 and 80 men respectively, having provided men to the 4ᵉ *escadron*. Out of the theoretical establishment of 659 men, the regiment had just 181 other ranks with 215 horses – 487 men and 444 horses were needed. Not an inch of cloth was in the *dépôt* or clothing – it had been used to clothe the new entrants to the regiment.[50] Alas, we know nothing more until the last days of the Empire.

The 9e *Cuirassiers* in August 1814 were wearing:[51]

Item	In Good Repair	In Need of Repair	Need Replacing	Items Missing
Habits	133			8
Vestes	131			10
Stable trousers			99	
Bonnets de police	133			8
Pairs of epaulettes	131			8
Gilets d'écuric	46		46	11
Pantalons de drap	45		54	32
Culottes de peau	131			8
Helmets	131			8
Manteaux	131			8
Gibernes	94			
Porte-gibernes	94			
Waistbelts	132			7
Sword knots	125			14
Pairs of boots	131			8
Pairs of gauntlets	131			8
Pairs of *cuirass fraise*	126			2
Banderole-porte-mousquetons	2			
Porte-manteaux	134			7
Trumpets	4			

The broadcloth *pantalons* are a non-regulation affection by the *cuirassiers*, which seem to have been in common use since 1810. In addition, the regiment was armed with 132 sabres, 132 pairs of pistols and 126 *cuirasses* – the 4 trumpeters were not armoured, along with the farriers. The men were issued with 421 shirts, 138 black stocks, 196 white stocks, 205 pairs of linen stockings – each man had a pair of socks but no underwear! – 18 pairs of woollen stockings, 124 pairs of shoes – we can only assume the lack of these was made up with clogs, or the *sous-officiers* had no need for shoes for stable duties as they could employ a groom to do this duty for them – and 125 pairs of black tricot gaiters. Brand new clothing in the *dépôt* comprised 6 *habits*, 130 *vestes*, 253 pairs of stable trousers, 284 *bonnets de police*, 107 helmets, 194 *manteaux*, 40 *gibernes* with belts, 54 waistbelts, 68 sword knots, 134 pairs of boots, 78 pairs of gauntlets, 2 *banderole-porte-mousquetons* and 146 *porte-manteaux*. Needing repair were 61 *habits*, 59 *vestes*, 23 *gilets d'écurie*, 6 pairs of *culottes de peau* and 11 helmets. To be written off were 10 *habits*, 10 *gilets d'écurie*, 1 pair of *culottes de peau*, 62 helmets and 19 *manteaux*. About the dress of the regiment, the inspector remarked:

We record that the dispositions of the clothing of the men by the decree of 19 January and 7 February 1812 have not yet been executed, nor have the modifications to the dress of the regiment by the Ministerial Circular of 23 April last; it will conform to article 63 of the instruction of 25 May … concerning the broadcloth and cloth parts of the uniform, the distinctions of the new 9ᵉ regiment of *cuirassiers* will be the colours carried by the former 13ᵉ *cuirassiers*. Those items of uniform which are to remain in use will have their facing colours changed.[52]

Trumpeter of the 9ᵉ *Cuirassiers* by Otto. This image is famous for showing the 9ᵉ *Cuirassiers*, or does it? We know the regiment's trumpeters wore *surtouts*: seven are recorded in June 1807 and these were still in service at the end of the year. Not a single *surtout* existed in the depot in 1805, with just six being made 1805 to 1807. More worryingly, however, not an inch of sky-blue cloth existed in regimental stores; conceivably this was dark blue and we have a colourist's error. Otto shows, it seems, a buff-coloured *surtout*, but yet again, the regiment had not an inch of buff-coloured cloth. Is it actually yellow? So, we have a yellow *surtout* with Imperial Blue facings? Indeed, this seems the case from the paper archive. But what of the bearskin? The 9ᵉ *Cavalerie* regiment never owned a single bearskin, nor the 9ᵉ *Cuirassiers* in the period 1803 to 1807. Could they have been purchased during 1808? If so then they left not a trace in the regiment's paper archive, and certainly, if they existed, were not replaced in 1809 after Wagram. Therefore, we are left with an enigma: Rousselot and Rigo both believe the image to be the 9ᵉ, yet the regiment's own archive would disagree. Who is right?

Rousselot's reconstruction of a trumpeter of the 9ᵉ *Cuirassiers*. The uniform is perfectly plausible: we know the regiment even had red cloth for the cut-out grenades on the coat tails. The only issue with the image is the bearskin: officially the regiment never possessed a single example. We also know the trumpeters were armoured, which again contradicts what is shown. Rousselot cites a now lost period engraving of the 9ᵉ as the source of his reconstruction.

Undeniable evidence that the 9ᵉ had not adopted Bardin regulation – the presence of *manteaux* affords further evidence – and still wore Imperial insignia somewhere on the clothing.

So, we ask, what was the regiment wearing? Thankfully the 9ᵉ has one of the most complete set of paper records for any *cuirassier* regiment. In 1807 the regiment was dressed in *habit à revers*.[53] Two years later, in 1809 over 750 new *habits à revers* were made.[54] Beyond reasonable doubt, the regiment had what is commonly known as the 1806 model *habit*, in use through to 1814. It also seems reasonable that the trumpeters were still in yellow *habits* faced blue.

Regimental accounts reveal that in the period 1 January 1811 to 1 January 1812, the regiment had spent 22,243fr 41 on uniforms, 736fr had been spent with the regiment's boot maker M. Thireul on repairs, and master boot maker M. Oger had charged 1,414fr 60 for making new boots, M. Doyen the breeches maker had charged 2,211fr to make *culottes de peau*, master tailor M. Fidel had charged 2,944fr 20 for his services and regimental workmen headed by Sergeant Maillot came to 450fr, some 9,183fr 46, when one included the services of 'piece workers' sewing up clothing in the form of kits in their homes managed by M. Schlessinger, who charged 1,427fr 68 for his services. In the year beginning 1 January 1812, a staggering 836,654fr 57 was spent on clothing, and in 1813 this fell to 148,583fr 25. In contrast just 723fr 35 was spent in all of 1814 between 2 January and 8 August. Under the 1st Restoration 14,205fr 06 was spent on clothing, which strongly suggests the regiment received new *habits* with *lieu de vin* facings as well as new trumpeters' kit. In the 100 days 15,363fr 37 was expended, which was no doubt spent on making kit for new entrants and I suppose also new trumpeters' kit, but this time in green with Imperial Livery. The 100 days also witnessed the first issue of new shirts and socks since 1812, when 3,186fr 88 was spent on shirts, socks and shoes. We also note 22,037fr 35 was spent on repairs and making new saddlery. Just 5,615fr 82 had been spent on repairs in the previous year.[55] In December 1815, when the regiment had the following cloth amounts:[56]

17m 47 yellow broadcloth
535m 60 *blanc picque de bleu*
0m *rouge-garance* broadcloth
0m yellow serge
0m blue tricot
0m linen

The *rouge-garance* broadcloth is not included in any earlier stores returns for cloth. We presume it was purchased sometime between October 1814 and December 1815 and entirely used for making clothing. The yellow milled serge was also purchased in the same time frame and was used to line and face the *habit* tails. Clothing in the magazine comprised:[57]

96 *habits*
514 *vestes en drap blanc*
249 *gilets d'ecurie*
305 *manteaux*
439 helmets

The high number of *vestes* in stores may indicate that these items were not worn on campaign. Equipment comprised:[58]

348 waistbelts
174 *gibernes*
174 *porte-gibernes*
572 *garnitures de cuirass*
325 sword knots
368 *porte-manteau*
313 pairs of boots
249 pairs of gauntlets
12 trumpets

It seems despite having 152 carbines in the *dépôt*, with 148 bayonets, none were issued or used on the campaign as no belts existed to hang the carbines from. We note the regiment

Tentative reconstruction of a trumpeter of the 9e *Cuirassiers* c.1805 in parade dress based on the regiment's archive. Our second image shows a trumpeter in campaign dress with armour. Thirdly a trumpeter as they appeared in 1813–14. Lastly, a reconstruction of a trooper of the 9e *Cuirassiers* in 1813–14 based on the regiment's paper archive.

Regulations in Practice 1812–15   115

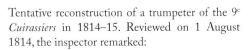

Tentative reconstruction of a trumpeter of the 9ᵉ *Cuirassiers* in 1814–15. Reviewed on 1 August 1814, the inspector remarked:

> We record that the dispositions of the of the clothing of the men by the decree of 19 January and 7 February 1812 have not yet been executed, nor have the modifications to the dress of the regiment by the Ministerial Circular of 23 April last; it will conform to article 63 of the instruction of 25 May … concerning the broadcloth and cloth parts of the uniform, the distinctions of the new 9ᵉ regiment of *Cuirassiers* will be the colours carried by the former 13ᵉ *Cuirassiers*. Those items of uniform which are to remain in use will have their facing colours changed.

Undeniable evidence that the 9ᵉ had not adopted Bardin regulation – the presence of *manteaux* affords further evidence – and it still wore Imperial insignia somewhere on the clothing. Not a word about green *habits* or Imperial Livery for trumpeters, but this is clearly inferred regarding the context of the 23 April 1814 decree, which ordered removal of Imperial insignia. Indeed, the only explicit Imperial insignia on a *cuirassiers*' uniform was the Imperial Livery worn by trumpeters; we therefore assume it was used.

Our hypothetical reconstruction is based on the war minister's recommendations to change the regiment's facing colour. In the year beginning 1 January 1812, 836,654fr 57 was spent on clothing – arguably every man was totally redressed, and in 1813 this fell to 148,583fr 25 and just 723fr 35 was spent in all of 1814 between 2 January and 8 August on making or mending clothing. Under the 1st Restoration 14,205fr 06 was spent on clothing, which strongly suggests the regiment received new *habits* – or they were simple changed – with *lieu de vin* facings as well as new trumpeters' kit. We assume Royalist Livery was adopted. Lastly is a tentative reconstruction of a trumpeter at Waterloo based on the war minister's recommendations to change the regiment's facing colour and the regimental accounts, which cover the production of new clothing in the 100 days and this surely includes trumpeters: assuming they were not dressed as rank and file. We note, that in the 100 days 15,363fr 37 was expended, which was no doubt spent on making kit for new entrants and I suppose also new trumpeters' kit, but this time in green with Imperial Livery.

Colonel de Murat-Sistrières of the 9ᵉ *Cuirassiers*: appointed in 1811 and left his post in 1813. He is wearing a *habit à revers*, and it is possible that the 9ᵉ were still wearing such garments in 1814.

had 519 sabres, 393 pistols and 604 *cuirasses*. Also in stores were 66 brand new shirts, and 46 pairs of black gaiters, which we assume were worn on foot duties.[59]

10ᵉ *Cuirassiers*

Reviewed on 31 May 1813, the 2ᵉ and 3ᵉ squadrons, the 302 men had been given 'their first issue' of clothing. Some 50 sets of harness were in the process of being made by the *dépôt* for the 176 troops' horses, a further 176 had been ordered from local contractors for 6,500fr. The major reported that 150 sabres had yet to be delivered from Strasbourg, and the two squadrons had no *gibernes*,

Martinet shows two figures from the regiment: firstly a *cuirassier* c.1805. Second is a trooper presumably at the end of the Empire as the trooper has pink – *lieu de vin*? – facings. Martinet shows no *giberne* and belt: in summer 1814 just eighty-two lacked these items and fifty-seven men had no epaulettes. No plumes were in use, but pompoms were. The troopers either had *surculottes* or *culottes de peau*, nobody had both as there simply wasn't enough of either for a man to have a pair of each. Martinet shows a red festoon to the *schabraque*: the regiment did indeed use scarlet broadcloth according to the regiment's paper archive, so we assume it was destined for this. Over 200m of scarlet broadcloth was used 1805 to 1807.

no *porte-gibernes* and no sabre belts! These were to be delivered on 6 April 1813 for the sum of 833fr.[60]

By 5 June 1813 the situation was little changed. The 6ᵉ company were missing 50 helmets, the clothing of the company had cost 4,500fr. Despite being clothed, the squadrons still had no sabres and were waiting for the delivery of 82 saddles and bridles. The major noted that 302 men were uselessly tied down for want of horses – just 88 for 302 men! – sabres and equipment.[61]

The 10ᵉ *Cuirassiers* had the following items of clothing and equipment on 6 August 1814.[62]

Item	In Good Repair	In Need of Repair	Need Replacing	Total Needed	Total Items	Items Missing
Habits	223	80	1	371	304	67
Gilets	312	0	2	371	314	57
Gilets d'écurie	193	71	44	371	308	63
Culottes de peau	146	0	168	371	314	57
Surculottes en drap gris	38	2	216	371	256	115
Stable trousers	33	0	281	371	314	57
Manteaux	271	1	40	371	312	58
Bonnets de police	300	0	10	371	310	61
Scarlet epaulettes	273	0	41	371	314	57
Helmets	274	25	15	371	314	57
Boots and spurs	235	63	16	371	314	57
Waistbelts	313	0	1	371	314	57
Gibernes et porte-gibernes	271	7	11	371	289	82
Sword knots	313	0	1	371	314	57
Porte-manteaux	284	0	30	371	324	57
Banderole-porte-mousquetons	The regiment has none					
Bayonets	0	0	0	0	0	0
Trumpets	6	3	0	12	9	3
Gauntlets	308	0	6	271	314	57
Fraise	276	0	12	371	288	83
Sabres	311	3	0	371	314	57
Pistols	191	8	0	371	199	172
Cuirasses	276	38	0	371	314	57
Shirts	929	0	0	371	929	0
Pantalons de toile	179	0	0	371	179	192
Black stock	319	0	0	371	319	52
White stock	638	0	0	371	638	0
Wool socks	885	0	0	371	885	0
Pairs of shoes	613	0	0	371	613	0
Black gaiters	195	0	0	371	195	176

Clearly the regiment in summer 1814 had no carbines. It also seems to have retained black gaiters for foot duties, along with shoes. The stores were completely empty of cloth, lace and other materials, although there were good quantities of uniform items in the magazines, ready for immediate issue. It would appear that the regiment made use of its stockpiles of cloth, etc. in the immediate cessation of hostilities, hence, in August 1814, the regiment had, ready for immediate issue:[63]

> 51 brand new *habits* (no distinction between those of troopers and *trompettes*)
> 91 brand new *manteaux*
> 140 brand new *gilets de drap*
> 343 brand new pompoms
> 238 brand new *bonnets de police*
> 289 brand new pairs of epaulettes
> 348 brand new *gibernes*
> 231 brand new sword belts and buckle plates
> 89 brand new helmets
> 200 brand new sword knots
> 67 brand new pairs of boots

The troopers either had *surculottes* or *culottes de peau*, nobody had both as there simply wasn't enough of either for a man to have a pair of each. The stores merely possessed 30 pairs of *culottes de peau*, which were *hors de service* and presumably kept merely to cannibalise for materials to be used to repair other existing pairs. There wasn't a single pair of *surculottes* in the stores. Similarly, there were no stable trousers at all in the stores. There were only 33 good pairs of stable trousers in use, plus another 281 pairs that were considered as *hors de service*, but for want of any others were still pressed into service. We have no information about the dress of trumpeters, as no details are listed for green cloth, lace or *habits*. The inspector summed up the August inspection by reporting:

> I remark that the regiment has not acted upon the dispositions for the clothing of the men of 19 January and 7 February 1812, and against all expectations have continued to not act upon the provisions of the ministerial circular of 23 April last. In conformity to the article 63 of the instruction of 25

Naïve self-portrait of a 10ᵉ *Cuirassier* c.1810.

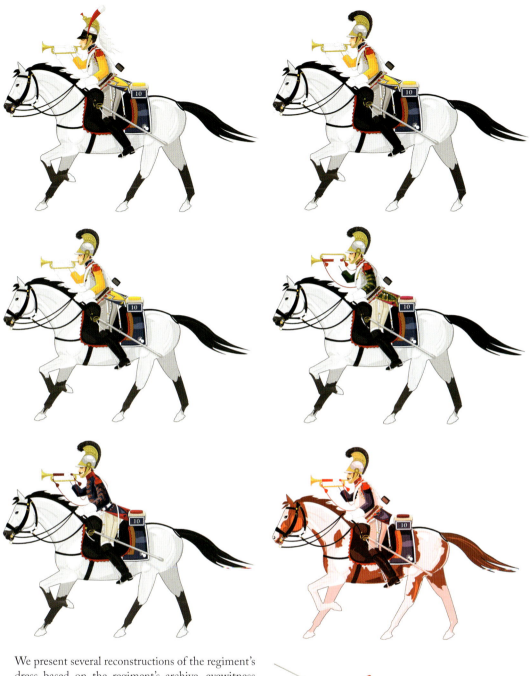

We present several reconstructions of the regiment's dress based on the regiment's archive, eyewitness images and extant items.

First is a trumpeter in the middle years of the Empire according to a naïve watercolour in Rousselot's papers. We are ignorant of his source of information. At the time of the 1807 inspections, the trumpeters were armoured, with 12 *cuirasses* clearly listed as for trumpeters. At the time of the 1807 inspection, we notice 45 felt *chapeaux* were in use: presumably for *sous-officiers* and trumpeters. We also note 843 plumes in use.

Secondly, a trumpeter *c.*1812 wearing the same uniform as before but with a helmet like the *Carabiniers*, of which an example is preserved in Ely

Museum, Cambridgeshire, recovered from the field of Waterloo with a *cuirass*. The latter has black leather *epaulières* that never carried copper scales. We assume the helmet was in service before 1815. Thirdly is a possible appearance of a trumpeter as they seem to have appeared in 1814. In summer 1814 we know the trumpeters were armoured as every man in the regiment was issued and wearing a *cuirass*. We have dressed the trumpeter in Imperial Livery as the inspector commented that the 10ᵉ had not removed Imperial iconography from use and dressed trumpeters in Royalist Livery, noting 'and against all expectations have continued to not act upon the provisions of the ministerial circular of 23 April last'. We assume the trumpeters were still adorned with Imperial Livery.

Fourthly is a tentative reconstruction of a trooper of the 10ᵉ *Cuirassiers* in 1815. In summer 1814 the War Ministry ordered 'concerning the duration of the broadcloth and other cloth items of uniform, there will be made the substitution of the colours of the 10ᵉ regiment of *Cuirassiers* with those of the 14ᵉ'. Thus, the 10ᵉ, in theory, adopted *lieu de vin* facings, rather than pink, but it is possible the regiment still had yellow. We have not a single piece of archive evidence to support this change taking place, although Martinet implies this did happen. The trumpeter is accompanied by a hypothetical reconstruction of a trumpeter during the 1st Restoration to Waterloo. Lastly is a hypothetical reconstruction of a trumpeter of the 10ᵉ *Cuirassiers* at Waterloo. We assume, as was practice in other regiments, that during the 100 days trumpeters wore troopers' *habits* rather than Royalist Livery, as we show here.

Major of the 10ᵉ *Cuirassiers* c.1805. The *cuirass* is of the first model and the *habit de cuirass* is closed by eleven buttons. (*Musée de l'Empéri, Collections du Musée de l'Armée, Anciennes collections Jean et Raoul Brunon*)

Trumpeter of the 10ᵉ *Cuirassiers* c.1812. The drawing is hugely problematical: firstly, the regiment had no bearskins in use in summer 1805, summer 1807 or winter 1807. Secondly, cloth-covered *chaperons* were entirely taken out of service in winter 1807, and the 174 pairs in use were replaced by sheepskin *schabraque*s. On this basis, the image dates from 1807 and earlier, which we can demonstrate is not supported by the paper archive. We are left to wonder therefore about the image's validity, especially as the image dates to 1824. The uniform shown is remarkably similar to the 5ᵉ *Cuirassiers*, therefore I suspect the image is of that unit and not the 10ᵉ.

May ... concerning the duration of the broadcloth and other cloth items of uniform, there will be made the substitution of the colours of the 10ᵉ regiment of *cuirassiers* with those of the 14ᵉ.[64]

Thus, the 10ᵉ, in theory, adopted *lieu de vin* facings, yet we have not a single piece of archive evidence to support this change taking place. It also seems the 10ᵉ continued with the *habit à revers* through to 1814. The inspector implied the regiment had green trumpeters' clothing and changed into blue with Royalist Livery.

For the dress of the regiment up to Waterloo very few pieces of archive paperwork exist. We note that during the 100 days, 100 *gilets sans manche*, 15 pairs of boots and 4 saddles were purchased new and 10 saddles were repaired for 1,800fr 17, along with 9 *bonnets de police* costing 4fr 88 each – hugely expensive and likely for *sous-officiers* as a trooper's example cost 1fr 50 – 1 *habit de cuirassier de modèle*, which cost 25fr 22, and 1 *porte-manteaux de modèle* for the sum of 12fr 72.[65] The need for such an item strongly suggests that the regiment had been using the larger 1801 type *porte-manteaux* or the earlier round pattern up to 1815. No further paperwork exists, and nothing from disbandment. One unusual distinction of the 10ᵉ, according to Rousselot, was that in June 1806 the helmet tuft was to be red as ordered by Colonel Lataye in the regimental standing orders, but alas does not present the actual orders themselves, which is deeply frustrating. We also note the *cuirass* had black leather *épaulières* to judge by an extant *cuirass* in the UK.

11ᵉ *Cuirassiers*

The paper archive of the regiment is incredibly sparse when it comes to dress and equipment. We know nothing virtually between Austerlitz and the 1st Restoration! The only document we can locate between these dates concerns the 3ᵉ squadron and the *dépôt* company reviewed on 5 June 1813. The 3 companies present mustered 424 other ranks with 135 horses. The major reported that production of clothing was ongoing, the *dépôt* held 93 *habits* and cloth to hand to complete 668 *habits* by the end of July, contracts having been issued on 13 May. Cloth for the *manteaux* was yet to be delivered. Equipment wise, stores held 355 carbines with just 93 *porte-carabines*, 336 sabres, 106 pistols, 361 *cuirasses*,132 helmets, 270 *gibernes*, 206 *porte-gibernes* and 154 waistbelts. The major reported that the regimental workmen were 'working hard' making the missing items of equipment and he noted that the new helmets were expected to be delivered before the end of July.[66]

We know nothing else until 1814, when the men were wearing:[67]

Martinet gives us two troopers from the 11ᵉ *Cuirassiers*, the first c.1805, the second from the 1st Restoration. In the second image, Martinet shows pink facings, which dates the image to the second half of 1814 through to Waterloo. We know this because at the time of the August 1814 inspection, the regiment had yellow facings and was in the process of swapping to pink when reviewed. The inspector noted that the regiment's clothing officer had purchased cloth and had issued contracts to change the collars and lining of the *habits* in a letter of 12 August 1814 to the War Ministry.

Item	In Good Repair	In Need of Repair	Need Replacing	Items Missing
Habits and epaulettes	130	48	3	4
Gilets	132	10		42
Gilets d'ecurie	106	9	3	2
Culottes de peau	175			5
Capotes	164	10	1	6
Surculottes	58	12	9	104
Pantalons de treillis	87		2	50
Bonnets de police	176	1	2	8
Pairs of gauntlets	172	1		7
Helmets	170	4		
Waistbelts	173			7
Waistbelt plates	173			7
Gibernes	111			
Porte-gibernes	111			

Item	In Good Repair	In Need of Repair	Need Replacing	Items Missing
Pairs of boots	100	34		46
Porte-manteaux	175	3		5
Trumpets	12			3
Sword knots	172			8

Capotes we assume to be the 1813 *manteau-trois-capote* and the *pantalons* are seemingly stable trousers. The magazine held the following amounts of cloth:[68]

0m 10 beige broadcloth
33m 52 blue broadcloth
90m 58 white broadcloth
24m 05 rose broadcloth
5m 89 green broadcloth
15m 22 yellow broadcloth
1,384m 25 broadcloth for *manteaux*
462m 75 blue tricot
696m linen for lining
783m 88 *treillis*
2,530m 80 yellow serge
98m 84 rose serge
46m 98 trumpeters' livery
84 sheepskins
48m 10 lace for chevrons
0m 80 lace for corporals' stripes
0m 40 silver lace for *sous-officiers'* stripes
367m 36 white worsted lace for *porte-manteaux*

The green broadcloth had been clearly used for the production of trumpeters' clothing along with what we assume was Imperial Livery. The inspector noted that the regiment had not changed its facing colours as decreed under the Bardin regulation, but remarked that the clothing officer had purchased cloth and had issued contracts to change the collars and lining of the *habits*: here is proof the 11e wore yellow facings in the campaigns of 1813 and 1814! The inspector also noted that the regiment had not acted upon the Bardin regulation with regards to the cut of the men's clothing nor the decree of 1814 concerning blue clothing for trumpeters: we assume the men were wearing their old *habit à revers*.[69]

It is often said that the 11e had no armour in the Waterloo campaign, about which *cuirassier* expert Ian Smith comments:

a report, dated 8th May 1815, from the dépôt of the 11e *Cuirassiers*, and written by the Major commanding the regimental dépôt, regarding the number of *cuirasses*,

We present several reconstructions of the trumpeters' dress from the 11e *Cuirassiers*' archive. Up first is a trooper at the time of the October 1804 inspection; second a trumpeter in 1808 when we know they were armoured, and a trumpeter wearing parade dress in 1809. Thirdly is a trumpeter in summer 1814. In a letter dated 12 August 1814 to the War Ministry, the official inspecting the 11e *Cuirassiers* noted that the regiment had not acted upon the Bardin regulation with regards the cut of the men's clothing, nor the decree of 1814 concerning blue clothing for trumpeters in place of the green items then in use. At the time of the 1814 review, the trumpeters and farriers were not armoured. Fifthly is a trumpeter in the second half of 1814 into 1815 wearing Royalist Livery, and lastly a trumpeter at Waterloo, assuming the regiment did indeed change facing colour as Martinet implies. On 15 June, the 11e had 308 other ranks in the field, and possessed 289 *cuirassiers*: 8 farriers were in the field, and were traditionally not armoured, so too the 2 veterinarians: this leaves 9 men not armoured, which we suppose were trumpeters, and 15 trumpeters excluding the trumpet major and corporal trumpeter were on regimental strength. Arguably therefore, at least some of the trumpeters in the field wore armour, excepting the trumpet major and corporal trumpeter, who traditionally it seems were not armoured.

sabres and pistols that they had in their regimental magazines. He states that the regiment had made numerous requests to acquire sufficient *cuirasses* and pistols to equip all the men of the dépôt, but to no avail.

He adds that **before** the 11e left their Thionville dépôt to join Lhéritier's division, the Arsenal of Thionville [only a few miles from the regimental dépôt of the 11e] still held 80 *cuirasses* and large stocks of pistols which could have been issued to the 11e, but the officer commanding the arsenal refused to cooperate. [Perhaps the officer commanding the Thionville dépôt had Royalist sympathies, so he withheld the armour and pistols?]

So, **after** the *escadron de guerre* had left Thionville, the Major informs the Minister of War that the 11e still held 168 *cuirasses* in its magazines, and 188 sabres, but **zero** pistols.

At their 1814 inspection, the 11e had the following armour stocks:

Still in the magazine: 73 *cuirasses* in good condition and 66 needing repairs.

Already issued to the rank and file: 142 *cuirasses* in good condition and 7 needing repairs.

That makes a **total for 1814 of 288 *cuirasses***. It is reasonable to assume that all the *cuirasses* needing repairs had been made fit for service by May 1815.

In 1814 they also had **no** stocks of pistols in the magazines, and only 89 altogether, which is only one pistol for every three men. The pistol situation had not improved at all by 8th May 1815, as the major still records **zero** in the magazines.

So, on 8 May 1815, **after** the regiment had left to join Guiton's brigade in the field, they still had 168 *cuirasses* left at their dépôt.

In the summer of 1814, the 11e Cuirassiers could boast over 300 officers and other ranks [which was quite high for this time, compared with, for example, the *carabiniers*], yet on 18 May, 1815, Guiton's brigade recorded the following returns:

11e *Cuirassiers*: 121 other ranks in the field
8e *Cuirassiers*: 384 other ranks in the field

That is a huge difference.

It's clear that when the 121 men of the *escadrons de guerre* had left the regimental dépôt at Thionville, they had left behind around two hundred men and 168 complete *cuirasses* and 188 sabres, but **zero** firearms of any description.

I believe that is for this reason alone that the Colonel of the 11e was unwilling to send any more men into the field. It wasn't for lack of *cuirasses* or sabres, but pistols.

Furthermore, it's now clear that the 11^e did **not** receive any armour between their review in the summer of 1814 and their departure for the front in early May 1815. Here's why I can prove this:

Despite being ordered to change regimental facings to pink in 1812, the regiment had clung tenaciously to yellow and only changed to pink during the 1st Restoration. We show a trooper as he appeared in summer 1814 and as they appeared at Waterloo complete with armour.

121 other ranks in the field plus 168 *cuirasses* still at the dépôt = 289 *cuirasses* altogether.

That's just **one** more *cuirass* than the 288 they had in 1814.

My guess is that the Major's letter to the Minister of War is a reply to Davout's question, 'Why haven't you sent more men to join their division?' I would then assume that Davout kicked someone's butt in the arsenal of Thionville, and so the 80 *cuirasses* and the stocks of pistols were indeed turned over to the dépôt of the 11ᵉ, which would give them precisely 248 more *cuirasses* and plenty of pistols ready to be issued.

On 15th June, the 11ᵉ had 308 other ranks in the field, which represents an additional 187 men who had arrived from the dépôt to join up with their regiment since 18th May.

So, the 11ᵉ would easily have had sufficient *cuirasses* to equip all their rank and file, and once the regiment had received sufficient pistols, the Colonel sent orders to the Major at the dépôt to send the 187 men to join him in the field.[70]

A cogent argument therefore that the 11ᵉ did indeed wear armour at Quatre-Bras and Waterloo. Alas, we do not have any disbandment records for the regiment to assess what was worn and how many *cuirasses* may have been in the *dépôt*.

12ᵉ *Cuirassiers*

The *dépôt* was inspected on 21 May 1812 and totalled 2 sergeant majors, 6 sergeants, 2 *fourriers*, 12 corporals, and 54 *cuirassiers* with just 22 horses. These were all old, experienced horses for teaching recruits to ride. The men were all well dressed and well equipped.[71] Inspected again on 22 July 1812, the regiment now had just 16 horses, and

Regulations in Practice 1812–15   127

was down to 53 men of all ranks. Since May, the *dépôt* had equipped just 18 men, and had no cloth or clothing to equip any further conscripts.[72] These 53 men became the cadre around which the regiment was re-formed on 30 January 1813.[73]

The clothing of the regiment in 1814 was in deplorable condition.[74] The bulk that in use was unserviceable. General Comte de Pully, who undertook the review of the 12ᵉ *Cuirassiers* in July 1814, wrote to the Minister of War 'it's easy to see that everything is poor or at best very mediocre with the 12ᵉ ...'[75] Nearly every item of clothing and equipment was poorly maintained in the 12ᵉ *Cuirassiers*: clearly resupply was an issue during the 1814 campaign:[76]

Item	In Good Repair	In Need of Repair	Need Replacing	Items Missing	Observations
Habits	40		101		Not one *habit* is in good condition, and all need repairs, not one has been delivered since the start of the last campaign.
Vestes sans manche	64	10	59		
Gilets d'ecurie					
Bonnets de police			133		
Manteaux	80	12	44		
Culottes de peau	The Corps has none and requires 145 pairs				
Surculottes	50		90		These are *pantalons*.
Pantalons treillis	The Corps has none				
Pairs of epaulettes	40		101		
Helmets	106	22	22		
Gibernes	88				
Porte-gibernes	88				
Waistbelts	133		4		
Belt plates	140				
Sabre knots	142				
Pairs of gauntlets	20		7		
Pairs of boots	42		28		
Pairs of spurs	42	3			
Trumpets	8				

The men missing boots we assume were wearing shoes, as 155 pairs were in use along with two pairs of gaiters. Also in use were 386 shirts, 61 black stocks – a lot of men wearing black linen neck cloths – 132 pairs of socks. The incredible thing is that at the very same time the stores were quite literally bursting at the seams with cloth:[77]

75m 63 beige broadcloth for *surculottes*
857m 90 of blue uniform cloth
418m 6 white broadcloth for front of *gilets*
334m 7 of yellow serge for *habit* linings

4m 80 green broadcloth for trumpeters
94m 11 yellow broadcloth for collar, cuffs and piping
1,034m 11 blue tricot for *gilets d'ecurie* and *porte-manteaux*
146m 20 linen for lining *habits*
281m 18 linen for lining the *housses*

In addition, the *dépôt* held over 280m of *treillis* cloth for stable trousers, which is incredible given that the regiment did not have any pairs at all in service! The *dépôt* also held over 380m of white *galon* for *porte-manteaux*. The inspector noted that the regiment had not adopted the provisions of the Bardin regulation and still wore yellow facings, and Imperial iconography was still in use. Furthermore, the regiment was ordered to take up rose facings, as decreed on 7 February 1812, and to dress its trumpeters in blue with Royalist Livery, as ordered to do so in April 1814.[78] No doubt because the regiment's administration was so chaotic, one can see how the Bardin regulation and later dictates from the War Administration were simply ignored. In many ways, the regiment's colonel simply did his own thing, his own way.

Officer of the 12e *Cuirassiers* wearing we assume a *surtout*. Oddly, his epaulettes show the rank for squadron commander, yet his plume suggests company commander.

Trooper of the 12e *Cuirassiers* in summer 1814. At the time of the 1814 review, the regiment had not yet changed their facing colour from yellow to pink, or adopted the provisions of the Bardin regulation. He is accompanied by a trooper of the 12e *Cuirassiers* as they appeared at Waterloo.

Martinet gives us two troopers of the 12ᵉ *Cuirassiers*, the first at the start of the Empire and the second from the last years.

Interestingly, at the disbandment review, 49 brand new plumes are listed: we wonder if these were bought for the 19 *trompettes* on the strength in the summer of 1814? That would be enough to issue one each and have some spares in the magazine. There's no other reference to either pompoms or plumes in 1815, either used or new, so the purchase must have been small-scale.[79]

Following Waterloo, the regiment's *dépôt* was largely still stocked with materials:[80]

274m 61 blue broadcloth
344m 6 broadcloth for *manteaux*
141m 49 rose broadcloth for facings
4m 80 green broadcloth for trumpeters
456m 72 blue tricot
123m 60 rose serge
294m 64 *treillis* for stable trousers
159m 89 linen for linings

In 1814, there was 4m 80 of green cloth in the stores. By the time of the disbandment review on 22 November 1815 the same amount of cloth is still there untouched in stores,

The paper archive of the 12ᵉ *Cuirassiers*, aligned with a period image, allows us to show the evolution of the trumpeter's uniform in detail. Wearing a bearskin is a trumpeter from October 1804 to June 1805, at which date they swapped into helmets. By August 1805, as we show, the trumpeter were armoured. For parades, rather than the *habit à revers*, they wore this elegant *surtout*, an original garment of which could be found in a private collection in the years prior to the Second World War. We then show a trumpeter as they appeared in summer 1814. We know they were wearing Imperial Livery and were not armoured. We show a tentative reconstruction of a trumpeter as they appeared during the 1st Restoration, and conclude with a reconstruction as they appeared at Waterloo.

whereas the quantity of blue in the stores has gone down by hundreds and hundreds of metres. Arguably therefore in the period 1812–14 the trumpeters had worn green *habits*, perhaps with Imperial Livery. Given no new green cloth was purchased or used, this leads me to deduce that no new green *habits de trompette* were made during the 100 days. Certainly, by the time of the 1814 inspection trumpeters wore blue *habits*. We must note, however, that as the regiment was so badly administered in 1814, and the clothing situation so chaotic, that it is highly likely that nobody organised or effected the removal or destruction of the green *habits de trompette*, and that they were simply chucked into a corner of the magazine, to be reissued upon Napoléon's return.

The *dépôt* held in addition 64 new *habits*, 197 in need of repair, 50 new *vestes* and 18 needing repairs, 103 new *gilets d'ecurie*, 65 new *bonnets de police*, 247 new helmets, 482 needing repairs and 68 fit only to be disposed of, 49 new *manteaux* and 280 needing repairs, 236 new pairs of *culottes de peau* and 10 pairs needing repairs. Furthermore, the *dépôt* held 48 new *housses* and 155 needing repairs, and 17 new *schabraques*, 160 needing repairs and 13 that were life expired.[81]

13ᵉ *Cuirassiers*

With the commencement of the Peninsular War, three provisional *cuirassier* regiments were formed. These were temporary groupings of companies from a motley assortment of regiments of the same arm. As part of this regeneration of the army post the Treaties of Tilsit, Napoléon also reorganised the cavalry reserve. Each brigade of heavy cavalry was to form two provisional regiments:[82]

Provisional Regiment	1 Company	2 Company	3 Company	4 Company	5 Company	6 Company
1	1 *carabiniers* 120 men	2 *cuirassiers* 120 men	1 *cuirassier* 140 men	2 *cuirassiers* 140 men	3 *cuirassiers* 140 men	
2	5 *cuirassiers* 140 men	12 *cuirassiers* 140 men	12 *cuirassiers* 140 men	9 *cuirassiers* 120 men	10 *cuirassiers* 120 men	11 *cuirassiers* 120 men

Each regiment was to be commanded by a major, with a staff to comprise an adjutant major, two lieutenant adjutant majors, and two adjutant *sous-officiers*. Each company was to have a captain, a lieutenant, two second lieutenants, a sergeant major, four sergeants, six corporals, two trumpeters and a farrier.[83] It was Napoléon's intention that each squadron of cavalry was to number 250 to 300 men drawn from the conscription classes of 1806 and 1807. By May 1808 the 1ᵉ *régiment provisoire de grosse cavalerie* mustered 620 men and 568 men formed the 2ᵉ *régiment provisoire de grosse cavalerie*. In addition, were 269 men from the 1ᵉ, 2ᵉ and 4ᵉ *Escadron du Marche* of *Cuirassiers*, a force of 1,578 *cuirassiers*.

Following the disaster at Baylen, the 1ᵉ *régiment provisoire de grosse cavalerie* and 2ᵉ *régiment provisoire de grosse cavalerie* were disbanded with the decree of 21 October 1808 and became the 13ᵉ *Cuirassiers*. The new regiment was commanded by Colonel d'Aigremont. We know very little about the dress of the regiment in any detail. It was

Officer and Trooper of the 13ᵉ *Cuirassiers* by Martinet.

dressed like the first twelve regiments and had wine lees facings. A report dated 17 September 1821 tells us that in 1809, 400 pairs of *pantalons* were purchased made in grey broadcloth with black leather reinforcement; 200 pairs of fringed epaulettes were obtained in December 1810; in lieu of plumes, 610 pompoms costing 3fr 80 had been purchased in new year 1813; the regiment's helmets were totally overhauled in new year 1813. Regiment archives report that 685 front plates, listed as *plaque de médusa* for the *cimier*, were purchased costing 3fr 80 each, 400 new turbans from bear pelt were made for the helmets at a total cost of 1,000fr, and 527 helmet *bossettes* were purchased costing 1fr 20. We assume therefore that the new plates for the *cimier* were adorned with '13' on the shield below the *médusa*, ergo until 1813 the regiment's helmet still bore the inscription of the various detachments that composed the regiment. In total 685 helmets were repaired in new year 1813, each costing 13fr 93.[84]

The clothing and equipment of the regiment were as follows at time of disbandment in August 1814, when it was taken in to the 9ᵉ *Cuirassiers*:[85]

Regulations in Practice 1812–15   133

Item	In Good Repair	In Need of Repair	To be Replaced	To be Written Off
Habits	65	137	203	
Vestes en drap blanc	36	15	278	
Pantalons de treillis	17		212	48
Bonnets de police	99	40	210	
Epaulettes	185	47	214	
Gilets d'ecurie	44	15	291	
Surculottes de drap	None, the corps needs 405 pairs			
Culottes de peau	81	2	314	
Helmets	269	128	8	
Manteaux	207	167	51	
Saddles	229	198		
Bridles	359	50		18
Filets	376	36		15
Bridons d'ecurie	None, the corps needs 427			
Headcollars and lead rope	268	126		66
Girths and surcingles	278	104	34	11
Housses	354	73		
Schabraques	137	210	55	25
Saddle blankets	231	15	70	81
Gibernes	The Corps has 18 *gibernes* and *banderoles*. It needs 332			
Porte-gibernes				
Waistbelts	360	45		
Pairs of boots	61	93	251	
Gauntlets	216	41	12	101
Garnitures de cuirass	78	70	165	60
Banderole-porte-mousquetons	The corps has none			
Porte-manteaux	169	192		44
Trompettes	8	1	4	

In addition the men were issued 859 shirts – easily enough for 2 shirts per man, 162 pairs of linen *pantalons*, 405 black stocks, 809 white stocks, 197 pairs of linen socks, 58 pairs of wool stockings, 405 pairs of shoes – 1 pair for every man – 25 pairs of black gaiters, 116 *sacs à distribution* – the large ration bag that measured 2ft wide and almost 4ft deep – and 181 pairs of *manchette du botte* – suggesting some men had knee breeches and others ankle-length *pantalons*, or perhaps more accurately most men had lost them. The *dépôt* held no stocks of cloth or other materials, but it did hold 49 *gilets d'ecurie* to be written off, 181 helmets in need of repair, 40 *manteaux* needing repairs and 16 that were to be written off, along with 66 waistbelts in need of repairs, 40 sword knots to be

134 Napoleon's Heavy Cavalry

written off and 12 more needing repairs. The *dépôt* also held 29 pairs of boots beyond repair and 57 *porte-manteaux* needing repairs. Due to supply issues, or more prosaically because of the lack of musketoons and thus no need to carry cartridges, the regiment had no *gibernes*. Yet the regiment had 355 pistols issued, and 50 needing repairs – so how did the trooper stow the cartridges for the pistol? The regiment also possessed 283 *cuirasses* in good condition and 132 in need of repairs, 335 sabres in good conditions and 70 needing repairs. The *dépôt* also held 60 sabres in good condition, and a further 100 needing repairs, 28 pistols needing repairs, 88 *cuirasses* in good condition and a further 60 needing repairs.[86]

The 5e *escadron* was taken into the 4e *Cuirassiers*:[87]

Item	In Good Repair	In Need of Repair	Need Replacing	Items Missing
Habits	69	31	10	
Gilets	92	2	6	4
Gilets d'ecurie	31	14	28	32
Culottes de peau	54	2	35	19
Surculottes en drap gris	87	5	12	6
Stable trousers	9	4	5	72
Manteaux	66	25	5	13
Bonnets de police	85	1		3
Scarlet epaulettes	70	2	5	14
Helmets	106	1		3
Boots and spurs	32	45	2	33
Waistbelts	81	20	5	4
Gibernes et porte-gibernes	The Corps has none			
Sword knots				
Gants à parament	99	4		1
Trumpets	2			

For the 106 men under arms, 106 sabres were issued, 94 pairs of pistols of 101 *cuirasses* – presumably the trumpeters were not armoured – and just 82 *fraise* were in use. Every man had a pair of shoes, and 88 pairs of black and 90 pairs of grey gaiters were issued and in use. Also in use were 189 pairs of *manchette du botte*, 72 night caps and 189 *rabats* for the stock, of which 98 examples were in use. A further 189 *rabats* – the detachable white piping from the stock – were in store, with 8 pairs of black gaiters, 45 of grey linen gaiters and 5 pairs of *manchette du botte*.
Cloth in stores comprised:[88]

7m 30 blue broadcloth
18m 20 white broadcloth
8m 80 *garance* broadcloth
0m *garance* serge

Regulations in Practice 1812–15   135

16m 70 blue tricot
148m 50 linen
148m of lace for the *porte-manteaux*
48m *blanc picquer de bleu*
55m *lieu de vin* serge
25m rose broadcloth
37m *treillis*

The *garance* was, we assume, used to make *fraise* for the *cuirass*. Brand new kit in stores included 59 helmets, 32 scarlet plumes, 8 *manteaux*, 24 white *vestes*, 9 *habits de modèle* – no doubt including the trumpeter and trumpet majors' items in green with Imperial Livery – 18 *habits*, 2 *capotes de modèle*, 1 *gilet de modèle* and 1 *banderole-porte-carabine de modèle*. None of the *effets de modèle* items seem to have been copied, and remained unused in stores. So, we must imagine the regiment had had plumes at some stage.

The regiment presented a very poor appearance. No *gibernes* and belts were in use bar those by the trumpeters. It is a common misconception that the regiment abandoned *culottes de peau* in favour of brown cloth overalls: we do note that not a single pair of *culottes de peau* were in use with the war squadrons, and instead the men were wearing their stable trousers tucked inside their riding boots. These were the only items of legwear the squadrons possessed. Some 11 pairs of *culottes de peau* were in store and 2 pairs of *pantalons* made from beige broadcloth. Again, it is often remarked that the regiment wore brown *habits*, this is certainly not the case. The inspector said nothing about the colour of the *habits*, and we are sure he would have done if they were brown and not blue. He did note however, that the men were wearing clothing that did not accord to the decree of 9 February 1812 and that everything was totally worn out. The inspector added that the regiment's uniform and equipment had been in use longer than the regulation

We reconstruct the dress of the 13ᵉ in summer 1814. The men had no *gibernes* and the *cuirassier* shoulder straps lacked copper scales. Myth tells us the regiment wore brown clothing: no archive evidence supports this. For comparison we present a trumpeter in summer 1814 based on the regiment's disbandment paperwork.

136   Napoleon's Heavy Cavalry

service life of garments. We can only assume the trumpeters wore reversed colours, and the men may well have been wearing *habits à revers*! Clearly, the last time the men had received any new clothing was in 1812 or earlier.[89]

14e *Cuirassiers* (3e *régiment provisoire de grosse cavalerie*)

For a sense of completeness, we include the 3e *régiment provisoire de grosse cavalerie* so we can say something about every *cuirassier* regiment that existed in the 1st Empire. The regiment was raised on 13 January 1808, with 2 officers and 100 men from the 4e *Cuirassiers*, 2 officers and 100 men from the 6e *Cuirassiers*, 2 officers and 80 men from the 7e *Cuirassiers* and 2 officers and 80 men from the 8e *Cuirassiers*. It was commanded by Colonel Antoine-Didier Guery. The regiment entered Spain in February 1808 and was garrisoned at Barcelona and mustered 430 men. It was reinforced with 150 men from the 3e *Escadron de Marche* of *Cuirassiers*, which was then based at Vittoria. At Perpignan, detachments in the cavalry dépôts from the 4e, 7e and 8e regiments of *Cuirassiers* were to form a *marche* squadron of 120 men to be sent to the Army of Aragon to reinforce the regiment. From 21 October 1808 the regiment was unofficially known as the 14e *Cuirassiers* with the formation of the 13e *Cuirassiers*.[90]

The regiment remained in Spain and served in Catalonia in January 1810, when the 2e squadron was totally overrun by the Spanish at Mollet del Vallès on 21 January 1810. To make up for losses, an *Escadron de Marche* was sent to Spain from Italy, some 6 officers with 12 horses and 255 other ranks with 255 horses drawn from the depots of the 4e, 6e, 7e and 8e regiments.[91] The reinforcements were inspected on 16 April 1810 prior to incorporation into the '14e *Cuirassiers*':[92]

	Habits de cuirassier	Stable coats	Bonnets de police	Culottes de peau	Epaulettes	Plumes	Gilets	Pantalons	Porte–manteaux	Manteaux	Housse et Chaperons	Helmets	Cuirasses	Sabres and belts
4e *Cuirassiers*	75	75	75	75	75	75	75	75	75	75	75	75	75	75
6e *Cuirassiers*	50	49	50	50	50	50	50	50	50	50	50	50	50	50
7e *Cuirassiers*	90	88	90	90	90	90	90	90	90	90	90	90	90	90
8e *Cuirassiers*	40	37	40	40	40	40	40	40	40	40	40	40	40	40
Total	255	249	255	255	255	255	255	255	255	255	255	255	255	255

Of note, every man had cloth *chaperons*, a plume and pair of epaulettes. The regiment was disbanded with the decree of 27 December 1810. The regiment was inspected for the last time on 31 January 1811 at Toulouse, with the men being sent to the 3e *Cuirassiers*. Clothing and equipment were as follows:[93]

	Habits	Surtouts	Stable coats	Bonnets de police	Linen pantalons	Epaulettes	Porte-manteaux	Manteaux	Schabraques	Housses	Chaperons	Helmets	Plumes	Cuirasses
4e *Cuirassiers*	119	12	108	127		127	127	127	54	54		145	106	47
Depot			7	4			48	78	56	61	12			78
6e *Cuirassiers*	118	99	130	126			168	159	122	126	15	169		135
Depot	2		8				16	14	18	57	107	41		101
7e *Cuirassiers*	131	16	140	150		150	150	55		55		148		53
Depot at Toulouse	125					20	47		48	76	30	18		71
Depot at Barcelona						26	44	49		104	119	68		122
8e *Cuirassiers*	105		100	126	130		119	126	80	86	4	127	126	86
Depot at Toulouse								33	66	52	8	52		75
Depot at Barcelona								7		65	47	7		57

The regiment had at the point of disbandment, 2 adjutant *sous-officiers*, 10 sergeant majors, 38 sergeants, 6 *fourriers*, 68 corporals, 10 trumpeters and 878 other ranks, with just 266 horses! Of interest, the men from the 4e *Cuirassiers* had both plumes and epaulettes, the 6e had neither, the men from the 7e had epaulettes but no plumes, and the 8e had plumes and no epaulettes – lest we assume that every regiment had these items! Did this reflect the dress of the parent regiment? Presumably so. Of interest is the continued use of *chaperons* and sheepskin half-*schabraques* in the same regiments. Also of comment is the differentiation between the *habit* and *surtout*. The regiment was formed in 1808, so the men would have been wearing the most recent issue of regulated clothing, i.e., the *habit à revers*, the so-called 1806 model we discussed earlier. Thus, the 3e when it marched to Russia, had we assume, its men in *habits à revers* or were they all redressed before heading to Germany?

14e *Cuirassiers*

Formed in 1810 from the 2e Dutch *Cuirassiers*, in November of that year the Minister for War authorised the regiment to adopt dark blue uniforms in lieu of white with 'wine lees' facings to accord with the 13e *Cuirassiers* in lieu of *bleu barbeau*. On 8 March 1811, 220fr was spent on the purchase of epaulettes for the *sous-officiers* – totally illegal purchase as the regulations did not allow *sous-officiers* anything other than red epaulettes like the troopers: clearly the regulations were 'overlooked'. During the same year 9,874fr was spent to harmonise Dutch uniforms with French ones.[94] The regiment's 4e squadron, which had been in Hamburg, was disbanded into the 10e in summer 1814. Of the French men in the regiment after the Dutch soldiers had been sent home, the handful were sent to the 10e *Cuirassiers*, and on 23 July were wearing almost brand-new uniforms:[95]

Item	In Good Repair	In Need of Repair	To be Replaced	To be Written Off
Habits	23		1	
Gilet sans manche	22		2	
Gilets d'ecurie	14		4	5
Bonnets de police	20		1	3
Culottes de peau	23		1	
Surculottes		2	21	
Pantalons de treillis			24	
Manteaux	23	1		
Pairs of epaulettes	23		1	
Helmets	24			

In addition, the men had between them 57 shirts, 24 black stocks, 48 white stocks and 23 pairs of shoes. The 1^e, 2^e and 3^e squadrons, once the Dutch soldiers had been sent home, were taken into the 12^e *Cuirassiers*. The clothing was entirely brand new and comprised 117 *habits-vestes*, 117 *gilets*, 116 stable coats, 119 *bonnets de police*, 116 *manteaux*, 117 pairs of *culottes de peau*, 116 pairs of *surculottes*, 115 pairs of stable trousers and 117 pairs of epaulettes. The Hamburg squadron arrived at Mayence on 3 July. The 18 men had 8 *habits-vestes* in good condition and 10 to be disposed of, 18 waistcoats, 18 *bonnets de police*, 16 *manteaux*, 11 pairs of *culottes de peau*, and 7 worn-out pairs of *surculottes*. No man had a pair of epaulettes, 17 men had a helmet, 14 a *giberne* and belt, 13 had a sabre and belt, and a pair of boots. Of '*petit* equipment' in use by the first three squadrons, we note the men had 195 shirts, 106 black stocks, 151 pairs of socks, 142 pairs of boots, 97 combes, 309 *habits* and cleaning brushes, 92 screwdrivers and 213 *rabats* for the stock – the *rabat* is the white piping inserted into the top edge of the stock. The *dépôt* held:[96]

294 brand new *habits-vestes* and 19 needing repairs
230 *vestes*
137 *gilets d'ecurie* with 7 more needing repairs
70 *bonnets de police*
294 *manteaux* with 20 needing repairs
249 pairs of *culottes de peau*
155 pairs of *surculottes* and 2 more pairs needing repairs
52 pairs of stable trousers
294 pairs of gauntlets
410 helmets
434 *gibernes*
435 *porte-gibernes*
407 *cuirasses*
408 *fraise de cuirass*

Regulations in Practice 1812–15   139

The inspector, General Comte de Pully, furthermore remarked that the following items had yet to be delivered to the regiment and were passed to the 12[e], all made to the new regulation:[97]

  118 *capotes-manteaux*
  128 *habits-vestes*
  24 *gilets d'Ordonnance* – white sleeveless round-cut waistcoats
  17 *bonnets de police*
  131 pairs of *culottes de peau*
  58 pairs of stable trousers
  103 pairs of *surculottes*
  165 *gibernes* and belts
  120 pairs of epaulettes
  58 old-pattern sleeveless waistcoats

Seemingly the regiment was at the point of converting to Bardin regulation when it was wound up. We suppose therefore that the *habits-veste* in use were in fact *habits à revers*. Lodged in stores were a further 147 pairs of shoes, 3 shirts and 3 pairs of socks.

Cloth in the *dépôt* was minimal, 188m 72 linen for lining *habits*, 38m 90 *treillis* to line the *housse*, *porte-manteaux* and make stable trousers and 93m 80 lace for *porte-*

Martinet gives us an officer and trooper of the 14[e] *Cuirassiers*.

Reconstructed from the regiment's archive is a trooper of the 14ᵉ *Cuirassiers* as they appeared at the time of the disbandment review in summer 1814, accompanied by a trumpeter.

manteaux. There is a note stating that the 14ᵉ *Cuirassiers'* *mousquetons* and bayonets were to be taken from them and redistributed directly to the 3ᵉ *Chasseurs à Cheval*. Another similar observation states that the 14ᵉ *Cuirassiers* had over a thousand *banderole-portemousquetons* and *crochets*, all in good condition, and only 210 needing repairs, and that all of these were also to be sent directly to the 3ᵉ *Chasseurs à Cheval*. With 188 spare, unissued *cuirasses* waiting in the magazines (in addition to those already currently issued), the entire regiment would have been armoured, including the trumpeter.[98]

15ᵉ *Cuirassiers*

Formed in Hamburg in 1814, the regiment drew its manpower from three provisional *cuirassier* regiments. The cadre of the regiment was formed at Hanover in January 1813. All twelve regiments of *cuirassiers* sent men to the central remount *dépôt* at Hanover, which by 11 July 1812 held 33 officers and 955 fully equipped and clothed *cuirassiers*.[99] The Emperor ordered General

Dismounted troopers and trumpeter of the 15ᵉ *Cuirassiers* in Hamburg. This is one of the few period artworks to show the regiment. The trumpeter in a colpack and Imperial Livery is unexpected, so too the men wearing *habits-vestes*.

Bourcier to dispatch from Hanover to Hamburg a force of 1,250 men, to be named the *Regiment de Marche de Hambourg*, and they were to leave Hanover by 5 July. All the men were dismounted and were ordered to carry with them their saddles and bridles, and the Emperor hoped the men would be mounted on horses provided by Marshal Davout.[100]

The detachment clearly made it to Hamburg and became the cadre for three new regiments of *cuirassiers*.

The regiment was fully organised on 11 September 1813. The 1e squadron was formed from the 4e squadron of 1e *Cuirassiers*, 2e squadron from the 2e *Cuirassiers*, 3e squadron from the 3e *Cuirassiers*, and 4e squadron from the 4e *Cuirassiers*. Clothing and equipment were as follows:[101]

	Habits de cuirassier	*Gilets de drap*	*Gilets d'écurie*	*Culottes de peau*	*Surculottes*	*Pantalons de treillis*	*Manteaux*	*Helmets*	*Pompoms*	*Bonnets de police*	*Gibernes et porte-gibernes*	*Banderole-porte-mousquetons*	*Epaulettes*	*Waistbelts*	*Cuirasses*
1e Squadron	85	85	79	85	85	0	85	85	0	85	77	77	85	85	83
	36	36	36	30	36	21	36	36	0	36	28	28	36	36	28
2e Squadron	69	69	63	69	69	69	69	69	0	69	60	60	69	69	66
	69	69	63	69	69	69		69	0	69	60	60	69	69	66
3e Squadron	98	98	93	98	98	98	98	98	0	98	93	93	98	98	97
	99	99	94	99	104	93	99	30	0	94	93	93	99	99	100
4e Squadron	99	99	93	99	99	99	99	99	0	99	91	91	99	99	96
	98	98	98	98	92	98	98	98	0	98	98	98	98	98	98

The lack of helmets in 7e company, part of 3e squadron, is remarkable: the inspector tells us the men wore *chapeaux* out of necessity. No man had a plume or pompom. We see that overall, the trumpeters did not have *cuirasses*, except 7e and 8e company, nor did they have *gibernes*, *porte-gibernes* and carbine belts. In addition, every man had a pair of shoes, and two shirts, a black stock, and a pair of socks as well as a sword knot.[102] No further paperwork for the regiment exists and therefore we simply have no way of progressing the history of the regiment any further.

We know little else about the dress of the regiment until in summer 1814 it was merged into the *Cuirassiers du Roi*. Items returned from the Hamburg magazine and taken into stores of the *Cuirassiers du Roi* were:[103]

	Habits de cuirassier	Habits de trompette	Gilets de drap	Gilets d'écurie	Pantalons de treillis	Bonnets de police	Surculottes gris	Culottes de peau	Manteaux	Casques	Bretelles	Garnitures	Plumes
New	0	0	0	0	0	0	0	0	0	0	0	0	0
Repair	0	0	0	0	0	0	0	0	34	30	0	0	0
To be Replaced	36	0	11	0	0	0	0	14	1	0	0	15	0
Total	36	0	11	0	0	0	0	14	1	30	0	15	0

Also, in the *dépôt* were 260 shirts, 95 black stocks, 164 white stocks, 155 pairs of socks, 93 pairs of shoes and 79 pairs of black gaiters. In stores were 53 *gibernes* with belts needing repairs, 53 *banderole-porte-mousquetons*, 63 sabre belts, 20 sword knots, 21 pairs of gauntlets and 59 pairs of boots fit only for disposal, 49 *cuirasses* needing repairs, 49 muskets needing repairs, 63 sabres, 43 bayonets and 44 pistols. No cloth and materials were held.[104]

16e *Cuirassiers* (2e *régiment provisoire de grosse cavalerie*)

Formed in Hamburg in 1813, the regiment was fully organised on 11 September 1813; the 1e squadron was formed of men assigned to the 4e squadron of 5e *Cuirassiers*, 2e squadron was formed from the 6e *Cuirassiers*, 3e squadron from the 7e, and the 4e from the 8e. Clothing and equipment were as follows:[105]

	Habits de cuirassier	Gilets de drap	Gilets d'écurie	Culottes de peau	Surculottes	Pantalons de treillis	Manteaux	Helmets	Bonnets de police	Gibernes et porte-gibernes	Banderole-porte-mousquetons	Epaulettes	Waistbelts	Cuirasses
1e Squadron	117	117	107	117	104	117	0	115	117	92	99	117	88	0
	102	6	93	56	74	93	1	77	104	10	0	104	27	1
2e Squadron	80	80	0	80	80	80	80	80	80	5	7	80	7	78
	89	78	84	89	89	89	89	89	89	36	28	89	36	89
3e Squadron	106	0	95	100	100	95	100	91	91	100	100	100	100	96
	72	0	66	72	72	72	66	72	72	64	64	72	72	20
4e Squadron	62	62	56	62	62	56	62	62	62	62	52	62	62	58
	61	61	55	61	61	55	61	61	61	61	58	61	61	58

We see that across the regiment, there was a chronic shortage of sabre belts, *gilets*, *gilets d'ecurie* and *cuirasses*! No squadron had a full complement of clothing and equipment. The 4ᵉ squadron was unique in having 119 plumes! One assumes the parent regiment, 8ᵉ *Cuirassiers*, also had plumes! We wonder if the *cuirassiers* shown by the Suhr brothers in Hamburg were men from the 5ᵉ *Cuirassiers*! It seems very likely. Every man in the regiment had two shirts, a pair of shoes, a pair of black twill gaiters, and a *sac à distribution*. Despite the lack of sabre belts, every man had a sabre.[106]

No paper further paperwork for the regiment exists. We simply have no way of progressing the history of the regiment any further. The regiment was disbanded in summer 1814 and we assume the men were taken into their parent regiments.

17ᵉ *Cuirassiers* (3ᵉ *régiment provisoire de grosse cavalerie*)

The regiment, like the other two formed in Hamburg under the orders of Marshal Davout, had four squadrons: the 1ᵉ formed from the 9ᵉ *Cuirassiers*, the 2ᵉ from the 10ᵉ *Cuirassiers*, the 3ᵉ from the 11ᵉ and the 4ᵉ from the 12ᵉ. Clothing and equipment were as follows:[107]

	Habits de cuirassier	Gilets de drap	Gilets d'ecurie	Culottes de peau	Surculottes	Pantalons de treillis	Manteaux	Helmets	Bonnets de police	Gibernes et porte-gibernes	Banderole-porte- mousquetons	Epaulettes	Waistbelts	Cuirasses
1ᵉ Squadron	119	119	119	119	119	119	95	119	119	100	0	111	2	119
	85	85	81	83	87	81	73	86	87	0	0	85	8	87
2ᵉ Squadron	59	0	59	59	59	55	59	41	59	55	53	59	59	57
	63	0	63	63	63	63	63	62	63	59	59	63	63	60
3ᵉ Squadron	61	55	55	61	61	55	61	61	61	55	55	61	61	61
	59	59	56	59	59	56	59	59	59	54	54	59	59	59
4ᵉ Squadron	88	87	82	46	88	82	64	0	88	78	78	87	88	0
	88	88	82	88	88	82	60	0	88	79	79	88	88	0

Every man was issued a sabre and had at least two pairs of socks, two shirts, a black stock, a pair of shoes, a pair of black gaiters – we wonder how the men with no sabre belts carried their sabres? The regiment had a shortage of *gilets*, *manteaux*, helmets, *cuirasses* and *gibernes*. No one squadron was fully equipped. We are left to wonder what headdress the 4ᵉ squadron used, presumably *chapeaux*.[108] No paper further paperwork for the regiment exists and we simply have no way of progressing the history of the regiment any further. The regiment was disbanded in summer 1814 and we assume the men taken into their parent regiments.

144 Napoleon's Heavy Cavalry

Cuirassiers du Roi

At the very end of the 1st Empire an 18th regiment – or should that be 19ᵉ given two 14ᵉ regiments existed? – of *cuirassiers* was formed: the *Cuirassiers du Roi*. It was recruited from Royalist volunteers and émigré on 23 April 1814. The regiment was dressed from stocks of clothing taken from the various *dépôt* of Paris. In August 1814 the clothing of the *Cuirassiers du Roi* was as follows:[109]

Item	Good Condition	Need Repairs	To be Replaced	Need Replacing	Items Missing
Habits	388	27	75	18	20
Habits de trompette	15				
Vestes blanche	149	11	14	1	368
Gilets d'ecurie	307	58	66	24	88
Pantalons de treillis	466	0	0	0	77
Bonnets de police	484	13	19	0	27
Surculottes gris	186	27	136	7	187
Culottes de peau	447	21	43	2	30
Manteaux	120	45	40	3	20
Capote manteaux	281	28	6	0	
Porte–manteaux	408	105	12	3	15
Casques	367	150	11	1	14
Garnitures de cuirass	439	5	55	0	44

The bulk of the clothing was new, and clearly a lot of it had been drawn out of stockpiles of clothing, hence we find both old- and new-pattern *manteaux* in use side by side. For a newly raised regiment, the lack of *vestes* is quite remarkable. The trumpeters' *habits* were clearly adorned with Royalist Livery. The stores contained:[110]

	Habits de cuirassier	*Habits de trompette*	*Gilets de drap*	*Gilets d'ecurie*	*Pantalon du treillis*	*Bonnets de police*	*Surculottes gris*	*Culotte de peau*	*Manteaux*	*Casques*	*Bretelles*	*Garnitures de cuirass*	*Plumets*
New	4	0	0	0	5	0	0	11	0	4	0	221	43
Repair													
Hors de service													
Total	4	0	0	0	5	0	0	11	0	4	0	221	43

Regulations in Practice 1812–15   145

We also note the presence of white epaulettes and aiguilettes, and embroidered *fleur-de-lys* for the tails of the *habits*. Based on contemporary iconography, the plumes were white. The unit was brought up to strength when the former 1ᵉ *Cuirassiers* were amalgamated with the regiment on 1 July 1814. The 548 officers and men, General Exelmans noted, were zealous in their devotion to the King when he organised the new regiment. We wonder how these young Royalists coped alongside the 187 survivors of the 1813 and 1814 campaigns? We know the regiment received new clothing and equipment based on the contents of the *dépôt* in 1815. Items in the *dépôt* at disbandment in December 1815 were as follows:[111]

	Habits de cuirassier	*Habits de trompette*	*Gilets de drap*	*Gilets d'écurie*	*Pantalons de treillis*	*Bonnets de police*	*Surculottes gris*	*Culottes de peau*	*Manteaux-capote*	*Casques*	*Bretelles*	*Garnitures*	*Plumes*	White epaulettes	*Aiguillettes*	*Porte-manteaux*
In Store Prior to Waterloo	482	7	632	434	598	482	1,076	375	758	842	0	707	180	499	168	482
Issued	481	5	576	409	573	252	1,075	348	202	240	0	487	120	99	150	132
Remaining in *Dépôt* to be Returned	1	2	0	25	25	230	1	27	556	602	0	220	60	400	18	350
Total	1	2	0	25	25	230	1	27	556	602	0	220	60	400	18	350

Clearly, along with white epaulettes and aiguillettes the trumpeters marched to Waterloo wearing Royalist Livery. Cloth in the magazine was as follows:[112]

	Blue broadcloth	White broadcloth	*Blanc picque de bleu* broadcloth	Scarlet broadcloth	*Gris-beige* broadcloth	Blue tricot for *porte-manteaux*	Scarlet serge	Linen	*Treillis*	Large buttons	Small buttons	Hooks and eyes	Lace for *portemanteau*	Lace for *porte-manteaux*	*Décorations du lys*
In Stores Prior to 100 Days	432m 89	216m 4	523m 32	82m 18	585m 13	736m 70	135m 96	1,593m 9	828m 91	772	1,298	159	67m	320m 68	819
Used	222m 63	142m 4	262m 50	7m 90	565m 94	736m 70	135m 96	1,354m 31	828m 91	225/ 9	776/ 6	159	67m	320m 68	819
Remaining	210m 26	216m 4	260m 82	92m 8	19m 19	0	0	238m 76	0	546/ 11	521/ 6		0	0	0

Of interest, the *surculottes* remained in *gris-beige* broadcloth. The old sleeveless and new sleeved model of cavalry *manteaux* were used side by side. Also, we have proof positive of the issue of white epaulettes and aiguillettes being worn by the regiment, along with *fleur-de-lys* badges for the turnbacks of the *habit*. The grenade on the saddle cloth may have also changed to a *fleur-de-lys*. Did the epaulettes revert back to scarlet in the 100 days? The colonel certainly made the request to Marshal Davout, noting the men in the regiment were being 'bullied' by other soldiers for being dressed as Royalists. Davout replied on 6 June that, yes, scarlet epaulettes could be used. Given the regiment had already left the barracks by this date, was the change carried out? Had the colonel packed up into a box all the scarlet epaulettes he could find in stores from the old 1ᵉ and placed them in a baggage waggon in case of need? We like to think so, but cannot be sure.[113]

Trooper of the *Cuirassiers du Roi* based on the regiment's paper archive, as well as period illustrations by Bassett and Martinet that show a black sheepskin *schabraque*. He is accompanied by a trumpeter. The clothing is reconstructed from original items preserved in a private collection in France, which accords with the regimental archive.

Chapter 10

Bardin and the *Cuirassiers* – Myth and Reality

As could be readily expected, many questions have arisen from our research and perhaps not many answers.

Habits

When we look at the inspection returns generated in summer 1814, it is clear that nearly half of the *cuirassier* regiments had not acted upon the Bardin regulations. So, what were they wearing? Between 1802 and 1815, the *cuirassiers* had three regulation garments:

1. 1803 *habit de cuirass* – single breasted, closed by a row of eight or nine or buttons to the front, three pointed pockets to the rear. Cuffs closed by flaps with three buttons. Short tailed. Variation on collar, cuff, piping and pocket direction to demark regiment.
2. *Surtout* – front closed by eight large buttons, two small buttons at the centre back. Long or short tails. Round cuffs, closed by two small buttons.
3. *Habit à revers* – old fashioned *habit* with *revers* fastened back by seven small buttons, cuffs closed by three small buttons, three pointed pocket flaps with three large buttons.

Ensemble of armour from the middle years of the Empire. The helmet is marked to the 5e regiment. This form of armour and helmet were used through to the Russian campaign, and we suspect were used as late as 1815 to make best use of stockpiles of equipment. (*Musée de l'Empéri, Collections du Musée de l'Armée, Anciennes collections Jean et Raoul Brunon*)

In the case of the 7e, 8e, 9e, 10e and likely the 14e they were, it seems, wearing the *habit à revers*. Of the others, which had taken up Bardin, we cannot say for certain what they were wearing as Bardin rather confusingly authorised two different garments!

From 1803, *cuirassiers* had both a *surtout* and a *habit* and this was allowed for again in 1806.[1] Such was the confusion about what was worn, that no one really knew what was worn – the *surtout* or *habit*, asked Nansouty in 1811. Bardin, with economy in mind, settled on the *surtout*.

Given the confused nature of the decree, as two separate garments are clearly described, we suspect that regiments simply continued to make the *surtout* and the *habit de cuirass*, both confusingly recorded in 1814 as *habits*!

Manteaux

Under Bardin, the old-pattern, three-quarter cloak was kept in service. It was made from *blanc piquer de bleu* broadcloth. The body measured 1m 35 deep at the front and 1m 40 deep at the back. The circumference of the bottom of the cloak was 6m 50. It was pleated

The Dresden manuscript gives us a very good idea of how *cuirassiers* looked at the end of the Empire. The grey overalls with the inner leg reinforced with black leather would become regulation in 1815. (*Collection KM*)

into the collar, which was 400mm wide and 90mm tall. To provide a second layer of cloth at the shoulder, a small shoulder cape (*rotonde*) was sewn into the collar, some 220mm deep at the front and 280mm deep at the back – very shallow indeed.[2]

On 18 April 1813 a War Ministry circular introduced the sleeved cloak (*manteaux-capote*) – the same as used by the light cavalry – for the *cuirassiers*.[3] On practical experimentation it is virtually impossible to wear this garment while wearing a *cuirass*; without a helping hand from friends it is totally impossible to get one's arms in the sleeves. It is totally unpracticable. Overwhelmingly in summer 1814, regiments used the old *manteau* with no sleeves as enshrined in the first edition of Bardin. Of the seventeen *cuirassier* regiments, only three regiments had *manteaux-capote*, and in limited numbers![4]

Helmets

Under the terms of Bardin, the *bombe* (skull) was made from steel, measured 190 to 200mm front to back, 160mm side to side and was 75mm tall. The bottom edge of the *bombe* was fitted with a rolled gutter, the leading edge of which was pieced with holes where it was sewn to the leather turban.

The *bombe* was surmounted by a *cimier*, the flanks being stamped from 'strong copper'. The cast front plate used in previous years was replaced a copper stamping, devoid of regimental number but to bear a head of *médusa* 110 by 40mm. The flanks/sides of the *cimier* were joined together by four bolts and spacing bars. These bolts were made from iron: they are shouldered and from 5 to 6mm in diameter and 35mm long with a turned-down projection 5mm long at each end that passed through the flanks of the *cimier* and were rivetted closed. The 1811 and Bardin helmet comes in for heavy critique by modern-day writers, particularly concerning the *cimier*. The thick casting of the front plate made getting a good soldered joint to the flanks difficult because of the heat exchange difference between the casting and stamped parts: for both 1811 and Bardin helmets the front plate was stamped, the edges were turned back 40mm, and being made from the same-grade copper plate made soldering far easier. Also, under Bardin a spacing bar and rivet held the front plate on, making a far more robust design.

Measured along the interior surface, the flanks measure 245mm, and over the top edge 325mm: it measured 110mm tall at the front, 70mm at the front and 15mm at the base. The body of the *crinière* measured 325mm long, and was lined with 'strong leather' measuring 245 by 35mm: at one end was a lanyard 380mm long by 20mm wide, and the opposite end a leather tab 25mm wide and 60mm long. The *crinière* – from examining an original this was literally a piece of horse's tail cut off the from the animal's dock and cured in salt – measured along the horse hair was to be 625mm. Bardin notes that the lanyard was pierced with a slot; the lanyard was passed around the internal brace at the base of the *cimier* by the buckle, the *crinière* was to pass through the slit in the lanyard and pulled tight, passed below the other three spacing bars and then passed between the spacer bar and the front plate. The *crinière* pulled tight and the tab fastened to an iron buckle placed on the turban set 25mm below the base of the *cimier*. The turban measured

110mm high and was made from 'strong cow hide'. It was faced with bear skin. The top edge of the turban where it fitted to the *bombe* had a rolled leather edge made from basane. The interior was lined with basane and a line draw string. The peak had a copper binding to allow the peak to keeps it shape. The chinscale rosettes measured 55mm in diameter. Each chinscale was 175mm long, and was cut from strong cow hide, with thirteen copper scales on the face held in place with iron staples and lined in basane. The chinscales fastened under the chin with black linen tapes.[5] No extant helmets that the author has examined have *crinières* attached in this method or a unique front plate to the *cimier*, so we wonder if these helmets were ever made!

However, Rousselot damns this helmet design through selective use of documents, relying on Comte de Saint-Germain's report solely, and quotes the statement 'the design which had been good in principle had become so faulty that all haste should be made to change almost all the helmets presently in service'.[6] As we have seen in 1801 and 1807, helmets then in use were considered useless, and made exactly the same comments in 1807. Poor research by Rousselot has left this notion unchallenged. The one item that came in for critique time and time again across the Empire was the helmet and most critics were almost unanimous in stating the design failings: therefore the 1811 and Bardin type – if they existed – were not better or worse than what went before. The issue in 1814 more than likely lay not with the design, but in their manufacture and materials.

Unknown *cuirassier* trooper from the 9e to 12e regiments witnessed in Germany in 1813. The collar patch is not recorded by other period artists as used by *cuirassier* regiments. It is therefore impossible to say which regiment is shown. The white *giberne* hints at stocks of Saxon equipment being pressed into use. The presence of shoulder straps rather than epaulettes is notable. (*Collection KM*)

Facing Colours

As could be expected by regiments not wearing Bardin regulation clothing, the desired changes to facing colours envision. In the Bardin regulation text we find table 1,017, which gives the facing colours for the various regiments: scarlet for 1e to 3e, aurore for 4e to 6e, yellow for 7e to 9e, rose for 10e to 12e, and wine lees for 13e and 14e.[7]

As with the changeover in clothing to the Bardin regulation from the 'old' pattern, some regiments had not acted upon other aspects of the decree, no doubt for pragmatic reasons. The 11e was in the process in summer 1814 of changing from yellow to pink. Perhaps understandably so, as when the regulations came into force, the regimental depots would have held metre upon metre of facing cloth, and buying new cloth and chucking the old material in a corner when it was still usable seemed 'a very bad idea' for many colonels facing a cash and supply shortage. The War Ministry realised that changing facings was not going to be done overnight if it was to be achieved with as little cost as possible. To this end, regiments were ordered to ensure that all stocks of existing broadcloth for facings were used before the new facing cloth was taken into use.[8] Thus, we can easily see how three regiments did not change their facings until the 1st Restoration. To make matters worse, under the 1st Restoration the 9^e was ordered into *lieu de vin* facings from yellow, and so was the 10^{e,} who had been ordered into pink under Bardin but had never replaced their yellow facings! We cannot tell if this change took place due to the lack of archive documentation.

The archive sources also tell us that that the festoon to the sheepskin *schabraque* was scarlet for all regiments and not in the regiment's facing colour, except the 10^e where period iconography shows yellow.

Officer of unknown *cuirassier* regiment in summer 1813. The scarlet collar patch with button is a unique observation made by the artist of the Freyburg manuscript. (*Collection KM*)

Carbines

It is supposedly fact that *cuirassiers* were encumbered with a sword, pistol and carbine. Well, that is a myth. The 7^e and 8^e had both carbine and belts in the depot in 1814, and the 11^e certainly had carbines, but never more than ninety-three belts to carry them in 1813, and we note not a single regiment in the field had carbines in 1814 or 1815. The 7^e, 8^e and 11^e may have equipped just a single company in 1813–14. The 8^e had just thirteen in October 1804 and no belts to carry them with, and they had disappeared by 1805.

Trumpeters

The call of the regimental trumpeters dictated the daily life of a regiment, and its movements in battle. So, how were these men dressed? Until October 1791 trumpeters had worn a blue *habit*, decorated with Royal Livery – seven chevrons on each arm, lace to the button holes, lace to long pockets on the tails and *retroussis*, collar and cuff.[9] The lace was removed in 1791, and thereafter trumpeters' *habits* were to be the same as other ranks. The regulation of 1802 implies drummers' *habits* had no lace as this was reserved

Reproduction trumpeter's *habit* respecting the Bardin regulation, made by Edouard Detaille. (*Musée de l'Empéri, Collections du Musée de l'Armée, Anciennes collections Jean et Raoul Brunon*)

for musicians.[10] With no official guidance from regulations, colonels had free rein in how to dress their trumpeters. We have to rely on scant archive sources and period iconography to recreate the dress of the trumpeters. Just the 8e and 11e did not armour their trumpeters in the period 1804–12.

One of the biggest myths about Bardin regulation is that *cuirassiers* universally wore Imperial Livery once Bardin regulation had come into use. Imperial Livery was actually not part of Bardin, and had been introduced to the army on 15 May 1811 when the War Ministry authorised a trumpeter's *habit* to have wool lace 24mm wide, and required 15m 30 of lace, of a model yet to be determined.[11] Something more formal about the dress of the trumpeters was enacted with the decree of 30 December 1811:

1. The *habits* of drummers and trumpeters are to be laced with 2m 70 of lace 27mm wide, to be sewn onto the *habit* conforming to the decree of 1 October 1786.

2. The *habits* of drum majors, trumpet majors and master musicians are to be no longer laced in gold or silver; the drum majors and trumpet majors will not be distinguished, but the master musicians will be by a double row of silver lace 22mm wide at the cuff, and the musicians by a single row in the same place.

The body of the *habit* will be green. The lining of the *habit*, the cuffs, the *revers*, the collar, *veste* or *gilet*, the *culottes* or *pantalons* will retain the colours of their corps and are not to be affected by these changes. No further changes to the remainder of the uniform, such as pompoms, *retroussis* etc are to be made.

However, upon consideration the uniform of the Light infantry will change concerning the lining of the *habit veste*, *gilet* and *pantalons*, which are blue. This colour has a disagreeable effect with green, it is therefore decided that that the lining of the *habit-veste*, the *gilet* and *pantalons* are to be green, and also the *habit*, for the drummers and musicians of this arm.[12]

Major Bardin notes that the 1811 decree was not enforced rigorously and that the lace amount and *habit* form was changed with the decree of 19 January 1812.[13] Bardin notes that new lace, of 'the Imperial pattern', was introduced on 17 September 1812.[14] We can only assume the 1811 lace was similar to that of 1812.

In order to test if *cuirassiers* adopted Imperial Livery, we have two markers in the written record: green broadcloth and the lace itself. Using inspection returns and regimental accounts from the seventeen regiments of *cuirassiers*, the only regiments we know who had clothing specifically for trumpeters were as follows:

1e *Cuirassiers/Cuirassier du Roi*:[15] In 1814, the regiment had 1 old trumpeter's coat in the dépôt, and 8 green trumpeters' *habits* with Imperial Livery in use. Between 23 April 1815 and 29 December 1815, seven trumpeters' *habits* in blue broadcloth with Royalist Livery were made, to be used alongside 15 identical garments from the *Cuirassiers du Roi*, of which 5 were issued.

2e *Cuirassiers*:[16] In October 1815, the regiment held 3m 27 of green broadcloth for trumpeters' *habits* and 30m of Imperial Livery, described at the time as new. No trumpeters' lace existed in 1814, but ten trumpeters' *habits* in need of repair did exist. These were either green with Imperial Livery or indeed reversed colours. No green cloth or Imperial Livery existed in 1814, so the green broadcloth and livery was clearly purchased in 1815.

3^e *Cuirassiers*:[17] In August 1814, the regiment had 51m of trumpeters' lace and no green broadcloth. At the time of disbandment in December 1815 the magazine held 5m of trumpeters' livery and 614m 37 of trumpeters' livery, which was presumably Royalist Livery that had never been used. Assuming no more Imperial Livery was purchased in 1815, that 46m of Imperial Livery had been used to decorate new trumpeters' *habits*, which were presumably blue, but the purchase and total use of green broadcloth is a distinct possibility, hence none was in the depot.

4ᵉ *Cuirassiers*:[18] Depot held on 6 August 1814 1m 95 of green cloth for trumpeters and not an inch of lace – it is likely that every inch of Imperial Livery the regiment possessed had been used to make trumpeters' *habits*. Purchased between 1 September 1814 and 1 April 1815 was 260m 10 of Royalist Livery for trumpeters, all of which was used to make 17 new *habits*. After 1 April 1815, 61m of Imperial Livery was purchased but never used. In the 100 days, eight trumpeters' *habits* were made, of which only four were issued. We can be sure that seven were blue, as only 5m 42 of green broadcloth was purchased, of which 1m 95 was used to make one trumpeter's *habit*, which never gained Imperial Livery. Clearly, blue *habits* were worn by the trumpeters at Waterloo and before.

Trumpeters wearing Bardin regulation clothing by Vernet.

6ᵉ *Cuirassiers*:[19] The inspection returns for 1814 itemised trumpeters' *habits*, but the regiment had none at all. Presumably at some stage they had existed and had been green with Imperial Livery.

7ᵉ *Cuirassiers*:[20] The inspecting general recorded Imperial Livery worn on green *habits* in August 1814.

9ᵉ *Cuirassiers*:[21] The inspecting general recorded that the regiment had Imperial iconography in use and had not adopted Royalist Livery; presumably he means that Imperial Livery was worn on green *habits* in August 1814.

11ᵉ *Cuirassiers*:[22] The depot held in October 1814, 5m 89 green broadcloth, but not an inch of lace for trumpeters.

12ᵉ *Cuirassiers*:[23] In August 1814 the depot held 4m 80 green broadcloth for trumpeters but not an inch of lace. None of this cloth used, and was still in the depot in December 1815 when the regiment was disbanded.

Bardin and the *Cuirassiers* – Myth and Reality

Parts of the '1811' helmet recovered archaeologically from the retreat from Moscow. (*Dmitry Rakov*)

At the start of the period 1790–1815, the *carabiniers*, contrary to Zix, Sauerweid and Hoffmann, had white metal plates to their bearskin caps. The plates were perhaps adorned with the arms of France. The white rather than scarlet lining to the coat tails is unusual: but with the shortages of cloth it is not unexpected.

Squadron commander of the 7e *Cuirassiers*. The *surtout* is closed by nine buttons, and the epaulettes are embroidered with fish scales. (*Private collection*)

This brief summary means that just nine out of 17 regiments in 1814 had trumpeters in green *habits* with Imperial Livery, and that, in reality many regiments probably dressed trumpeters as rank or file or retained reversed colours!

For the *cuirassiers*, it is often commented upon that the trumpeters did not have armour. However, it is clear that all the regiments from 1803 through to the 100 days had sufficient armour for the men and trumpeters.

Green *habits* with Imperial Livery as universal across the arm is a myth. The famous *cuirassier* trumpeters' coat at the Musée de l'Empéri is actually made from original lace on a totally new *habit* made for Edouard Detaille, yet today the garment is understood to be authentic. The evidence for *cuirassier* trumpeters actually having these *habits* and white epaulettes is actually very minimal indeed.

Chapter 11

The *Carabiniers* 1802–10

The two regiments of *carabiniers* were formed in the middle years of the sixteenth century. They were cavalry armed with rifles – in French *carabine* – and at the Battle of Neerwinden in 1693 the corps was commanded by Prince de Conti. The men were drawn from each regiment of cavalry into a provisional formation. Formed into an independent regiment in 1693, 13 May 1758 witnessed the regiment renamed *Royal carabiniers de monsieur le Comte de Provence*. In 1762 the Corps of *Carabiniers* was some 30 squadrons strong, formed in five brigades, which was reduced to a single regiment of eight companies in 1776 – each company comprising 145 troopers and five officers. In 1779 the regiment was reorganised into two brigades, each of five squadrons. In 1788 the Corps was renamed the *Carabiniers de Monsieur*, comprising two regiments, each of four squadrons. From then on, both regiments would serve side by side as a single cohesive brigade.

Trooper of *Carabiniers c.*1800 by Zix.

With the outbreak of the Revolution, the privileged Royal Corps and regiments were abolished; yet with King Louis XVI still nominally monarch, the *carabiniers* were retained. On 18 August 1790 the National Assembly voted to retain the two regiments and their traditions, and they were renamed the '*Grenadiers des troupes à cheval*', literally the grenadiers of the mounted troops, and were fitted out with scarlet-fringed epaulettes and bearskin caps. The two regiments had seniority over the rest of the cavalry. Always a hotbed of Royalists, the officers of the corps owed more allegiance to the crown than the state or Emperor. In the wars of the revolution the *carabiniers* fought mostly in the army of Germany. In 1804 Louis Bonaparte was named Colonel General of *Carabiniers*; the two regiments led the coronation procession from the Tuileries to Notre-Dame, much to the chagrin of the *Grenadiers à Cheval* of the Imperial Guard.

We commented upon the dress regulations for both regiments in earlier chapters, suffice to say they wore blue *habits* with red facings, red grenadier epaulettes and swaggered under tall bearskin caps. Drawn up at some stage in 1806 was a uniform specification for the *carabiniers*:[1]

158 Napoleon's Heavy Cavalry

Item	Cloth	Quantity
Habits	Blue broadcloth	2m 3
	Facing cloth	0m 23
	Facing colour milled serge	3m 26
	Linen for lining	0m 89
	Large buttons	11
	Small buttons	22
Surtouts	Blue broadcloth	1m 73
	Facing cloth	0m
	Facing coloured milled serge	3m 26
	Linen for lining	0m 89
	Large buttons	8
	Small buttons	2
Vestes	White broadcloth	1m 19
	White milled serge, including sleeves	2m 52
	Linen for lining	0m 29
	Buttons	12
Manteaux	*Blanc picque de bleu*	5m 75
	Facing colour milled serge	1m 48
Housse et *Chaperons*	Blue broadcloth	0m 59
	White lace 0m 40 wide	0m 59
Porte-manteaux	Blue tricot	1m 34
	Treillis	1m 78
	White lace 0m 22 wide	2m 97

The dress of the two regiments underwent only minor modifications during the course of the Empire. The cut of the *habits* evolved as fashion dictated, and the bearskins gained chinscales in later summer 1809. We now trace the dress of the two regiments from their paper archives.

1ᵉ *Carabiniers*

The 1ᵉ *Carabiniers* were inspected on 22 September 1798. Clothing and equipment in use comprised:[2]

Item	Total Items	Items Missing	Good	Need Repairs	To be Written Off	To be Replaced	Total
Habits	529	144	518		11	11	673
Vestes	537	136	520		17	17	673
Culottes de peau		673					673
Manteaux	418	250	321	44	57	57	668

Item	Total Items	Items Missing	Good	Need Repairs	To be Written Off	To be Replaced	Total
Surtouts	497	176	446	15	36	36	673
Gilets d'ecurie	15	617	12		3	3	632
Chapeaux	142	531	107		35	35	673
Bearskin	400	273	400				673
Bonnets de police	510	163	478	10	22	22	673
Pantalons d'ecurie	9	664			9	9	673
Waistbelts	496	177	395	9	92	92	673
Gibernes	254	370	250		4	4	624
Porte-gibernes	254	370	254				624
Pair of boots	385	283	334	38	13	13	661
Selles completes	375	293	350	23	2	2	668
Brides complete	376	293	363	1			668
Schabraques	374	294	324	19	31	31	668
Couvertures	306	362	274	4	31	31	668

The depot held 80 *habits* needing to be repaired, along with 320 *manteaux* and 75 *porte-manteaux*. The regiment was inspected again on 20 April 1802:[3]

Item	Good Conduction	In Need of Repair	To be Written Off	Total	Number Made Since 23 September 1800
Standards	4				
Habits	185	200	169	554	125
Surtouts	206	81	148	539	347
Manteaux	189	196	117	496	95
Gilets	228	143	186	537	565
Gilets d'ecurie	135	71	287	493	209
Culottes de peau	532			532	1,104
Pantalons d'ecurie	554			554	838
Chapeaux	123	76	352	550	617
Bonnets à poil	284	94	136	614	225
Bonnets de police	133	15	348	550	617
Ceinturons	271	128	132	531	104
Gibernes	328	69	93	400	138
Porte-gibernes	336	84	70	490	244
Bretelles de fusil					
Porte-manteaux	256	182	119	667	131
Bottes	181	178	166	525	135
Sword knots	560			560	574

Item	Good Conduction	In Need of Repair	To be Written Off	Total	Number Made Since 23 September 1800
Selles completes	202	82	82	416	86
Brides complete	332	49	70	451	51
Housses	288	69	93	450	294
Chaperons	32			32	32
Schabraques	235	43	117	395	

In terms of armament the regiment had 560 musketoons, 404 pistons and 530 sabres, of which 100 sabres were to be written off and 38 needed repairs. The depot had held in 1800, 351 brand new pairs of scarlet-fringed epaulettes, of which 318 pairs had been issued and 28 remained in stores. For the 560 musketoons, just 50 were issued with 50 *banderole-porte-mousquetons*, to 1st company, 1st squadron and 193 brand new *banderole-porte-mousquetons* were in store. In addition, 488 pairs of gauntlets were in use. The depot also held 136 new pairs of *chaperons*. In order to repair the regiment's clothing the inspecting officer authorised materials be purchased. One stand-out item is scarlet broadcloth, 56mm wide to make the boards of the fringed grenadier epaulettes. For the trumpet major and sergeant majors, 9m of 24mm wide silver lace was purchased, for sergeants 20m of silver lace, and 8m for *fourriers*, again 24mm wide. Some 22mm wide white lace was purchased for the rank stripes of corporals, 24mm wide for *bonnets de police* and *porte-manteaux*, and 440m 48mm for *housse*s and *chaperons* costing 936fr 50. Also, 8 of 22mm wide lace was purchased for the farriers to make horse shoe arm badges. Not an inch of lace was purchased for trumpeters; the only item they were allocated was grenadiers' epaulettes – presumably scarlet – so we can say nothing definite about their uniform.

Trooper of the 1ᵉ *Carabiniers* by Hoffmann. Of interest is the scarlet collar.

Nearly a year passed until the regiment was inspected again on 24 June 1803, when the regiment's clothing was as follows:[4]

Item	Good Conduction	In Need of Repair	To be Written Off	Total	Number Made Since 20 April 1802
Standards	4				
Habits	456	64	94	608	
Surtouts	267	87	227	588	94
Manteaux	453	85	88	556	47

The *Carabiniers* 1802–10   161

Item	Good Conduction	In Need of Repair	To be Written Off	Total	Number Made Since 20 April 1802
Gilets en drap blanc	567	49	222	608	102
Gilets d'ecurie	196	83	446	584	8
Culottes de peau	608		8	616	606
Pantalons d'ecurie	563		6	569	569
Chapeaux	354		230	584	569
Bonnets à poil	463	32	96	584	64
Bonnets de police	209	10	383	576	48

Materials and clothing made between 24 June 1803 and 27 September 1804 were as follows:[5]

Item	In Depot 24 June 1803	Purchased Since 1803	Total	Amount Used	Remaining in Depot
Blue broadcloth	973m 52	564m 60	1,533m 12	1,104m 17	433m 95
White broadcloth	322m 46	153m 51	476m 96	397m 16	78m 81
Scarlet broadcloth	86m 97	29m 67	116m 64	149m 97	6m 97
Blanc picque de bleu	283m 52		283m 52	283m 52	
Blue tricot	13m 59	198m 40	216m 79	216m 79	
Scarlet serge	9m 99		9m 99	9m 99	
White serge	1,343m 22	325m 93	1,688m 50	1,241m 43	446m 87
Treillis for *pantalons*	120m 49		120m 49	120m 49	
Treillis for *porte-manteaux*	The regiment has none				
Silver lace	4m 73	55m 50	60m 23	56m 13	4m 10
Lace for *housses*	240m 84		240m 84	209m 76	31m 08
Lace for *porte-manteaux*	41m 82	560m 71	602m 52	441m 06	161m 47
Tassels for *bonnets de police*	49	300	349	320	29

In the same period 48 *habits* were made, 139 *surtouts*, 48 *manteaux*, 574 *gilets*, 378 stable coats, 624 pairs of *culottes de peau de* mouton, 475 pairs of stable trousers, 625 *chapeaux*, 222 bearskins and 319 *bonnets de police*. As in previous inspection returns, we have no clue as to the dress of trumpeters. The total lack of blue milled serge and the small amount of scarlet broadcloth used is proof positive that reverse colours were not used by both regiments. We can only assume they wore the same uniform as rank and file, but perhaps with lace to the collar and cuff of the *habit*. The lack of any period iconography is also a hinderance in making any comments about the uniform beyond it was not reversed colours.

Reviewed following Heilsberg, every man had a *habit, surtout, gilet en drap, gilet d'ecurie* and bearskin but lacked plumes. The *culottes de peau* were all life expired, and

Lieutenant Schauenbourg of the 2ᵉ *Carabiniers* by Zix. Of interest is the open collar.

Lieutenant Bassigny of the 2ᵉ *Carabiniers* at Wagram. Of interest, the bearskin has chinscales.

the sabres likewise, which needed brand new blades. Fit only for the dustbin was every single bearskin.[6]

Six months later, the clothing in use with the regiment on 15 December 1807 was as follows:[7]

Item	Good Conduction	In Need of Repair	To be Written Off	Total	Number Made Since 15 July 1805
Standards	5			5	
Habits	532	200	240	972	532
Vestes	800		176	976	1,243
Surtouts	400	100	476	976	1,155
Manteaux	600	100	75	775	664
Gilets d'ecurie	300	200	400	900	1,394
Culottes de peau	675			675	1,416
Pantalons d'ecurie	300		170	470	831
Chapeaux			110	110	
Bonnets à poil	400	230	140	770	566
Bonnets de police	568	100	308	976	1,252
Ceinturons	500	300	100	900	413
Gibernes	500	250	135	885	479
Porte-gibernes	500	250	135	885	476

The *Carabiniers* 1802–10   163

Item	Good Conduction	In Need of Repair	To be Written Off	Total	Number Made Since 15 July 1805
Bretelles de Fusil					
Porte-manteaux	550	250	176	976	746
Bottes	450	150	175	775	799
Selles completes	520	180	75	775	513
Bridles complete	520	180	75	775	567
Housses	739		36	775	891
Chaperons	Nil				
Schabraques	400	200	175	775	277
Couvertures	520	150	105	775	682

Of interest, the regiment had changed to the *demi-schabraque* in sheepskin sometime after July 1805 in replace of the cloth *chaperons*. These discontinued items were presumably stored in the depot.

Cloth used since 1805 and in December 1807 was as follows:[8]

Item	In Depot 1805	Purchased Since 1805	Total	Amount Used	Remaining in Depot
Blue broadcloth	261m 11	3,399m 47	3,660m 58	3,660m 58	
Blanc picque de bleu	223m 25	3,762m 75	3,986m	3,841m	145m
White broadcloth	226m 76	501m 84	728m 60	728m 60	
Scarlet broadcloth	29m 90	126m 88	156m 18	140m 35	15m 88
Blue tricot		1,103m 90	1,103m 90	1,103m 90	
Silver lace	1m 72	61m 13	62m 85	32m 85	30m
Galon pour housses	31m 08	2,900m 24	2,931m 32	2,931m 32	
White serge	769m 07	1,930m 72	2,699m 79	2,435m 85	263m 94
Scarlet serge	480m 04	2,289m 18	2,769m 22	2,728m 68	40m 54
Linen		4,383m 05	4,385m 05	4,281m 45	101m 60

A huge amount of lace had been used to make new *housses*. The silver lace was no doubt used for *sous-officiers'* rank stripes. Clothing purchased, repaired and issued between 1805 and 1807 was as follows:[9]

Item	In Depot 1805	Purchased Since 1805	Total	Issued	New in Depot	To be Written Off
Habits		568	568	532	36	
Vestes	22	1,345	1,867	1,243	124	
Surtouts	16	1,139	1,155	1,155		
Manteaux		664	664	664		
Gilets						

164   Napoleon's Heavy Cavalry

Item	In Depot 1805	Purchased Since 1805	Total	Issued	New in Depot	To be Written Off
Gilets d'ecurie	1	1,378	1,379	1,374	5	
Culottes de peau		1,416	1,416	1,416		
Pantalons d'ecurie	53	786	839	831	8	
Chapeaux						400
Bonnets à poil	86	480	566	566		
Bearskin cords		600	600	566	34	
Bonnets de police	37	1,219	1,256	1,252	4	
Ceinturons		413	413	402	11	
Gibernes	18	485	503	479	24	
Porte-gibernes		501	501	476	25	
Bretelles de fusil						
Porte-manteaux	77	669	746	746		
Bottes	61	806	867	799	68	
Sword knots	87	458	545	545		

We know nothing of the trumpeters, other than supposing reversed colours. Our next point of reference is not until the process of armouring the regiment had begun.

2[e] *Carabiniers*

The early paperwork for the 2[e] *Carabiniers* cannot be located at the time of writing. Following Heilsberg, every man had a *habit*, *surtout*, *gilet*, *gilet d'ecurie*, bearskin and pair of *culottes de peau*, every pair of which needed replacing.[10] Six months later, the clothing in use with the 2[e] *Carabiniers* on 17 December 1807 was as follows:[11]

Martinet presents this study of the 1[e] *Carabiniers*. The collar is blue piped scarlet, the inverse of Hoffmann in 1805.

Item	Good Conduction	In Need of Repair	To be Written Off	Total	Number Made Since 14 July 1805
Habits	900	107	3	1,010	506
Surtout	110			110	1,196
Manteaux	800	50	50	900	592

The *Carabiniers* 1802–10   165

Item	Good Conduction	In Need of Repair	To be Written Off	Total	Number Made Since 14 July 1805
Gilets	1,004			1,004	1,586
Gilets d'ecurie	600	150	228	978	1,111
Culottes de peau	276		724	1,000	1,672
Pantalons d'ecurie	150		691	841	1,307
Chapeaux	13	300	208	521	13
Bonnets à poil	900	50	60	1,010	969
Bonnets de police	900		78	978	703
Ceinturons	949			949	452
Gibernes	900		59	959	452
Porte-gibernes	900		59	959	301
Bretelles de fusil	924			924	364
Porte-manteaux	1,010			1,010	1,015
Bottes	800	50	52	52	883
Selles completes	900	113		1,013	595
Bridles complete	900	113		1,013	595
Bridons d'abreuvoir	900	113		1,013	597
Licol et longe	900	113		1,013	640
Sangles					
Housses	987			987	490
Chaperons	194			194	194
Schabraques	800			800	
Couvertures	794		100	894	461

Of interest, the regiment had changed to the half-*schabraque* in sheepskin sometime after July 1805 in replace of the cloth *chaperons*. These discontinued items were presumably stored in the depot.

Cloth used since 1805 and in December 1807 was as follows:[12]

166   Napoleon's Heavy Cavalry

Item	In Depot 1805	Purchased Since 1805	Total	Amount Used	Remaining in Depot
Blue broadcloth	211m 51	3,289m 30	3,500m 81	3,468m 87	31m 94
White broadcloth	14m 14	736m 44	750m 58	750m 58	Nil
Scarlet broadcloth	128m 84	184m 18	313m 02	255m 82	57m 20
Blanc picque de bleu	Nil	2,923m	2,923m	2,923m	Nil
Blue tricot	267m	2,057m 2	2,324m	2,324m	Nil
Scarlet serge	1,608m 27	1,478m 68	3,086m 95	3,035m 95	51m
White serge	301m 68	994m 72	1,296m 40	1,296m 40	Nil
Treillis	Nil				
Linen	246m 01	5,587m	5,833m 01	5,806m 86	26m 15

Clothing purchased, repaired and issued between 1805 and 1807 was as follows:[13]

Item	In Depot 1805	Purchased Since 1805	Total	Issued	New in Depot	To be Written Off
Habits	Nil	506	506	506	Nil	
Surtouts	Nil	1,196	1,196	1,196	Nil	
Manteaux	103	489	592	592	Nil	
Gilets	341	1,245	1,586	1,536	50	100
Gilets d'ecurie	Nil	1,167	1,167	1,141	26	
Culottes de peau	Nil	2,207	2,207	1,672	535	
Pantalons d'ecurie	557	750	1,307	1,307		
Chapeaux	Nil	313	313	13	300	
Bonnets à poi	Nil	969	969	869	100	
Bonnets de police	147	556	703	703		
Ceinturons	14	384	398	388	10	
Gibernes	152	300	452	452		
Porte-gibernes	1	300	301	301		
Bretelles de fusil	Nil	364	364	364		
Porte-manteaux	Nil	1,015	1,015	1,015		
Bottes	53	880	933	883	50	100
Selles completes	Nil	645	645	595	50	
Brides complete	Nil	665	665	615	50	
Licol et longe	12	678	690	640	50	
Bridons d'abreuvoir	9	789	798	566	232	
Sangles	Nil					
Housses	Nil	497	497	490	7	
Chaperons	Nil					

The *Carabiniers* 1802–10

Item	In Depot 1805	Purchased Since 1805	Total	Issued	New in Depot	To be Written Off
Couvertures	59	470	529	461	68	
Pairs of scissors and combs						
Oat bags						
Wallets						
Body brushes				Nil		
Curry combs						
Shirts						
Black stocks						
Pair of gaiters						
Linen bags						
Cockades						

The regiment was dressed as we suppose according to the regulations. We know nothing of the trumpeters, other than supposing reversed colours.

Trooper of the 1ᵉ *Carabiniers* in a naïve self-portrait. (*Musée de l'Empéri, Collections du Musée de l'Armée, Anciennes collections Jean et Raoul Brunon*)

The dress of the trumpeters of the *carabiniers* is not recorded by any archive documents. We assume they wore reversed colours, which is what Rousselot shows, copied from Hoffmann in 1805. (*Collection KM*)

In undress, trumpeters wore *surtouts*, which again we assume were in reversed colours as Rousselot shows. (*Collection KM*)

Chapter 12

The *Carabiniers* 1810–15

The great innovation for the heavy cavalry was the total transformation of the *carabiniers* following the Battle of Wagram.

As a result of the heavy losses sustained by the two regiments of *carabiniers* during the campaign of 1809, the Emperor resolved to afford better protection to these, the elite of the cavalry regiments, by equipping them with the *cuirass* and on 24 December of the same year he signed the following decree:

FIRST ARTICLE
Our two regiments of *Carabiniers* will be *cuirassed*. A style of *cuirass* and helmet will be proposed which, whilst maintaining a difference between the *Carabiniers* and the *Cuirassiers*, will offer equal protection to the former.

To this effect, as soon as the aforementioned regiments receive their *cuirasses*, their musketoons will be abolished.[1]

Thus, the appearance of the *carabiniers* was profoundly modified and 1811 saw the appearance of the *carabinier* in his dazzling new uniform.

Although the Emperor had chosen the type of armour to be worn, nothing had been decided with regard to the colour of the uniform. After some hesitation he adopted the colour madder-red, but the Minister of War decided, probably for reasons of economy, that the basic colour of the uniform should be white, contrasted with sky-blue (*bleu de ciel*). It would seem that, from the time the *cuirass* was issued, the *carabiniers* wore the jacket that was to become regulation wear later with the decree of 7 February 1812, the *habit de cuirassier*. The jacket was made from white cloth, with *bleu de ciel* collar piped white, the turnbacks were made from *bleu de ciel* serge with white grenades, the false pockets were simulated with white piping and decorated with three large buttons, the front of the *habit* was piped with *bleu de ciel* and fastened with a row of nine buttons; moreover, two large buttons marked the waist. The epaulettes were scarlet, with 10mm

Printed by Basset in 1814, we see a trooper of the 1ᵉ *Carabiniers*.

The *Carabiniers* 1810–15   169

wide white lace around the perimeter of the epaulette strap; they were kept in place by white epaulette brides piped *bleu de ciel* and two small uniform buttons, one on each shoulder. The tails bore grenades cut from white broadcloth. The front was closed by a row of nine large uniform buttons, with two at the small of the back. The *habit* was cut in three sizes: 380mm collar to waist, 410mm collar to waist and 440mm collar to waist. The tails measured 405, 430 or 455mm long and ranged from 215, 230 and 245mm wide at the base. The regulation for the *carabiniers' habit* referred to makes no mention of pockets on the tails, but the accompanying plates show long pockets on the tails, nor is any comment made about the cuffs.[2] The specification was as follows:[3]

Item	Cloth	Old Specification	New Specification
Habits	Blue broadcloth	2m 3	
	White broadcloth		1m 55
	Facing cloth	0m 23	0m 45
	Facing colour serge	3m 26	
	Linen for lining	0m 89	1m 45
	Large buttons	11	17
	Small buttons	22	8
Stable coats	Blue tricot	1m 73	
	Bleu de ciel broadcloth		1m 19
	Linen for lining	1m 34	1m 34
	Small buttons	22	22
Bonnets de police	White broadcloth		0m 25
	Bleu de ciel broadcloth		0m 2
	Linen for lining		0m 12
Vestes	White broadcloth	1m 19	1m 15
	White serge	2m 52	
	Linen for lining	0m 29	1m 40
	Buttons	12	12
Manteaux	*Blanc picque de bleu*	5m 75	5m 75
	Facing colour serge	1m 48	1m 48
Housse et *chaperons*	Blue broadcloth	0m 59	0m 59
	White lace 0m 40 wide	0m 59	0m 59
Porte-manteaux	Blue tricot	1m 34	
	Bleu celeste tricot		1m 34
	Treillis	1m 78	1m 78
	White lace 0m 22 wide	2m 97	1m 34

As with the *cuirassiers*, at some point after the committee met and agreed upon the clothing of the *carabiniers* the *habit* specification was changed to give the regiments pockets on the tails. Of interest, the previous design of *habit* had no tails on the pockets – so we assume that initially Bardin merely confirmed existing practice.

The regiments were distinguished from each other by the cuff-patch, which was white with sky-blue edging for the 1ᵉ regiment and sky-blue with white edging for the 2ᵉ regiment. The rest of the uniform remained as before. The stable coat was made from broadcloth, but this changed to tricot under the Bardin regulation. The *porte-manteaux*, originally dark blue, became *bleu de ciel* in 1810 and became white in 1812 – presumably the lace colour changed or was eliminated and replaced with piping. According to Les Gupil, the *housse* remained Imperial Blue, and changed to *bleu de ciel* in 1812![4]

The helmet was made from brass; the head-band, chinstraps and rosettes in the form of sun rays from white metal. The thin crest, raised and placed well back, was surmounted by scarlet *chenille*. The crowned « N » and the star of the rosettes were cast in yellow brass. The *cuirass* was made from beaten iron, embellished with brass studs and covered almost entirely with brass plate except for a 25mm wide border that was left bare. It was kept in place by a belt of natural leather with a brass buckle and two leather shoulder pieces embellished with two small brass chains that terminated in a brass plate having two fixing holes. As with the *cuirassiers*, the breast and back plates of the *cuirass* were decorated around the edges with a fabric trim- the *fraise* – which, while not visible at the shoulders and the sides, showed clearly at the neck, the arm holes and the waist. This trimming or ruff of the *cuirass* was made from a dark blue cloth, finished around the edge with white *cul-de-dé* lace edging.

Martinet presents this *carabinier* trooper *c.*1812.

Bardin

Coming two years later, the Bardin regulation covers the *carabiniers* twice, in part 1 of the work and in part 3. The text specifically dealing with the *carabiniers* was heavily edited on 10 April 1813:

> Section 2 *Carabiniers*.
> **Art 1er. Clothing**
> 771.
> The clothing of the *sous-officiers* and *carabiniers* will comprise a *habit* made from broadcloth, a sleeveless waistcoat, a *gilet d'écurie* made from tricot, a pair of *culotte de peau* in deer hide, a pair of *culotte de peau* in sheepskin, a pair of *surculottes* in grey

The *Carabiniers* 1810–15   171

~~broadcloth, a pair of stable trousers, a *manteau*, a *cuirass* conforming to the model,~~ ~~a *bonnets de police* ...~~ will conform to the general dispositions viz. No 297, and the form of the *cuirass* will conform to the model No. 783.

772.
The *habit veste* ~~will be made from white broadcloth and have no revers~~ will have no *revers* and conform to table 1916. The buttoned portion will measure 380, 410, 440mm depending on the height of the men and will close with 9 evenly spaced large buttons. The top most button will be placed 20mm from the top edge, and the bottom button will be placed 20mm from the piping. The length of the tails will be 405, 430 and 455mm; their width at the base will be 215, 230 and 245mm. ~~The turnbacks will be garnished with a grenade in white broadcloth. The distinctions of the regiments will be the cuffs, viz see table of uniforms No. 1016. The *habit* is garnished with 17 large buttons.~~

773.
The epaulettes are of the same form as those for the grenadiers of the line infantry except they will be decorated around the outside edge with linen lace 10mm wide.

774.
The waistcoat will be made from white broadcloth and have no sleeves. It will be lined in linen, the collar likewise, which will have no hooks and eyes, will arrive 25mm from the opening.

775.
The *gilets d'ecurie* will be made from *bleu celeste* tricot and will conform to the general model viz. No. 302.

776.
The buttons are made from white metal, and will carry a grenade in relief. The *habit* will have 17 large buttons and 8 small.

777.
The *culotte de peau* will be made from sheepskin and will conform to the general model No ...

778.
The braces will conform to the general model, viz No. 22.

779.
The *surculotte* made in grey broadcloth will conform to the model No. 305.

780.

The stable trousers ~~will be the same height as the *pantalons* made from broadcloth, and cut the same; they will descend to within 110mm from the ankle and be cut ample to be worn over the boots.~~ Will conform to the general model, viz. No. 311.

781.

The *manteau* will be made from white broadcloth and conform to the general model viz No. 312.

Art 2. Headdress

782. The headdress of the *sous-officier* and *carabiniers* will comprise a helmet of the dimensions given and a *bonnets de police* in white broadcloth and which will conform to the general model viz. No. 45. In the middle of the escutcheon will be a grenade in *bleu de ciel* broadcloth, the piping being the same.

Art 4. Armament and Equipment

796. Weaponry

The armament of the brigade of *carabiniers* will compose a *mousqueton*, a sabre, a pair of pistols all conforming to the models and will be delivered from the arsenals of the empire. The sergeants, *fourriers* and trumpeters will not carry the *mousqueton*.

797. Equipment

The equipment of the *carabiniers* will compose a *porte-manteau*, a *giberne* and *banderole*; the *banderole-de-mousqueton*, the sabre belt, sword knot, trumpet, boots and spurs [illegible]. The buff work of the regiment will be coloured yellow and will be decorated with a white lace 10mm wide.[5]

Concerning the *habit*, based on the original text this was cut in three sizes: 380mm collar to waist, 410mm collar to waist and 440mm collar to waist. The tails measured 405, 430 or 455mm long and ranged from 215, 230 and 245mm wide at the base. Infantry *habits* had three pointed pockets on the tails. The regulation for the *carabinier's habit* referred to makes no mention of pockets on the tails, but the accompanying plates show long pockets

An elegant officer of *carabiniers* by Martinet.

on the tails, and sufficient buttons are issued for the pockets and cuffs.⁶ Therefore as it stood, *carabinier* and *cuirassier habits* had round cuffs with flaps closed by three buttons, the front closed by eight buttons and two at the small of the back. When were pockets added? We note the smallest size were discontinued from April 1813, if any of the smaller size had been made.

As part of the Bardin regulations, the *carabiniers* adopted the white sheepskin *schabraque* in lieu of *chaperons*. The *housse* remained unchanged. The regulation notes the lining was to stop 10mm from the leading edge. The white *cul-de-dé* lace went around the extremity of the *housse*. In the rear corner was a flaming grenade device with five flames. For *cuirassiers*, the grenade was replaced by a regimental number figured in white lace.⁷ For footwear, *carabiniers* retained the rigid *botte forte*.

Portrait of an officer of *carabiniers* c.1812. (*Private collection France*)

Officers of *carabiniers* were forbidden from adopting the *schabraque* used by the troopers, instead they retained the cloth *chaperons*. The width of the silver lace to the *housse* and *chaperons* varied according to rank; 53mm for the colonel and squadron commanders, 45mm for captains, 40mm for lieutenants and 35mm for *sous lieutenants*. The colonel had a second row of lace, 20mm set inside the thicker row of lace. The major had the same distinction but in gold lace, the same as his epaulette boards.⁸

The regulation has another surprise in that officers had Imperial Blue saddle furniture and not *bleu de ciel* and were forbidden from using a sheepskin *schabraque*. Of interest, Bardin added in a pencil note signed 'Bdn' to the officers' clothing allowance, which allowed them a long-tailed *habit veste* like officers of infantry. We assume it had *bleu de ciel revers* closed to the waist! This would have been a very eye-catching garment indeed.

Chapter 13

Regulations in Practice

The decree for the *carabiniers* clothing was published on 7 February 1812 in the *Journal Militaire*, yet it seems the *carabiniers* were not authorised to start producing new clothing until late summer 1812. The decree of 17 September 1812 mentioning this is frustratingly vague: it makes no mention of cloth, but does mention the adoption of trumpeters' lace, grenadiers' scarlet epaulettes, helmets with red *chenilles* and a pompom, the waistbelt, *porte-giberne* with copper buttons to attach it to the *banderole-porte-mousqueton*, all in yellow lace edged with white lace, the *giberne*, sword knot and gauntlets.[1] On 30 August cloth *chaperons* were officially supressed in favour of sheepskin *schabraques*. Not a word is mentioned about adopting Bardin regulation clothing! A new *manteau-capote* was authorised from 18 April 1813.[2] A decree of 10 July allowed both cloth *chaperons* and sheepskin *schabraques*, along with *housses* of the old and new model.[3]

Not a word officially was made that ordered the *carabiniers* to adopt Bardin regulation clothing. We are left to wonder therefore what the reality of the situation was. The only paperwork that deals with the *carabiniers* in armour dates from the very end of the Empire. We reproduce the totality of information about the dress of both regiments.

A squadron commander of the *carabiniers* in a dated portrait from 1812. The grenades to the *chaperons* are unexpected, so too the tassels. (*Private collection France*)

1e *Carabiniers*

On Bastille Day 1810, Marshal Davout gave the regiment a shake-down inspection. The regiment mustered 790 officers and men with 95 officers' mounts and 683 troop horses. Every piece of clothing was 'written off'. The serviceable items were:[4]

Item	In Good Repair	In Need of Repair	To be Written Off	Total
Pairs of boots	700		87	787
Porte-manteaux	652		136	788
Waistbelts	782			782
Gibernes et porte-gibernes	696		22	718
Pairs of gauntlets	660		116	776
Sword knots	786			786
Musket slings	688			688
Lock covers	570		116	686
Saddles	686			686
Housses	686			686
Schabraques	500	124	59	684
Muskets	685			685
Sabres	786			786
Pistols	720			720

Troopers of *carabiniers* observed in summer 1813. Of note they are wearing white *habits* and grey *pantalons*, which the regimental archives wholly support. (*Collection KM*)

176   Napoleon's Heavy Cavalry

Not an inch of clothing in the depot was considered serviceable, or any stocks of material. The depot did hold 6 pairs of boots, 6 *porte-manteaux*, 14 waistbelts, 7 *gibernes* and belts, 17 pairs of gauntlets, 8 sword knots, 37 musket slings, 40 lock covers, and 34 saddle blankets. Davout ordered the production of 960 helmets and *cuirasses* and, asked for tariffs to be drawn up as soon as possible and began the production of new clothing: the famous white *habit* with sky-blue facings. We have no date for the formal adoption of armour or the new white *habit*. Our next point of information is at the close of the 1st Empire sadly.

An idea of what the 1[e] regiment wore when it adopted armour can be gleaned from the following inspection return of October 1814. Many artists, historians and re-enactors all ascribe the *carabiniers* as having sky-blue undress *habits* to wear on campaign. These never existed. Of note, no sky-blue undress *habits* are listed when the regiment was inspected in summer 1814:[5]

Item	In Good Repair	In Need of Repair	Need Replacing	Items Missing
Habits en drap blanc	284	72	91	0
Gilet en drap blanc	181	56	216	0
Gilets d'ecurie	65	106	195	65
Culottes de peau	155	34	242	0
Surculottes	99	14	318	0
Pantalons d'ecurie	73	0	291	67
Manteaux	271	52	103	5
Bonnets de police	260	13	174	0
Scarlet epaulettes	224	71	91	
Helmets	248	78		
Boots and spurs	103	137	191	
Waist belts	225	206		
Gibernes and belts	229	108		
Sword knots	311	8		112
Gauntlets	228			177
Garnitures de cuirass	205	6		176
Sabres	235	128		
Pistols	331	102		
Cuirasses	171	86	0	174
Shirts	753			
White stock	167			
Black stock	165			
Linen *pantalons*	31			
Wool socks	85			
Pairs of shoes	260			
Black gaiters	120			
Grey gaiters	39			

One oddity of the regiment was the presence of 195 *housses* and *chaperons* in good condition, 81 in need of repair, and 43 needing to be replaced, along with 223 *schabraques* in good condition, 31 needing repairs and 38 needing to be replaced. The *schabraque* is no doubt the half-*schabraque* that covered the saddle and pistol holsters. The *housse* is also the *demi-croupelin* style, which covered the horse's quarters. The *chaperons* are unexplainable. The regiment had the following stocks of material in the depot:[6]

Item	Newly Made or Materials	Good Condition	To be Repaired	To be Replaced
Beige broadcloth	Nil			
Bleu celeste broadcloth	4m			
White broadcloth	27m			
Scarlet broadcloth	Nil			
Green	Nil			
White tricot	1m			
Habits	32			
Helmets	303		145	
Waistbelts	100		80	
Gibernes	300		80	
Giberne belts	138		248	
Sword knots	124			
Pairs of gauntlets	16			
Porte-mousquetons	300		300	

The regiment's magazine held 600 *banderole-porte-mousquetons*, none were issued and no *mousquetons* were issued at this date. The beige broadcloth was destined for making *surculottes*, the green – though none existed in the magazine, was clearly destined for the clothing of the trumpeters. At disbandment in 1815 the cloth in the depot was as follows:

211m 66 white broadcloth
160m 60 *blanc picquer de bleu* for *capotes*
36m 97 *bleu celeste* broadcloth
7m 40 scarlet broadcloth
60m *gris-beige* broadcloth for *surculottes*
2m 71 green broadcloth for trumpeters
308m *bleu celeste* serge

The depot also held 46 *habits* needing repairs and 14 to be written off, 10 *gilets* to be written off, 100 stable coats needing repairs and 50 be written off and 30 pairs of *culottes de peau*. New clothing in the depot included 42 *habits*, 50 pairs of epaulettes, 77 *gilets*, 23 stable coats, 155 helmets, 100 *crinières* (surely *chenille*?), 40 *bonnets de police*, 22 *manteaux* and 9 pairs of *surculottes*.[7]

Officers of *carabiniers* observed in summer 1813. (*Collection KM*)

2ᵉ *Carabiniers*

In 1813, the relatively few *carabiniers* who returned from Russia were not given uniforms from the depot at Luneville, but were allotted 40fr per man from regimental funds to get new uniforms made in Berlin! The same went for their basic equipment – I assume: boots, gauntlets, *ceinturons, housses, porte-manteaux*, etc. Presumably Berlin military tailors were given a dirty, torn and sweaty surviving *habit de cuirass* to copy! From the settling of unpaid bills on the regimental accounts, drawn up in 1820, the Ministry of War refused to settle the bill![8] We wonder how these uniforms looked, and what sort of lace was used on the *housses, porte-manteaux* and epaulettes, as well as where the armour, helmets and sabres came from! Presumably these were forwarded on from Luneville.

Trooper of *carabiniers* c.1812 observed by the German artist Weiland.

Regulations in Practice   179

In summer 1814 the regiment had the following clothing and equipment in use:

Item	In Good Repair	In Need of Repair	To be Written Off	Need Replacing	Items Missing
Habits en drap blanc	236	32	36	25	16
Gilets en drap blanc	111	7	19		208
Gilets d'ecurie	189	43	28		85
Bonnets de police	183	4	19		139
Culottes de peau	96	1	25		233
Pantalons d'ecurie					345
Manteaux-capote	206	23	18	5	77
Epaulettes	173		33		120
Surculottes en drap gris	136	5	22		182
Helmets	241	84			
Chenilles	345				
Boots and spurs	146	29	18	25	111
Porte-mousquetons	189	88		71	
Waist belts	197	62		13	33
Gibernes	297	12		5	
Porte-gibernes	217	92		5	
Sword knots	137				192
Gauntlets	119				210
Garnitures de cuirass	159				165
Porte-manteaux	150	120			

In addition, the depot held 612 brand new shirts, 205 black stocks, 47 white stocks, 255 pairs of shoes, 115 pairs of black gaiters, 160 new helmets and 50 needing to be written off, 160 *chenilles* to be disposed of, 19 new *gibernes*, 19 new *porte-gibernes*, and 155 new *banderole-porte-mousquetons*. The regiment had no stocks of clothing or materials: the regiment needed reclothing almost as new. We can only assume these defects in clothing and equipment were made up in the months leading to Waterloo.

180 Napoleon's Heavy Cavalry

Complete ensemble of an officer of *carabiniers*. The *habit* is a trooper's example. (*Musée de l'Empéri, Collections du Musée de l'Armée, Anciennes collections Jean et Raoul Brunon*)

At the end of the 100 days campaign the regiment had the following stocks of material in the *dépôt*, which attests to a great restocking of the regiment's effects having taken place:[9]

Item	Newly Made or Materials	Good Condition	To be Repaired	To be Replaced
White broadcloth	1,343m 42			
Blanc picque de bleu broadcloth for *manteaux*	Nil			
Bleu celeste broadcloth	60m 80			
Scarlet broadcloth	Nil			
Gris-beige (grey-brown) broadcloth	69m			
Green broadcloth	Nil			
Bleu celeste tricot	525m 30			
White lace for *porte-manteaux*	102m			
Habits	20			41
Vestes	21			
Stable coats		14		126
Bonnets de police	Nil			
Culottes de peau	Nil			
Stable trousers	Nil			
Manteaux	4	107	4	28
Helmets	50		270	60
Chenilles	96	50	50	184
Surculottes	Nil			
Pairs of epaulettes	50			
Pairs of boots			28	63
Porte-manteaux			34	
Waistbelts		10	200	10
Gibernes		200		18
Giberne belts		40	160	18
Porte-mousquetons	170	30	178	
Sword knots		106		
Pairs of gauntlets		50		20
Waistbelts plates		220		
Spurs	Nil			
Trumpets		4		4
Saddles	1	95	197	8
Bridles	1	164	71	11
Housses	1	126	46	50
Pistol lanyards in buff leather		25		

182 Napoleon's Heavy Cavalry

Officer's sumptuous helmet and armour. (*Photograph and collection of Bertrand Malvaux*)

Item	Newly Made or Materials	Good Condition	To be Repaired	To be Replaced
Bottes de mousqueton	200			
Cuirasses	100	100	255	
Garnitures de cuirass	100	86		
Pairs of pistols	51	88½	10½	
Sabres	145	50	175	15

From the return, the items listed as in need of repair and to be replaced entirely as worn out or damaged beyond economic repair were all items from the 1815 campaign.

Chapter 14

Carabiniers – Myth and Reality

The dress of the *carabiniers* is not as easily understood as many think, and indeed the appearance of the regiments is not 100 per cent certain. Several myths have developed about the dress of the two regiments, which we discuss.

Undress *Habits*

Popular opinion argues that the *carabiniers*, once they adopted armour, wore sky-blue undress *habits*. So, let's look at the evidence as it stands in December 2023:

1. MAT No. 39 Jean Etienne Godfroi Guillot, born 30 December 1786 joined the 1ᵉ *Carabiniers* 15 November 1806, promoted to corporal 11 February 1811 and sergeant 16 March 1814. Awarded the legion of honour 1 October 1814. Discharged November 1815, he died 15 August 1862. He served in 5ᵉ company, 1ᵉ squadron. In the collection of General Vanson's papers in the Musée de l'Armée we find a portrait of sergeant Guillot, who is wearing a *bleu celeste habit*, possibly in imitation of the officers. This was clearly made between March 1811 and August 1814. We cannot assume because a *sous-officier* had such a garment that the private men had these. It merely informs us *sous-officiers* did so.[1]
2. MAT No. 865 Joseph Abeel of the 2ᵉ regiment records at some time pre-September 1811 that he received 'a white *habit* with red cuffs, a blue *habit* with no cuffs, a *cuirass* in red cooper weighing 20 to 22 livres, a roman style helmet in red copper weighing 6 to 7 livres and a stiff pair of riding boots'.[2]
3. MAT No. 1926 Charles Schehl, trumpeter of the 2ᵉ *Carabiniers* notes:

   > The regiment possessed a double equipment: a uniform in *bleu celeste* for the march and a white uniform for parade with collar and cuffs in *bleu celeste*, as well as a pair of overalls in grey cloth reinforced with basane and another pair which were white … the horses were adorned with heavy German saddles garnished with white sheepskin *schabraque*, in the angles were embroidered grenades.[3]

   Regimental paperwork confirms Schehl volunteered to the regiment directly as a trumpeter on 7 January 1812. He served in 7ᵉ company of 3ᵉ squadron and was made a prisoner of war on 20 October 1812. He died in 1862.[4] As a trumpeter, is he actually just describing the dress of the trumpeters? An undress blue garment

Carabiniers – Myth and Reality

Trooper's helmet and armour. (*Photograph and collection of Bertrand Malvaux*)

186   Napoleon's Heavy Cavalry

and a parade white *habit*? In the famous painting of General Lariboisière bidding farewell to his son, the trumpeters are adorned in white, which would mean a more sombre campaign garment would be used, and certainly one that marked the trumpeters out as easily visible. The painting shows the trumpeters in armour, with red *chenilles* to the helmet.

4. No archive paperwork attests to the exists of these *habits*. Certainly in 1814 and 1815 the men had one white *habit* and one stable coat. The *habits* are clearly inventoried and identified as such in stores returns and inspections. At disbandment a mix of stable coats and white *habits* – clearly identified was such – were worn side by side.

We have three points of reference for the existence of these sky-blue *habits* that we can consider primary sources. Albrecht Adam and Faber de Faur suggest *bleu celeste habits* were worn in 1812: these artworks were completed in the 1820s as coloured engravings and are not primary sources.

We don't doubt the regiment wore an undress garment likely to be *bleu de ciel*, but its shape and form is totally unknown, and we may well be literally dealing with wearing stable coats on campaign. If a second *habit* existed, they did categorically not exist by summer 1814? We have to ask, were these merely the stable coat? Nothing in the eyewitness evidence proposes anything other than use of the stable coat. Indeed, the regimental accounts of the 2ᵉ *Carabiniers*, which runs from 1809 to 1815, lists the purchase of green cloth in December 1811 for the trumpeters, the purchase of twenty trumpets in 1813, expense of fire wood, harness, saddles etc. Not once is any mention made of a second undress *habit*.[5] If these garments were not the stable coat, we can be absolutely sure that regimental funds were not used to buy them.

To summarise: *bleu de ciel* undress *habits* – likely the stable coat – worn in the Russian campaign, and later, giving rise to the myth of undress *habits* continuing beyond 1812. Certainly, on the night before Waterloo in torrential rain and mud the *bleu celeste* stable coat was a much more practical garment to be wearing! IF a second *habit* existed in addition to the stable coat – *a big if!* – we have no idea of its appearance, and we can be certain not a single garment existed in 1814 and 1815: if they existed, it is likely all were lost in the Russian campaign!

Fraise

Around the armour, the *carabiniers* had a cloth decoration called a *fraise*. This was fixed to the *cuirass* lining, called a *matelassure*. The colour of this item is open to some debate:

1. Gericault, in his painting of a trooper, dated 1818–19, shows an Imperial Blue *fraise*; Vernet shows likewise a dark blue *fraise*. Officers' portraits consistently show dark blue; Martinet shows dark blue *fraise* for officers. Bardin, in his regulation, states the *fraise* was red, at least for officers:

Carabiniers – Myth and Reality

1138. *Cuirass*. The armour of a *carabinier* officer will be of the same metal, shape, design, dimensions and ornaments as that of the troop. A steel edge will appear around the edge; its armholes will be trimmed with scarlet cloth bordered by a silver lace, placed to fold over the edge of the cloth, so that 5 millimetres will be visible one each side (see the engraved drawing No. 1138). That of the senior officer will be gilded.[6]

Bardin makes no mention of the sunburst device for officers, which accords with period iconography.

2. In the painting of General Lariboisière, the trumpeters have *bleu de ciel fraise*; Sauerweid shows the same detail for officers and men in the camp at Dresden in summer 1813; a portrait of sergeant Guillot shows *bleu de ciel fraise*; a portrait of trooper Catarzi of the 2ᵉ regiment shows a *bleu de ciel fraise;* Martinet shows a *bleu de ciel fraise*. In 1814 and 1815 neither regiment possessed any dark blue broadcloth, ergo the *fraise* was *bleu de ciel*.
3. Weiland in his print of a *carabinier* trooper shows a red *fraise*. A contemporary image of corporal Marteau of 8ᵉ company, 1ᵉ regiment, shows a red *fraise*.

It seems therefore that officers, when armour was adopted, had Imperial Blue *fraise*, changed to red under Bardin. But what of the men? Did the men copy the officers? It would make sense for all armoured troops to have the same *fraise* and *matelassure* for ease of production. It seems reasonable to suggest – this is an educated guess and not fact – that based on iconography from the epoch 1810–12, the 1ᵉ regiment had red *fraise*, and the 2ᵉ *bleu de ciel* or even Imperial Blue. From 1813, in both regiments it seems the *fraise* was *bleu de ciel*. The absence of dark blue cloth could also mean that it had all been used to make new *fraise*, and the same argument can be made in 1815. This is clutching at straws somewhat, but is a logical argument for the retention of dark blue *fraise*.

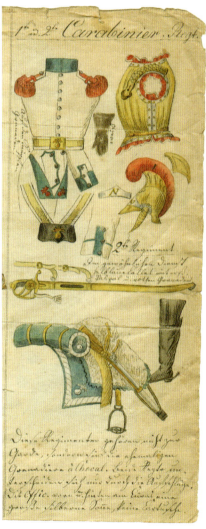

Notes on the dress of the *carabiniers* made by Westphalian Artillery Officer Breitenbach in 1813. (*Collection KM*)

Overalls

To save the very costly parade breeches, the regiment was issued undress overalls made from broadcloth. Bardin calls these *surculottes* or literally over-breeches. These closed down the outside leg with a row of eighteen buttons and fastened below the knee. However, the assumption that the *surculottes* listed in stores appeared exactly as described by Bardin is problematical:

Nothing is written down concerning the dress of the *carabiniers'* trumpeters when they adopted armour. Reversed colours is assumed, which is what Rousselot shows. This reconstruction may be incorrect. (*Collection KM*)

1. MAT No. 1926 Charles Schehl, trumpeter of the 2ᵉ *Carabiniers*, notes he was issued 'a pair of overalls in grey cloth reinforced with basane and another pair which were white …'[7]
2. Sauerweid shows grey overalls with black basane reinforcing the inner leg and *bleu de ciel* side stripes. In one drawing he hints that these were closed by buttons on the outside seam just like light cavalry *pantalons à cheval*.
3. Contrary to what Bardin states in his text, the plates by Vernet accompanying the regulation clearly show light cavalry-style *pantalons à cheval*. These close down each leg with eighteen bone buttons. The lower leg is reinforced with a leather cuff. The inner leg is reinforced with black basane, and the garment secured under the instep by a leather tab.

We can be sure, therefore, that under the tall riding boots, the men on campaign wore the same legwear as the light cavalry, made from beige broadcloth with basane reinforcement. The *bleu de ciel* side stripe is a perfectly acceptable embellishment. It is doubtful if these garments were worn over the tall boots as Vernet shows.

Porte-manteaux

When we look at period iconography, the two regiments were using two forms of *porte-manteau*: the old 1790s circular pattern and the later 1801–12 regulation square example. The earliest images we have of the *carabiniers* in armour show the square *porte-manteau*, Martinet is the sole source for the use of the round example. The use of *bleu celeste* facings to the *habit* and also *fraise* suggests a date of 1814–15. Did the regiment revert back to the circular pattern at the Restoration? It seems so. Before Bardin, the *housse* seems to have been Imperial Blue. While on the subject of saddle furniture, officers did not have bearskin pistol holster covers or black *schabraques* under Bardin regulation. IF these existed, they were used in the Russian campaign only. The sole period image of a black *schabraque* is by Gericault.

Sky-blue?
What colour were the uniforms of the *carabiniers* once they adopted armour? The regimental archive states the men wore '*bleu celeste*'. This we assume to be sky-blue.

Artists and re-enactors like to show this as a very light blue, literally sky-blue; akin to a pastel or powder blue. But was this actually the colour of the two regiments?

Period iconography shows two colours:

1. Martinet shows a very light blue, arguably '*bleu celeste*', so too a portrait of MAT No. 1834 Trooper Catarzi of the 2ᵉ regiment, who was killed in the Russian campaign.
2. When we examine undoubtably period illustrations by Gericault, as well as artwork of Guillot mentioned, and other naïve self-portraits and original garments, the colour of the facings is far darker than modern interpretation and other period images allow. The original *carabinier habit* in the Musée de l'Empéri could be forgiven to have Imperial Blue facings. In actuality it is a deep mid blue, almost exactly the same colour as used by the 5ᵉ *Hussard*. Indeed, a sample of cloth provided by M. Brunon for comparison to the 5ᵉ *Hussard* ensemble in the museum reveals an almost exact match. M. Brunon reported that this cloth sample was '*carabinier* blue'. The cloth sample is a visual match to the known original *habit*, confirming M. Brunon's description. In order to identify what colour this cloth actually is, we turn to French army cloth samples from the epoch:

    1. A French army sample book of cloth colours from 1796 housed in the A.S.K. Brown Library, Providence, Rhode Island, in the USA.
    2. A cloth sample book dated 1814 housed in the British Library, London.
    3. An official French army cloth sample book sealed and dated 1823.

Rousselot presents this trumpeter in 1812, but fails to give a source for his drawing. (*Collection KM*)

Comparison of our sample with these three references reveal it to be an exact match for all three '*bleu de ciel*' cloth samples. Therefore, without a shadow of a doubt the *carabiniers* used mid-blue cloth. Further confirmation comes when we check Bardin. He states the *carabiniers* had *bleu de ciel* facings. Case closed? Not really. Under flash this cloth is indeed a bright blue, but is certainly not the colour shown by Martinet and not comparable to known examples of *bleu celeste*!

We note, however, that the archive paperwork for the *carabinier* regiments lists the cloth they used as *bleu celeste*. Two possibilities arrive:

1. The *bleu de ciel* broadcloth was recorded incorrectly as *bleu celeste* as this is how the regiment referred to this colour.
2. The regiments by 1814 did indeed wear *bleu celeste* AND *bleu de ciel*.

Quite clearly two different colours were used by the pair of regiments.

The first reference to *bleu de ciel* comes with Bardin. The 1810 decree lists *bleu celeste*, which is exactly what the portrait of MAT No. 1834 Catarzi of the 2^e regiment shows. The regiments were ordered to make 200 examples of items of Bardin regulation kit on 21 July 1812.[8] These garments would have had *bleu de ciel* facings. The depot would have held metres and metres of *bleu celeste* cloth and, rather than it go to waste, the War Ministry ordered that 12 September 1812 old stocks of facing cloth was to be used before any new cloth was purchased.[9]

Thus, without shadow of a doubt brand new Bardin garments with *bleu de ciel* facings were issued in late 1812 into 1813. Meantime, the regiments would be churning out new clothing using the cloth in the depot, and it seems quite logical that the adjutant simply ordered more of the same, i.e. *bleu celeste*!

Thus the *carabiniers* wore two different shades of blue, and quite possibly side by side!

Officers we do note as recorded by Martinet in posed portraits and also from extant items dated 1814, did indeed wear a much lighter blue.

2e Carabiniers - Timbalier. Revue à Dusseldorf - 1811.

Rousselot presents this kettledrummer. We know the brigade had such a person, but he was a child, and we have no knowledge at all from the epoch on how they were dressed. This image by Rousselot, based on notes by Roger Forthoffer, may well be total fiction as it cannot be verified with other sources and is in direct contradiction to known facts in showing an adult kettledrummer. (*Collection KM*)

Kettledrummers

Artists like to show the regiment having kettledrummers, however not a single piece of archive paperwork confirms their existence. However, MAT No. 1926 Charles Schehl, trumpeter of the 2[e] *Carabiniers*, notes 'the brigade of *Carabiniers* had an *enfant de troupe* as kettle drummer'.[10]

Lucien Rousselot notes that when drawn up in Dusseldorf in 1811, the kettledrummer wore a *bleu celeste habit de cuirassier*. At five of the nine buttons to the front appeared white lace Brandenburgs, with seven white lace chevrons to each sleeve. The drum banners are *bleu celeste* with silver embroidery, his *chenille* is *bleu celeste* rather than white. No trace whatsoever has been found of the kettledrums themselves in any archive paperwork, nor do any of the regimental muster lists record the name of the kettledrummer. The drums were likely lost in the snows of Russia and were in use for no more than eighteen months.

Trumpeters

So, what of trumpeters? If we judge the painting of General Lariboisière to be reliable it seems a white *habit* with armour was one order of dress, likely campaign use.

Rousselot notes that when the brigade was drawn up for review in Dusseldorf in 1811 the trumpeters were adorned with *bleu celeste habits* with the front closed by a single row of nine buttons, with five white lace Brandenburg loops, white fringed epaulettes with scale shoulder boards, and the helmet had a white *crinière*. He also notes the sheepskin *schabraque* was black and the trumpeters' *culottes de peau* were buff/yellow ochre.

Charging into battle are the *carabiniers* at Borodino by Lejeune. Of interest, they have white *habits* on campaign, as shown by Sauerweid and Breitenbach in 1813.

Sergeant Guillot shows us his uniform in 1813. Of note, he wears a blue undress *surtout*: is this the origin of the blue campaign *habit*?

In December 1811 Imperial Livery and green *habits* were adopted.[11] We know just over 17m of green broadcloth was purchased by the 2^e regiment in 1811 in accordance with the decree. However, as the regiment was miles from the Luneville depot and in the field in Germany, we are sure that:

A) Green *habits de trompette* were made in the depot.
B) It is doubtful that they made it to the squadrons already in the field before the regiments crossed the Nieman.
C) The green *habits de trompette* made at Luneville in 1812 were worn by the war squadrons from 1813 to 1814, and likely again in the 100 days.

Carabiniers – Myth and Reality

The dress of a trumpeter before the adoption of Imperial Livery is shrouded in mystery. This painting executed in 1814 shows white *habits* for the trumpeters in parade dress, the same garments as worn by the troopers, and is the sole period depiction of a trumpeter before Imperial Livery was taken up.

Trumpeter in campaign dress. It is copied from a naïve drawing executed in summer 1813 – we are told by Rousselot, but it may date to after the epoch. Richard Knoetel presented a similar uniform based on the Album Theatre de Berlin, which is a source not from the epoch but the 1850's. Rousselot relied on Knoetel a great deal, and we can see that Knoetel's dating and assumptions that soruces were from the epoch is wrong on accessing the primary sources Knoetel used. Both Rousselot and Knoetel - remembering the caviats mentioned earlier – gives a trumpeter a *bleu de ciel habit* with white collar, cuffs and turnbacks. The artist gives a red *chenille* to the helmet. The garment shown may be the undress coat that trumpeter Schehl speaks of. Therefore, this uniform may well have been worn from 1811 through to disbandment, keeping the costly Imperial Livery garments for parade dress?

We cannot say what the trumpeters wore in the 1st Restoration. Likely they wore white *habits*, or reversed colours. Green *habits de trompette* existed during the 100 days.

The 1ᵉ regiment had green cloth in the depot, but no lace: perhaps the *habits* were simply green? The presence on the list of green cloth on the list of cloth in the dépôt of the 2ᵉ regiment has two conclusions:

1. No green cloth existed before or after September 1815.
2. None remaining in summer 1815 is indicative that the trumpeters indeed wore green *habits* in 1815, but we are ignorant of the lace used on these garments.

Trumpeters wearing Bardin regulation uniforms. On the left is the brigadier *trompette* with red rank stripes and white *chenille* to his helmet, on the right a trumpeter with red *chenille*. Armour was worn on campaign.

Both are likely, but on balance of evidence it seems the regiments' trumpeters wore green *habits*. Green cloth existed in the depot since 1811. Therefore, the trumpeters from the time armour was adopted wore green *habits*.[12]

Notes

Chapter 1

1. Service Historique de la Armée du Térre [hereafter SHDDT] Xc 107 8e Cavalerie. Dossier AnX. Merlin au Ministre de Guerre 10 Frimaire AnX.
2. SHDDT Xc 94 1e Cavalerie. Dossier AnX. Margaron au Ministre de Guerre 2 Frimaire AnX.
3. SHDDT Xc 263 régiments provisoire.
4. SHDDT Xs 525 PROJET D'ARRÊTÉ Relatif à l'Habillement des troupes pour l'An X.
5. SHDDT Xs 525 PROJET D'ARRÊTÉ Portant établissement d'une Masse générale destinée à l'Habillement et à l'Entretien des Troupes. 1er vendémiaire An 11.
6. Les Gupil Note 5 Surtout.
7. Bibliotheque Musée de l'Armée, Manuscripts and printed books, Volume 1 du projet de règlement sur l'habillement du major Bardin, pp.27–31.
8. Etienne Alexandre Bardin (1808) Manuel d'infanterie, ou Résumé de tous les règlements, décrets, usages, renseignements concernant l'infanterie , dans lequel se trouve renfermé tout ce que doivent savoir les sergents et caporaux. Paris: Chez Magimel, p.335.

Chapter 2

1. SHDDT Xc 108. Dossier AnX. Margaron au Ministre de Guerre 18 Frimaire AnX.
2. SHDDT Xs 525.
3. SHDDT Xs 525. 1 Vend An XII.
4. Ian Smith Pers Comm 6 January 2018.
5. Ian Smith Pers Comm 30 August 2019.
6. SHDDT Xc 91 1e Cavalerie Cuirassiers. Dossier AnX. Rapport 17 Germinal AnX.
7. SHDDT Xc 91 1e Cavalerie Cuirassiers. Dossier AnIX. Rapport 23 Messidor AnXI.
8. SHDDT Xc 95 1e Cuirassiers. Dossier An XIII. Rapport 26 Juillet 1805.
9. SHDDT Xc 97 2e Cuirassiers. Dossier An XII. Rapport 20 Thermidor An13.
10. SHDDT Xc 97 2e Cuirassiers. Dossier An XII.
11. SHDDT Xc 97 2e Cuirassiers. Dossier An XIII.
12. SHDDT Xc 99 3e Cuirassiers. Dossier An XI. Rapport 10 Fructidor AnXI.
13. SHDDT Xc 99 3e Cuirassiers. Dossier An XII. Rapport 1 Vendémiaire An XII.
14. SHDDT Xc 99 3e Cuirassiers. Dossier An XIII. Rapport 11 Thermidor An XIII.
15. SHDDT GR 1M 1927 Registre Preval.
16. SHDDT Xc 100 4e régiment de Cuirassiers. Dossier An XI. Rapport 13 Messidor AnXI.
17. SHDDT Xc 100 4e régiment de Cuirassiers. Dossier An XIII. Rapport 26 Vend AnXII.
18. SHDDT Xc 100 4e régiment de Cuirassiers. Dossier An XIV. Rapport 16 Vend AnXIV.
19. SHDDT Xc 103 5e régiment de Cuirassiers. Dossier An XI. Rapport 25 Thermidor AnXI.
20. SHDDT Xc 103 5e régiment de Cuirassiers. Dossier An XIII. Rapport 1 Vendémiaire An XIII.
21. SHDDT Xc 103 5e régiment de Cuirassiers. Dossier An XIII. Rapport 8 Thermidor An XIII a.
22. SHDDT Xc 103 5e régiment de Cuirassiers. Dossier An XIII. Rapport 8 Thermidor An XIII b.
23. SHDDT Xc 104 6e Cuirassiers. Dossier An XI. Rapport 20 Floréal Year XI.
24. SHDDT Xc 104 6e Cuirassiers. Dossier An IV. Rapport 19 Vendémiaire An XIV.
25. SHDDT Xc 104 6e Cuirassiers. Dossier 1808. Rapport 13 Janvier 1808.
26. SHDDT Xc 106 7e Cuirassiers. Dossier An XIII. Rapport 9 Vend An13.
27. SHDDT Xc 106 7e Cuirassiers. Dossier An XIV. Rapport 18 Vend An14.

196 Napoleon's Heavy Cavalry

28. SHDDT Xc 108 8e Cuirassiers. Dossier An XI. Rapport 17 Prairial AnXI.
29. SHDDT Xc 108 8e Cuirassiers. Dossier An XIV. Rapport 20 Vend An14.
30. SHDDT Xc 108 8e Cuirassiers. Dossier 1808. Rapport 1 Janvier 1808.
31. SHDDT 2C 247 Bis Habillement.
32. SHDDT Xc 110 9e Cuirassiers. Dossier AnXI. Rapport 28 Prairial AnXI.
33. SHDDT Xc 110 9e Cuirassiers. Dossier An13. Rapport 17 Thermidor An13.
34. SHDDT Xc 112 12e Cuirassiers. Dossier An13. Rapport 9 Thermidor An13.
35. SHDDT Xc 113 11e Cavalerie. Dossier An 12. Rapport 22 Vend An 12.
36. SHDDT Xc 114 11e Cuirassiers. Dossier AnXI. Rapport 4 Vend An13.
37. SHDDT Xc 114 11e Cuirassiers. Dossier AnXI. Rapport 1 Thermidor An13.
38. SHDDT Xc 116 12e régiment de Cuirassiers. Dossier An XIII. Rapport 24 Vendémiaire An XIII.
39. SHDDT Xc 116 12e régiment de Cuirassiers. Dossier An XIII. Rapport 20 Thermidor An XIII.
40. SHDDT Xc 95 1e Cuirassiers.
41. SHDDT Xc 100 4e régiment de Cuirassiers. Dossier 1815.
42. Anon (1791). Instruction provisore sur l'Habillement des troupes 1 Avril 1791. Paris: Imprimerie Royale, pp.4–5.
43. SHDDT Xaa 3. Garde du Directoire. Habillement Grenadiers à Cheval.
44. SHDDT Xab 34. Grenadiers à Cheval. 1804 a 1814. Habillement.
45. Les Gupil (1812) No. 31 Devis de Cuirassiers.
46. Carnet de la Sabretache 1904, p.623.
47. Ian Smith Pers Comm 6 January 2018.
48. Bibliotheque Musée de l'Armée. Fonds Rousselot. Fiche Dragons 1e Empire.
49. Anon (1791), p.5.
50. Anon (1791), p.13.
51. SHDDT Xc 108. Dossier An X. Rapport 22 Floréal AnX.
52. SHDDT Xc 108. Dossier An X. Merlin au Ministre de Guerre 26 Floréal AnX.
53. Ian Smith Pers Comm 6 January 2018.
54. Ibid.
55. Ibid.
56. SHDDT Xc 111 10e Cuirassiers. Dossier An XI.
57. SHDDT Xc 113 11e Cavalerie. Dossier An 12. Rapport 22 Vend An 12.
58. SHDDT Xc 116 12e Cuirassiers. Dossier AnXI.
59. Bibliotheque Musée de l'Armée. Fonds Rousselot. Fiche Dragons 1e Empire.
60. SHDDT GR 1M 1927 Registre Preval.
61. Anon (1791), p.7.
62. Bibliotheque Musée de l'Armée. Fonds Rousselot. Infanterie de la Ligne. Extraits Journal Militaire, p.59.

Chapter 3

1. Jacques Baselian Gassendi (1819) Aide-mémoire à l'Usage des officiers d'artillerie de France. Chez Magimel, Paris. Tome 2, pp.636–68.
2. Collection Bertrand Malvaux.
3. Jacques Baselian Gassendi. Aide Memoires des Officicers d'Artillerie. Paris: Chez Magimel, 1817, p.638.
4. SHDDT GR 1M 247 Bis Habillement.
5. Bibliotheque Musée de l'Armée. Fonds Rousselot. Dossier Cuirassiers.
6. SHDDT Xc 23 pièce 10. Rapport 10 Janvier 1815.
7. Ian Smith Pers Comm 13 November 2020.
8. SHDDT Xc 95 1e Cuirassiers. Dossier An X.
9. SHDDT Xc 97 2e Cuirassiers. Dossier An XII. Rapport 20 Thermidor An13.

Notes 197

10. SHDDT Xc 97 2e Cuirassiers. Dossier An XII. Rapport 15 Vendémiaire An XIII.
11. SHDDT Xc 97 2e Cuirassiers. Dossier An XII. Rapport 20 Thermidor An XIII.
12. SHDDT Xc 99 3e Cuirassiers. Dossier An XI. Rapport 10 Fructidor AnXI.
13. SHDDT Xc 99 3e Cuirassiers. Dossier An XIII.
14. SHDDT Xc 100 4e régiment de Cuirassiers. Dossier An XI.
15. SHDDT Xc 100 4e régiment de Cuirassiers. Dossier An XIII.
16. SHDDT Xc 103 5e régiment de Cuirassiers. Dossier An XII.
17. SHDDT Xc 103 5e régiment de Cuirassiers. Dossier An XIII.
18. SHDDT Xc 104 6e Cuirassiers. Dossier An XI.
19. SHDDT Xc 104 6e Cuirassiers. Dossier An IV. Rapport 19 Vendémiaire An XIV.
20. SHDDT Xc 106 7e Cuirassiers. Dossier An XI.
21. SHDDT Xc 108 8e Cuirassiers. Dossier An XI. Rapport 17 Prairial AnXI.
22. SHDDT Xc 108 8e Cuirassiers. Dossier An XIII. Rapport 14 Vend An13.
23. SHDDT Xc 108 8e Cuirassiers. Dossier An XIV. Rapport 20 Vend An14.
24. SHDDT Xc 110 9e Cuirassiers. Dossier An XI.
25. SHDDT Xc 112 12e Cuirassiers. Dossier An13. Rapport 9 Thermidor An13.
26. SHDDT Xc 114 11e Cuirassiers. Dossier An XI.
27. SHDDT Xc 114 11e Cuirassiers. Dossier AnXI Rapport 1 Thermidor An13.
28. SHDDT Xc 116 12e régiment de Cuirassiers. Dossier An XIII. Rapport 24 Vendémiaire An XIII.
29. SHDDT Xc 116 12e régiment de Cuirassiers. Dossier An XII.

Chapter 4

1. SHDDT Xc 525 Circulaire 17 Fevrier 1807.
2. Ian Smith Pers Comm 18 December 2019.
3. SHDDT Xc 95 1e Cuirassiers. Dossier 1808. Rapport 1 Janvier 1808.
4. SHDDT Xc 97 2e Cuirassiers. Dossier 1807. Rapport 23 Décembre 1807.
5. SHDDT Xc 99 3e Cuirassiers. Dossier An XII. Rapport 1 Vendémiaire An XII.
6. SHDDT Xc 99 3e Cuirassiers. Dossier An XIII. Rapport 11 Thermidor An XIII.
7. SHDDT Xc 103 5e régiment de Cuirassiers. Dossier An XI.
8. SHDDT Xc 103 5e régiment de Cuirassiers. Dossier An XIII. Rapport 1 Vendémiaire An XIII.
9. SHDDT Xc 104 6e Cuirassiers. Dossier An IV. Rapport 19 Vendémiaire An XIV.
10. SHDDT Xc 104 6e Cuirassiers. Dossier 1808. Rapport 13 Janvier 1808.
11. SHDDT Xc 106 7e Cuirassiers. Dossier 1808. Rapport 31 Décembre 1808.
12. SHDDT Xc 108 8e Cuirassiers. Dossier 1808. Rapport 1 Janvier 1808.
13. SHDDT Xc 110 9e Cuirassiers. Dossier 1807. Rapport 14 Décembre 1807.
14. SHDDT Xc 114 11e Cuirassiers. Dossier 1808. Rapport 30 Janvier 1808.
15. SHDDT Xc 116 12e régiment de Cuirassiers. Dossier An XIII. Rapport 26 Vendémiaire An XIII.

Chapter 5

1. SHDDT Xs 525.
2. Journal Militaire 6 Juillet 1806.
3. Les Gupil (1812) No. 31 Devis de Cuirassiers.
4. Ian Smith Pers Comm 6 January 2018.
5. SHDDT Xc 111 10e Cuirassiers. Dossier 1815. Rapport 1 Juin 1819.
6. SHDDT GR 1M 1962 Fonds Preval.
7. Ibid.
8. Ibid.
9. SHDDT GR 1M 247 Bis Habillement.

Chapter 6

1. SHDDT Xc 95 1e Cuirassiers. Dossier 1808. Rapport 1 Janvier 1808.
2. SHDDT Xc 97 2e Cuirassiers. Dossier 1807. Rapport 23 Décembre 1807.
3. SHDDT Xc 99 3e Cuirassiers. Dossier 1807. Rapport 20 Décembre 1807.
4. SHDDT Xc 101 4e Cuirassiers. Dossier 1807. Rapport 30 Décembre 1807.
5. SHDDT 2C 247 Bis Habillement.
6. SHDDT Xc 103 5e régiment de Cuirassiers. Dossier 1807. Rapport 4 Décembre 1807.
7. SHDDT Xc 104 6e Cuirassiers. Dossier 1808. Rapport 13 Janvier 1808.
8. SHDDT Xc 106 7e Cuirassiers. Dossier 1808. Rapport 31 Décembre 1808.
9. SHDDT Xc 108 8e Cuirassiers. Dossier 1808. Rapport 1 Janvier 1808.
10. SHDDT Xc 110 9e Cuirassiers. Dossier 1807. Rapport 14 Décembre 1807.
11. SHDDT Xc 110 9e Cuirassiers. Dossier 1807. Rapport 14 Décembre 1807.
12. SHDDT Xc 110 9e Cuirassiers. Dossier 1807. Rapport 14 Décembre 1807.
13. SHDDT Xc 110 9e Cuirassiers. Dossier 1815. Rapport 10 Septembre 1815.
14. SHDDT Xc 110 9e Cuirassiers. Dossier 1815. Rapport 10 Septembre 1815.
15. SHDDT Xc 110 9e Cuirassiers. Dossier 1815. Rapport 10 Septembre 1815.
16. SHDDT Xc 110 9e Cuirassiers. Dossier 1810. Rapport 1 Janvier 1810.
17. SHDDT Xc 112 10e Cuirassiers. Dossier 1808. Rapport 31 Décembre 1807.
18. SHDDT Xc 114 11e Cuirassiers. Dossier 1808. Rapport 30 Janvier 1808.
19. SHDDT Xc 116 12e Cuirassiers. Dossier 1808. Rapport 6 Janvier 1808.
20. SHDDT Xc 95 1e Cuirassiers. Dossier 1808. Rapport 1 Janvier 1808.
21. SHDDT Xc 97 2e Cuirassiers. Dossier 1807. Rapport 23 Décembre 1807.
22. SHDDT Xc 99 3e Cuirassiers. Dossier 1807. Rapport 20 Décembre 1807.
23. SHDDT Xc 101 4e Cuirassiers. Dossier 1807 Rapport 30 Décembre 1807.
24. SHDDT Xc 103 5e régiment de Cuirassiers. Dossier 1807. Rapport 4 Décembre 1807.
25. SHDDT Xc 104 6e Cuirassiers. Dossier 1808. Rapport 13 Janvier 1808.
26. SHDDT Xc 106 7e Cuirassiers. Dossier 1808. Rapport 31 Décembre 1808.
27. SHDDT Xc 108 8e Cuirassiers. Dossier 1808. Rapport 1 Janvier 1808.
28. SHDDT Xc 110 9e Cuirassiers. Dossier 1807. Rapport 14 Décembre 1807.
29. SHDDT Xc 112 10e Cuirassiers. Dossier 1807 Rapport 31 Décembre 1807.
30. SHDDT Xc 114 11e Cuirassiers. Dossier 1808. Rapport 30 Janvier 1808.
31. SHDDT Xc 116 12e Cuirassiers. Dossier 1808. Rapport 6 Janvier 1808.
32. SHDDT Xc 97 2e Cuirassiers. Dossier 1807. Rapport 23 Décembre 1807.
33. SHDDT GR 1M 247 Bis Habillement.

Chapter 7

1. Ian Smith Pers Comm. Digital copy of letter dated Paris 19 October 1810 from Nansouty to the War Minister.
2. AN, AF/IV/1179. RAPPORTS ET PROJET DE DÉCRET Relatifs à une nouvelle Fixation de la Masse générale d'Habillement. 11 Mars 1811.
3. Les Gupil (1812) No. 31 Devis de Cuirassiers.
4. Les Gupil (1812) No. 31 Devis de Cuirassiers.
5. Document in personal collection of Ian James Smith.
6. Francois Guy Hourtoulle. Soldats et Uniforms du Premier Empire. Clamart, France: Editions Graphipho, 1990), pp.120–122.
7. François Guy Hourtoulle. (1990) Soldats et Uniformes du Premier Empire. Clamart, France: Editions Graphipho, pp.120–122.
8. SHDDT Xc 101 4e Cuirassiers. Dossier 1807. Rapport 30 Décembre 1807.
9. SHDDT Xc 101 4e Cuirassiers. Dossier 1807. Rapport 9 Fevrier 1808.
10. Les Gupil (1812) No. 31 Devis de Cuirassiers.
11. SHDDT 2C 400 fol. 404 Lauriston to Napoléon. 19 March 1812.

Notes   199

12. SHDDT 2C 400 fol. 401 Lauriston to Napoléon. 6 March 1812.
13. SHDDT 2C 400 fol. 401 Bourcier to Napoléon. 6 March 1812. See also SHDDT 2C 400 fol. 401 Lauriston to Napoléon. 7 March 1812; SHDDT 2C 400 fol. 401 Lauriston to Napoléon. 20 March 1812.
14. SHDDT Xc 111 10e Cuirassiers. Dossier 1815. Rapport 1 Juin 1819.

Chapter 8
1. AN, AF/IV/1326/A.
2. Bibliotheque Musée de l'Armée, Manuscrits and printed books, Volume 1 du projet de règlement sur l'habillement du major Bardin. p.214.
3. SHDDT Xs 525 Tariff Cuirassier 1813.
4. Les Gupil (1812) No. 31 Devis de Cuirassiers.
5. Bibliotheque Musée de l'Armée, Manuscripts and printed books, Volume 1 du projet de règlement sur l'habillement du major Bardin. p.222.
6. Les Gupil (1812), p.239.
7. SHDDT Xs 528 Ordre Comte de Cessac 21 Juillet 1812.
8. AN, AF/IN/1179. Ordre [illegible]. The order states the reserves made in July 1812 were to be issued and replenished. For the infantry, this reserve would consist of 200 capotes, 200 habits-veste, 200 gilets-manche 200 pairs of pantalons, 200 bonnets de police, 200 schakos, 200 gibernes and belts and 200 musket slings. From the sequence of orders, the paper in question is attached to, it must date from between 20 November 1812 and 6 January 1813.
9. SHDDT Xs 528 'Devis des quantités d'etoffes, toiles et boutons nécessaires pour confection des différentes parties de l'Habillement.', p.3.
10. Journal Militaire, 3e Tremestre 1812. Décret 17 Septembre 1812.
11. SHDDT Xs 526. Circulaire 30 Aout 1812.
12. Bibliotheque Musée de l'Armée, Manuscripts and printed books, Volume 1 du projet de règlement sur l'habillement du major Bardin, p.217.
13. Ibid.
14. Ibid., pp.95–96.
15. SHDDT Xs 526. Circulaire 10 Avril 1813.
16. Journal Militaire 2e Semester 1814, p.28.
17. Ibid.
18. SHDDT Xc 23. Pièce 10. Rapport 10 Janvier 1815.
19. SHDDT Xc 23. Décret 23 Avril 1814.

Chapter 9
1. SHDDT Xc 95 1e Cuirassiers. Dossier 1813. Rapport 31 Mai 1813.
2. SHDDT Xc 95 1e Cuirassiers. Dossier 1814. Rapport 1 Juillet 1814.
3. SHDDT Xc 95 1e Cuirassiers. Dossier 1814. Rapport 1 Juillet 1814.
4. SHDDT Xc 95 1e Cuirassiers. Dossier 1814. Rapport 1 Juillet 1814.
5. SHDDT Xc 97 2e Cuirassiers. Dossier 1810. Rapport 24 Décembre 1810.
6. SHDDT Xc 97 2e Cuirassiers. Dossier 1813. Rapport 1 Juin 1813.
7. SHDDT Xc 97 2e Cuirassiers. Dossier 1813. Rapport 5 Juin 1813.
8. SHDDT Xc 97 2e Cuirassiers. Dossier 1814. Rapport 3 Octobre 1814.
9. SHDDT Xc 97 2e Cuirassiers. Dossier 1814. Rapport 3 Octobre 1814.
10. SHDDT Xc 97 2e Cuirassiers. Dossier 1814. Rapport 3 Octobre 1814.
11. SHDDT Xc 97 2e Cuirassiers. Dossier 1815. Rapport 8 Décembre 1815.
12. SHDDT Xc 97 2e Cuirassiers. Dossier 1815. Rapport 8 Décembre 1815.
13. SHDDT Xc 97 2e Cuirassiers. Dossier 1815. Rapport 8 Décembre 1815.
14. SHDDT Xc 99 3e Cuirassiers. Dossier 1814. Rapport 3 Octobre 1814.
15. SHDDT Xc 99 3e Cuirassiers. Dossier 1814. Rapport 3 Octobre 1814.

200   Napoleon's Heavy Cavalry

16. SHDDT Xc 99 3e Cuirassiers. Dossier 1814. Rapport 3 Octobre 1814.
17. SHDDT Xc 99 3e Cuirassiers. Dossier 1814. Rapport 3 Octobre 1814.
18. SHDDT Xc 99 3e Cuirassiers. Dossier 1814. Rapport 3 Octobre 1814.
19. SHDDT Xc 99 3e Cuirassiers. Dossier 1815.
20. SHDDT Xc101 4e Cuirassiers. Dossier 1814. Rapport 1 Aout 1814.
21. SHDDT Xc 100 4e régiment de Cuirassiers. Dossier 1814. Rapport 4 Aout 1814.
22. SHDDT Xc 100 4e régiment de Cuirassiers. Dossier 1815. Rapport 8 Septembre 1815.
23. Dark crimson.
24. Bright pink.
25. SHDDT Xc 100 4e régiment de Cuirassiers. Dossier 1815.
26. Ibid.
27. SHDDT Xc 100 4e régiment de Cuirassiers. Dossier 1815.
28. SHDDT Xc 103 5e régiment de Cuirassiers. Dossier 1814. Rapport 11 Aout 1814.
29. SHDDT Xc 103 5e régiment de Cuirassiers. Dossier 1815. Rapport 6 Avril 1819.
30. SHDDT Xc 103 5e régiment de Cuirassiers. Dossier 1814.
31. SHDDT Xc 103 5e régiment de Cuirassiers. Dossier 1814.
32. SHDDT Xc 103 5e régiment de Cuirassiers. Dossier 1814.
33. SHDDT Xc 103 5e régiment de Cuirassiers. Dossier 1814.
34. SHDDT Xc 103 5e régiment de Cuirassiers. Dossier 1815. Rapport 6 Avril 1819.
35. SHDDT Xc 104 6e Cuirassiers. Dossier 1814. Rapport 3 Aout 1814.
36. SHDDT Xc 104 6e Cuirassiers. Dossier 1814. Rapport 3 Aout 1814.
37. SHDDT Xc 104 6e Cuirassiers. Dossier 1814. Rapport 3 Aout 1814.
38. SHDDT Xc 104 6e Cuirassiers. Dossier 1814. Rapport 3 Aout 1814.
39. SHDDT Xc 104 6e Cuirassiers. Dossier 1815. Rapport 21 Novembre 1815.
40. SHDDT Xc 104 6e Cuirassiers. Dossier 1815. Rapport 26 Mars 1821.
41. SHDDT Xc 106 7e Cuirassiers. Dossier 1814.
42. SHDDT Xc 106 7e Cuirassiers. Dossier 1814. Rapport 3 8bre 1814.
43. SHDDT Xc 106 7e Cuirassiers. Dossier 1815. Rapport 19 Décembre 1815.
44. SHDDT Xc 106 7e Cuirassiers. Dossier 1815. Rapport 19 Décembre 1815.
45. SHDDT Xc 108 8e Cuirassiers. Dossier 1815. Rapport 5 Octobre 1814.
46. SHDDT Xc 108 8e Cuirassiers. Dossier 1815. Rapport 5 Octobre 1814.
47. SHDDT Xc 108 8e Cuirassiers. Dossier 1815. Rapport 5 Décembre 1815.
48. SHDDT Xc 108 8e Cuirassiers. Dossier 1815. Rapport 5 Décembre 1815.
49. Ibid.
50. SHDDT Xc 110 9e Cuirassiers. Dossier 1813. Rapport 28 Fevrier 1813.
51. SHDDT Xc 110 9e Cuirassiers. Dossier 1814. Rapport 1 Aout 1814.
52. SHDDT Xc 110 9e Cuirassiers. Dossier 1814. Rapport 9 Aout 1814.
53. SHDDT Xc 110 9e Cuirassiers. Dossier 1807. Rapport 14 Décembre 1807.
54. SHDDT Xc 110 10e Cuirassiers. Dossier 1815. Rapport 10 Septembre 1815.
55. SHDDT Xc 110 9e Cuirassiers. Dossier 1815. Rapport 12 Mai 1817.
56. SHDDT Xc 110 9e Cuirassiers. Dossier 1815. Rapport 15 Janvier 1816.
57. SHDDT Xc 110 9e Cuirassiers. Dossier 1815. Rapport 12 Mai 1817.
58. SHDDT Xc 110 9e Cuirassiers. Rapport 25 7bre 1815.
59. Ibid.
60. SHDDT Xc 111 10e Cuirassiers. Dossier 1813. Rapport 31 Mai 1813.
61. SHDDT Xc 111 10e Cuirassiers. Dossier 1813. Rapport 5 Juin 1813.
62. SHDDT Xc 111 10e Cuirassiers. Dossier 1815. Rapport 6 Aout 1814.
63. SHDDT Xc 111 10e Cuirassiers. Dossier 1815. Rapport 6 Aout 1814.
64. SHDDT Xc 111 10e Cuirassiers. Dossier 1815. Rapport 6 Aout 1814.
65. SHDDT Xc 111 10e Cuirassiers. Dossier 1815. Rapport 1 Juin 1819.
66. SHDDT Xc 114 11e Cuirassiers. Dossier 1813. Rapport 5 Juin 1813.

67. SHDDT Xc 114 11e Cuirassiers. Dossier 1814. Rapport 12 Aout 1814.
68. SHDDT Xc 114 11e Cuirassiers. Dossier 1814. Rapport 12 Aout 1814.
69. SHDDT Xc 114 11e Cuirassiers. Dossier 1814.
70. Ian Smut Pers Comm 11 July 2020.
71. SHDDT Xc 116 12e régiment de Cuirassiers. Dossier 1812. Rapport 21 Mai 1812.
72. SHDDT Xc 116 12e régiment de Cuirassiers. Dossier 1812. Rapport 22 Juillet 1812
73. SHDDT Xc 116 12e régiment de Cuirassiers. Dossier 1813. Rapport 30 Janvier 1813.
74. SHDDT Xc 116 12e régiment de Cuirassiers. Dossier 1814. Rapport 30 Juillet 1814.
75. SHDDT Xc 116 12e régiment de Cuirassiers. Dossier 1814. Rapport 30 Juillet 1814.
76. Ibid.
77. SHDDT Xc 116 12e régiment de Cuirassiers. Dossier 1814. Rapport 30 Juillet 1814.
78. SHDDT Xc 116 12e régiment de Cuirassiers. Dossier 1814. Rapport 30 Juillet 1814.
79. SHDDT Xc 116 12e régiment de Cuirassiers. Dossier 1814. Rapport 30 Juillet 1814.
80. SHDDT Xc 116 12e régiment de Cuirassiers. Dossier 1815. Rapport 8 Octobre 1815.
81. SHDDT Xc 116 12e Cuirassiers. Dossier 1815. Rapport 8 Octobre 1815.
82. SHDDT Xc 263 1e régiment provisoire de grosse cavalerie rapport 16 8bre 1807.
83. SHDDT Xc 263 1e régiment provisoire de grosse cavalerie rapport 16 8bre 1807.
84. SHDDT Xc 118 13e Cuirassiers. Rapport 17 7bre 1821.
85. SHDDT Xc 110 9e Cuirassiers. Dossier 1814. Rapport 3 8bre 1814.
86. SHDDT Xc 110 9e Cuirassiers. Dossier 1814. Rapport 3 8bre 1814.
87. SHDDT Xc 110 9e Cuirassiers. Dossier 1814. Rapport 3 8bre 1814.
88. SHDDT Xc 110 9e Cuirassiers. Dossier 1814. Rapport 3 8bre 1814.
89. SHDDT Xc 110 9e Cuirassiers. Dossier 1814. Rapport 3 8bre 1814.
90. SHDDT Xc 263 3e régiment provisoire de grosse cavalerie rapport 21 Juillet 1808.
91. SHDDT Xc 263 3e régiment provisoire de grosse cavalerie rapport 21 Fevrier 1810.
92. SHDDT Xc 263 3e régiment provisoire de grosse cavalerie rapport 16 Avril 1810.
93. SHDDT Xc 263 3e régiment provisoire de grosse cavalerie rapport 31 Janvier 1811.
94. SHDDT Xc 120 14e Cuirassiers. Rapport 25 Juin 1819.
95. SHDDT Xc 111 10e Cuirassiers. Dossier 1815. Rapport 6 Aout 1814.
96. SHDDT Xc 116 12e régiment de Cuirassiers. Dossier 1814. Rapport 30 Juillet 1814.
97. Ibid.
98. SHDDT Xc 116 12e régiment de Cuirassiers. Dossier 1814.
99. SHDDT 2C 545 fol. 301, Bourcier to Clarke, 1 Juillet 1813.
100. SHDDT 2C 545 fol. 301, Clarke to Bourcier, 28 Juin 1813.
101. SHDDT Xc 263 1e régiment provisoire de grosse cavalerie rapport 11 7bre 1813.
102. SHDDT Xc 263 1e régiment provisoire de grosse cavalerie rapport 11 7bre 1813.
103. SHDDT Xc 95 1e Cuirassiers. Dossier 1814. Rapport 1 Juillet 1814.
104. SHDDT Xc 95 1e Cuirassiers. Dossier 1814. Rapport 1 Juillet 1814.
105. SHDDT Xc 263 2e régiment provisoire de grosse cavalerie rapport 11 7bre 1813.
106. SHDDT Xc 263 2e régiment provisoire de grosse cavalerie rapport 11 7bre 1813.
107. SHDDT Xc 263 3e régiment provisoire de grosse cavalerie rapport 11 7bre 1813.
108. SHDDT Xc 263 3e régiment provisoire de grosse cavalerie rapport 11 7bre 1813.
109. SHDDT Xc 95 1e Cuirassiers. Dossier 1814. Rapport 1 Octobre 1814.
110. SHDDT Xc 95 1e Cuirassiers. Dossier 1814. Rapport 1 Juillet 1814.
111. SHDDT Xc 95 1e Cuirassiers.
112. SHDDT Xc 95 1e Cuirassiers. Dossier 1815. Rapport 15 Décembre 1815.
113. Bibliotheque Musée de l'Armée, Fonds Rousselot. Dossier 1e Cuirassiers.

Chapter 10
1. Journal Militaire 6 Juillet 1806.
2. Bibliotheque Musée de l'Armée, Manuscripts and printed books, Volume 1 du projet de règlement sur l'habillement du major Bardin, pp.71–72.

202 Napoleon's Heavy Cavalry

3. SHDDT Xc 525 Décret 18 Avril 1813.
4. Regiments with manteaux-capote were the 1e, 3e and 7e.
5. Bibliotheque Musée de l'Armée, Manuscripts and printed books, Volume 1 du projet de règlement sur l'habillement du major Bardin, pp.214–217.
6. Bibliotheque Musée de l'Armée. Fonds Rousselot. Dossier Cuirassiers.
7. Bibliotheque Musée de l'Armée, Manuscripts and printed books, Volume 1 du projet de règlement sur l'habillement du major Bardin, p.222.
8. Journal Militaire 2e Tremestre 1812, p.111.
9. Bibliotheque Musée de l'Armée, Fonds Rousselot photocopy of p.7 from 1779 dress regulations.
10. Bibliotheque Musée de l'Armée, Fonds Rousselot.
11. Etienne Alexandre Bardin (1813) Mémorial de l'officier d'infanterie. Chez Magimel Paris. 2 Volumes. 2 Tome. p.695.
12. Les Gupil, p.219.
13. Bardin, Tome 2, p.703.
14. Bardin, Tome 2, p.695.
15. SHDDT Xc 95 1e Cuirassiers.
16. SHDDT Xc 97 2e Cuirassiers. Dossier 1815.
17. SHDDT Xc 99 3e Cuirassiers. Dossier 1815.
18. SHDDT Xc 100 4e régiment de Cuirassiers. Dossier 1815.
19. SHDDT Xc 104 6e Cuirassiers. Dossier 1814.
20. SHDDT Xc 106 7e Cuirassiers. Dossier 1814. Rapport 3 8bre 1814.
21. SHDDT Xc 110 9e Cuirassiers. Dossier 1814. Rapport 9 Aout 1814.
22. SHDDT Xc 114 11e Cuirassiers. Dossier 1814.
23. SHDDT Xc 116 12e régiment de Cuirassiers. Dossier 1814.

Chapter 11

1. Les Gupil (1812) No. 30 Devis de Carabiniers.
2. SHDDT Xc 90 1e Carabiniers. Dossier An 7. Rapport 1 Vendémiaire An VII.
3. SHDDT Xc 90 1e Carabiniers. Dossier An X. Rapport 30 Germinal An X.
4. SHDDT Xc 90 1e Carabiniers. Dossier An XI. Rapport 5 Messidorl An XI.
5. SHDDT Xc 91 1e Carabiniers. Dossier An XII. Rapport 5 Vendémiaire An XIII.
6. SHDDT 2C 247 Bis Habillement.
7. SHDDT Xc 91e Carabiniers. Dossier 1807. Rapport 15 Décembre 1807.
8. SHDDT Xc 91 1e Carabiniers. Dossier 1807.
9. SHDDT Xc 91 1e Carabiniers. Dossier 1807.
10. SHDDT 2c 247 Bis Habillement.
11. SHDDT Xc 93 2e Carabiniers. Dossier 1807. Rapport 17 Décembre 1807.
12. SHDDT Xc 93 2e Carabiniers. Dossier 1807.
13. SHDDT Xc 93 2e Carabiniers. Dossier 1807.

Chapter 12

1. SHDDT Xc 91 1e Carabiniers. Dossier 1809. Rapport 24 Décembre 1809.
2. Bibliotheque Musée de l'Armée, Manuscripts and printed books, Volume 1 du projet de règlement sur l'habillement du major Bardin, p.220.
3. Les Gupil (1812) No. 30 Devis de Carabiniers.
4. SHDDT Xs 525.
5. Bibliotheque Musée de l'Armée, Manuscripts and printed books, Volume 1 du projet de règlement sur l'habillement du major Bardin, pp.157–165.
6. Ibid., p.220.
7. Ibid., pp.200–201.
8. Ibid., p.210.

Notes   203

Chapter 13

1. Journal Militaire 2e Tremestre 1812, p.111.
2. Journal Militaire 1e Tremestre 1813, pp.148–149.
3. Journal Militaire 2e Tremestre 1813, p.81.
4. SHDDT Xb 91 1e Carabiniers. Dossier 1810. Rapport 14 Juillet 1810.
5. SHDDT Xc 91 1e Carabiniers.
6. SHDDT Xc 91 1e Carabiniers.
7. SHDDT Xc 91 1e Carabiniers. Dossier 1815. Rapport 25 7bre 1815.
8. SHDDT Xc 93 2e Carabiniers. Dossier 1815. Rapport 30 Mars 1820.
9. SHDDT Xc 93 2e Carabiniers.

Chapter 14

1. Ian Smith Pers Comm 4 December 2020.
2. Ian Smith Pers Comm 4 December 2020.
3. Karl Schehl (1912) Vom Rhein zur Moskwa, 1812. Düsseldorf: Verlag von L. Schwann.
4. Ian Smith Pers Comm 4 December 2020.
5. SHDDT Xc 93 2e Carabiniers. Dossier 1815. Rapport 30 Mars 1820.
6. Bibliotheque Musée de l'Armée, Manuscripts and printed books, Volume 1 du projet de règlement sur l'habillement du major Bardin. pp.206–207.
7. Karl Schehl (1912) Vom Rhein zur Moskwa, 1812. Düsseldorf: Verlag von L. Schwann.
8. SHDDT Xs 528 Ordre Comte de Cessac 21 Juillet 1812.
9. Journal Militaire 2e Tremestre 1812, p.111.
10. Karl Schehl (1912) Vom Rhein zur Moskwa, 1812. Düsseldorf: Verlag von L. Schwann.
11. Les Gupil (1812) Administrations du Masses, Paris, Chez Magimel, p.219.
12. SHDDT Xc 93 2e Carabiniers.

Bibliography

Printed Works

Etienne Alexandre Bardin (1808) *Manuel d'infanterie, ou Résumé de tous les règlements, décrets, usages, renseignements concernant l'infanterie, dans lequel se trouve renfermé tout ce que doivent savoir les sergents et caporaux.* Paris: Chez Magimel.

Etienne Alexandre Bardin (1813) *Mémorial de l'officier d'infanterie.* Chez Magimel, Paris. 2 Volumes.

Honoré Hugues Berriat (1812) *Legislation militaire.* Pairs, Chez-Magimel.

Francois Guy Hourtoulle (1990) *Soldats et Uniformes du Premier Empire.* Clamart, France: Editions Graphipho.

Gassendi (1819) *Aide-mémoire à l'Usage des officiers d'artillerie de France.* Chez Magimel, Paris.

Les Gupil (1812) *Administrations du Masses.* Paris, Chez Magimel.

Karl Schehl (1912) *Vom Rhein zur Moskwa*, 1812. Düsseldorf: Verlag von L. Schwann.

Archives Nationales de France

AF/IV/1119.
AF/IV/1479.

Bibliotheque Musée de l'Armée

Fonds Rousselot.
Volume 1 du projet de règlement sur l'habillement du major Bardin.
Volume 4 du projet de règlement sur l'habillement du major Bardin.

Service Historique Armée du Térre

Xc 23 *Cavalerie*
Xc 90 1ᵉ *Carabiniers*
Xc 91 1ᵉ *Carabiniers*
Xc 93 2ᵉ *Carabiniers*
Xc 94 1ᵉ *Cavalerie*
Xc 95 1ᵉ *Cuirassiers*
Xc 97 2ᵉ *Cuirassiers*
Xc 98 3ᵉ *et* 4ᵉ *Cavalerie*
Xc 99 3ᵉ *Cuirassiers*
Xc 101 4ᵉ *Cuirassiers*
Xc 102 5ᵉ *Cuirassiers*
Xc 104 6ᵉ *Cuirassiers*
Xc 106 7ᵉ *Cuirassiers*
Xc 108 8ᵉ *Cuirassiers*
Xc 109 9ᵉ *Cavalerie*
Xc 110 9ᵉ *Cuirassiers*

Xc 110 10ᵉ *Cavalerie*
Xc 112 10ᵉ *Cuirassiers*
Xc 113 11ᵉ *Cavalerie*
Xc 114 11ᵉ *Cuirassiers*
Xc 115 12ᵉ *Cavalerie*
Xc 116 12ᵉ *Cuirassiers*
Xc 118 13ᵉ *Cuirassiers*
Xc 120 14ᵉ *Cuirassiers*
Xc 263 *provisoire de* grosse *cavalerie*
Xs 525 Habillement
Xs 526 Habillement